Trauma and Its Impacts on Temporal Experience

This unique text develops an original theoretical framework for understanding the relationship between trauma and time by combining phenomenological and psychoanalytical traditions.

Moving beyond Western psychoanalytical and phenomenological traditions, this volume presents new perspectives on the assessment and treatment of trauma patients. Powerfully illustrating how the temporal dimension of a patient's symptoms has until now been overlooked, the text presents a wealth of research literature to deepen our understanding of how trauma disrupts individual temporal experience. Ultimately, the resulting phenomena that occur (including dissociation and cognitive distortions) position time as a transdiagnostic psychological dimension, closely connected to the subject's sense of self.

This text will benefit researchers, academics, and educators with an interest in psychoanalysis, phenomenology, and trauma and dissociation studies more broadly. Those specifically interested in the philosophy of the mind, Freud, and psychotherapy will also benefit from this book.

Selene Mezzalira obtained her Ph.D. in Philosophy (2016) and Clinical Psychology (2018) from the University of Padova, Italy, and Ryokan College, USA, respectively. She has been a visiting scholar at Columbia University in the city of New York and at the University of California, Irvine, USA.

Explorations in Mental Health

For more information about this series, please visit www.routledge.com/Explorations-in-Mental-Health/book-series/EXMH

Trauma and Its Impacts on Temporal Experience

New Perspectives From Phenomenology and Psychoanalysis

Selene Mezzalira

Routledge
Taylor & Francis Group

NEW YORK AND LONDON

First published 2022
by Routledge
605 Third Avenue, New York, NY 10158

and by Routledge
2 Park Square, Milton Park, Abingdon, Oxon, OX14 4RN

Routledge is an imprint of the Taylor & Francis Group, an informa business

Library of Congress Cataloging-in-Publication Data
Names: Mezzalira, Selene, author.
Title: Trauma and its impacts on temporal experience : new
  perspectives from phenomenology and psychoanalysis / Selene
  Mezzalira.
Description: New York, NY : Routledge, 2022. | Series:
  Explorations in mental health | Includes bibliographical
  references and index.
Identifiers: LCCN 2021039119 | ISBN 9781032137292
  (hardback) | ISBN 9781032137315 (paperback) |
  ISBN 9781003230601 (ebook)
Subjects: LCSH: Psychic trauma. | Time perception. |
  Consciousness.
Classification: LCC BF175.5.P75 M49 2022 | DDC 155.9/3—dc23
LC record available at https://lccn.loc.gov/2021039119

ISBN: 978-1-032-13729-2 (hbk)
ISBN: 978-1-032-13731-5 (pbk)
ISBN: 978-1-003-23060-1 (ebk)

DOI: 10.4324/9781003230601

Typeset in Sabon
by Apex CoVantage, LLC

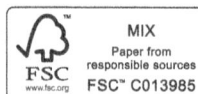

MIX
Paper from
responsible sources
FSC
www.fsc.org   FSC™ C013985
Printed in the United Kingdom
by Henry Ling Limited

Contents

About the Author

Selene Mezzalira obtained her bachelor's and master's degrees in philosophy from the University of Padova, Italy, in 2010 and 2012, respectively. She also obtained a diploma from the Galilean School of Excellence in the same city in 2013. She got her first Ph.D. in Philosophy in 2016 from the University of Padova. In 2017, she graduated in Piano performance at the Conservatory of Music in Vicenza, Italy. She obtained her second Ph.D. in Clinical Psychology from Ryokan College, Los Angeles, USA, in 2018. She has been a visiting scholar at Columbia University in the city of New York in 2014, and at the University of California, Irvine, in 2015. Currently, she works as a teacher and translator.

Introduction

Trauma and the Elusive Nature of Psychic Time

Time is probably the most elusive and enigmatic phenomenon the human mind is called to understand. Whereas our senses are connected to specialized sensory receptors, the human brain has no receptors for time (Ornstein, 1997). Yet time is present in us. As Buonomano (2018) stated, the brain is literally a "time machine." Time features everywhere in human experience – one can *feel* it passing, with no understanding of its origin, nor of its nature in ordinary experience. The nature of "duration" seems equally enigmatic, as centuries – and even millennia – of philosophical conjectures have demonstrated.

What is first and foremost jumping to the eyes of those who intend to describe time or, more profoundly, to question its intrinsic nature is an inexorably elusive aspect, precisely what is by nature unobservable, ungraspable, and unmanageable. The famous Augustinus's ([397–398] 1972) affirmation, "What, then, is time? If no one asketh me, I know. If I wish to explain it to one that asketh, I know not,"[1] best describes the enigmatic nature of time. Anticipating contemporary phenomenology, Augustinus was already aware that neither the past nor the future, nor even the present exist as pieces of outer reality, but are instead represented as memory, expectation, and perception, respectively. Time is so elusive and pervasive in our everyday life that Socrates's dictum, "The unexamined life is not worth living," can be assumed to ground our inquiry on the nature of time in human existence.[2] Our ordinary experience tells us that all psychic functions are temporal in nature (Loewald, 1962). They exist and develop in time, and imply an active relationship between the dimensions of past, present, and future. The awareness of succession and duration of mental events grounds our subjective experience of time (Arlow, 1986). The series of instantaneous and contingent perceptions of temporal objects cannot be assimilated to points in an ideally linear arrow supposed to be homogeneous and monodirectional (Knöll et al., 2013).

Typically, we experience ourselves living in a series of "nows" that are qualitatively distinct from past (i.e., memory) and future (i.e., expectation).

DOI: 10.4324/9781003230601-1

Also, we tend to experience time as continuously moving forward. However, human experience contains plenty of situations when time does not seem to move according to our common understanding of it. For instance, as we shall articulate throughout this work, "the consciousness of time can be significantly altered by the experience of psychological trauma" (Frewen & Lanius, 2015, p. 71). In fact, traumatized individuals tend to experience a "loss of time," along with symptoms such as the reexperiencing of the traumatic shock, and trauma-related intrusive thoughts and emotions as well. The temporal perception of trauma also produces a disruption in the person's sense of identity and reality (Mann, 1982). Trauma seems to represent an aspect so irreducible of our *Zeitgeist* that we might say, as Selzer (1997) pointed out, that "the modern subject has become inseparable from the categories of shock and trauma" (p. 18). As Hinton (2015) put it:

> [E]verything that we experience has a temporal dimension, and temporality is at the core of subjectivity, especially the process of remembering. Time drives us, inspiring both our nobility of purpose and our destructiveness, and it is strangely elusive, appearing to vanish as soon as we try to describe it. . . . We enter the world helpless, immersed in an enigmatic flood of messages, faced with the task of becoming subjects through the establishment of memories that anchor our sense of self. Thus, though entering time frequently involves an experience of disruption and loss, it also gives us substance and reality.
>
> (pp. 353–354)

Post-traumatic stress disorder (PTSD), the psychopathological expression of traumatic experience, is defined in the *Diagnostic and Statistical Manual of Mental Disorders (DSM-5)* as a condition stemming from the experience of (or exposure to) actual or threatened death, serious injury, or sexual violence (American Psychiatric Association [APA], 2013). Dissociation and cognitive distortions affect not only non-traumatized individuals, but also and specifically trauma patients, and are often regarded as defensive mechanisms associated with responses to traumatic events (McLean et al., 2007). In this view, dissociation is thought to maintain the individual's experiential schemas by preventing the acquisition of new information that might hinder the person's preexisting cognitive and emotional patterns. Accordingly, individuals are more likely to suffer from new information entering their existential domain if their acquired schemas are rigid and hardly modifiable. As a result, both dissociation and cognitive distortions can work as useful mechanisms that serve the goal to prevent subjects to be traumatized by new information entering their existential domain. Furthermore, both phenomena are more likely to occur among people who underwent trauma than in people who have not. Thus understood, dissociation and cognitive distortions affecting traumatized individuals might be regarded as useful mechanisms, which evolution has endowed human beings with in order to survive threat. If this is true, then a clear and consistent definition of trauma in terms of temporal and cognitive distortions would promote the development of common metrics for research and evaluation and guide the development of best practices that might serve the process of healing from trauma.

We hinted at cognitive and temporal "distortions" occurring in diverse situations, especially when trauma is present. Distortions of the sense of time, which characterize traumatic experience, also occur when using substances such as lysergic acid diethylamide (LSD), marijuana, and alcohol, and in certain psychiatric illnesses as well. The rationale for this is that, as contemporary neuroscience has shown, our perception of the temporal properties of objects and events often shows to be "out of phase" when compared to its measurement made possible by high-precision scientific instruments (Libet, 2004). The discordance exhibited by the subjective reports about the temporal perception of stimuli, when compared to the experimental measurement of their occurrence, has led to the idea that the world, insofar as our action and perception are concerned, is an "illusion" generated by our cognitive apparatus.[3] The idea that the general representation of the world, which we achieve based on the temporal processing of perceptual inputs, is something distorted or illusory, particularly when compared with the "scientific" model of reality, has made its way predominantly within the sciences of mind developed in the recent decades. Indeed, "the assumption that everything that people experience is, in reality, a construction or even an illusion created by their brains is one of the common convictions of neuroscientists and neurophilosophers" (Fuchs, 2018, p. 3).

From a phenomenological perspective, however, time and the *experience* of time are inseparable, as all meaningful subjective events are temporal in nature. Of note, to think of a "real" time as opposed to some other kind of (subjective) time amounts to forgetting the phenomenological roots of temporal experience. The so-called "objective time" is in fact a symbolic construction that can be exhibited in the form of a spatial intuition (the clock). Every measure of time refers to time as a spatialized quantity (length). This requires that time be "stopped" by a conceptual freezing that immobilizes events, as a consequence of the conscious objectification of perception in its translation into conceptual language. Therefore, to characterize conscious time as a "distortion" of objective time implies that the former be reduced to the latter. Notwithstanding, when we refer to temporal, mnestic, and cognitive "distortions" while speaking of the traumatic effects that shocking situations can produce on human subjects, we will do so only *metaphorically*. Indeed, (conscious or unconscious) experience represents the bedrock of our discourse, which refers to the phenomenological features of experience as the foundation of all scientific conceptualizations of subjectivity. In other words, far from being a mere illusion, human experience is to be regarded as it is lived by subjectivity and analyzed as such – not based on conceptual constructions that forget its very foundation.

Therefore, time can be understood as an intellectual construction, depending on processes of mental organization unifying thought and action (Whitrow, 1980). As such, the conceptualization of time can be thought of as a late product of human evolution, possibly associated with the development of language. One might also speculate that time is not an agent, but refers instead to a "positional" idea, that is, to a way of ordering things and events in the flow of an individual's life. Far from being a "container," time seems rather to be a *function* that permits us to distinguish past from present and present from future. Thus understood, time serves as an *organizing principle* that provides individuals with psychological structure, that is, a screening function for all experience.

In this work, I propose a theoretical framework for understanding the link between trauma and its temporal dimensions, exploring different conceptualizations of temporality as well as different experiences of time sense. As to these different modes of experiencing time, the distinction between the two Greek forms of time, that is, *Chronos* (Χρόνος) and *Kairos* (Καιρός), will help us in this journey. *Chronos* is the measurable and traceable time, represented on a straight line. *Kairos* is the time of human activity and opportunity – the time of the event that can be grasped in the "here and now" (Jaques, 1998). Subjective time is a constant flow of relationships, unable to be petrified or anatomically analyzed. In this perspective, rather than referring to different kinds of time, its objective and subjective determinations, that is, *Chronos* and *Kairos*, refer to different forms of experiencing the world, that is, to different ways of organizing the individual experience over time.

Consciousness and Temporality: Phenomenology, Psychoanalysis, and the Neuroscience

Historically, phenomenology and psychoanalysis surfaced in the post-positivistic cultural atmosphere, when radically new, original conceptions of time developed out of scientists' and philosophers' efforts to overcome the Newtonian conception of time and to place subjective experience in the foreground.[4] As to phenomenology, it was Edmund Husserl (1859–1938) who analyzed the fundamental structure of time as constituted by the reality of the "present" (the only dimension really existing), which is distinct from the past, which no longer is (and exists only in memory), and the future, which is yet to come (and exists only in our expectations). The present is delineated as a synthesis of "protention" of yet-to-come events and "retentions" of just-passed events, as well as by the limit that links them together, that is, the "now" – the true original dimension of temporality, in which the original perception is given.

As a matter of fact, the rise of twentieth-century psychiatry was marked by both psychoanalysis and phenomenological theorizations of psychopathology (Leoni, 2019), which developed to the point that Stolorow and Atwood (1984), several decades later, would have spoken of an actual "psychoanalytic phenomenology." It has been argued that psychoanalysis and phenomenology share "symmetrical intellectual pursuits," in that "they share a deep concern for the relation between science and subjectivity" (Csordas, 2012, p. 55). In this view, phenomenology consists of the effort of establishing a rigorous science grounded in the subjective conditions of knowledge, whereas psychoanalysis attempts to understand psychic life on the basis of rigorous principles concerning our conscious and unconscious mind. The common denominator of both branches of human science is the conviction that any science that eschews the subjective nature of experience is inadequate *as* science (Csordas, 2012). Also, both phenomenology and psychoanalysis have evolved, thanks to the consideration of the crucial importance of the relational system (D'Agostino et al., 2019), which shapes the curves of human existence.

Today, a crucial integration of phenomenology and neuroscience is being implemented (e.g., Mezzalira, 2019), and ever new perspectives on temporal consciousness are being proposed. As we shall see, the history of psychoanalysis also features some of the deepest theorizations of the temporal dimensions that characterize the intertwining of consciousness and temporality, both grounded in the "first-person," subjective perspective of human experience. In contemporary neuroscience, however, the reality of subjective (temporal) experience is often jeopardized by what is often named as an illusion. We will see how the so-called temporal "distortions," which appear as one of the hallmarks of this presumed "illusory" reality (Mezzalira, 2018a, 2018b), occur especially when traumatic experience is present.

It ought to be kept in mind that apparent temporal distortions are *not* exclusive of traumatic phenomena. In fact, psychic events are generally not temporally linear (Brena, 2009). When scientists and philosophers claim that "instant" temporal acts of perception appear "distorted" when compared to clock time, they refer to the specific temporal dimension that rules the laws under which we organize action and perception (Knöll et al., 2013). If this were true, then it should certainly be agreed that the subjective time *tout court* is, as it were, "de-formed" in relation to objective time. However, time seems not to be a "container," as Van der Hart et al. (2004) argued, but rather a *function* that permits us to distinguish past from present and present from future. Of note, not only the neural correlates of time sense are yet to be discovered (Frewen & Lanius, 2015), but they are also tentative in nature.

Back in the late 1970s, B. Libet and his neuroscientific team began to demonstrate that conscious awareness makes its entry on the stage with a consistent delay compared to brain activation in perception and sensorimotor processes, and intentional action as well (Libet et al., 1979; Libet et al., 1983; Libet, 1999, 2007). In fact, in human perception and action, there seems to be a discrepancy between the subjective temporal evaluation of experience and the experimental measurement of the time required to produce it. From a phenomenological perspective, we are indeed *immediately* aware of a specific sensory experience; however, the measurement of the objective times for its production shows instead that awareness is delayed by at least 500 milliseconds (msec) with respect to the sensory or motor event. This has facetiously led to the question as to whether consciousness could be regarded as "mentally retarded" (Chiereghin, 2008).

Although awareness appears about 500 msec after neural activation of the sensory or motor areas associated with perception or action, respectively, we are never aware of this crucial delay, but believe to perceive events at the instant of their actual appearance, and to become aware of our willingness to act precisely when our brain areas linked to the body parts involved in the wanted movement become activated (Libet, 2004). How can we bridge the gap between these two facts? How can we explain our belief that we perceive the world "in real-time," when our awareness always comes "late" in relation to the physical activation of the brain regions involved in our perception and action? How can we overcome the substantial *gap* between experimental measurement of time and subjective temporality? How can we make sure that the two experiences do not contradict each other, but find an explanation that validates both as different aspects of the same phenomenon?

In order to bridge the temporal gap between the two events, Libet (2004) introduced the concept of a "backdating." The timing of subjective experience would be backdated by the amount of time necessary for the brain activity to become in effect adequate to produce conscious experience. Based on this hypothesis, awareness of present perception and action is *actually* delayed; however, the *content* of conscious experience is "realigned" with the timing of brain activation through a subjective reference backward in time, which leads conscious awareness to adhere to the "true" moment when the brain became activated. It seems indeed that the temporal discrepancy between our conscious awareness and the related neural activity is not an aleatory fact, deduced as a hypothesis from experimental results, but grounded on the very neurophysiology of human beings. From an evolutionary point of view, for instance, the priority of the detection of spatial and temporal aspects of action and perception is due to the possibility of triggering attack/defense mechanisms, which leads to greater chances of survival.

These results show ways of *temporizing* experience that are irreducible both to the classical conception of time as a "monodirectional" series of instants and to the thematization of time as something that manifests itself in a succession of moments based on a "linear" cause–effect relationship (Chiereghin, 2011). In this regard, the concept of "field of presence" allows us not only to articulate, without separating them, different moments in time. It also allows for an *intersubjective* consideration of time (Brena, 2009). From this perspective, we can consider the 500 msec necessary for the emergence of awareness as constituting a single field of presence, within which no delay breaks the subjective "extended contemporaneity" of experience. The discontinuous, "digital" time measured by scientists articulates a field of simultaneity of interpersonal experience without disrupting it. Otherwise stated, if perception and action are *not* independent, subjective experience and experimental observation would appear not only compatible but also mutually confirmed.

The temporal unity of consciousness implies that in order to remember, we need to admit the existence of a retentional function of subjectivity, as memory always implies a dragging of the past into the present – and a punctual present is not enabled for this dragging. In fact, if the event were not in some way held in the preconscious domain it could never become conscious. This seems to contradict every monodirectional and linear conception of time. In fact, it is no longer a matter of establishing an order between events according to what comes before and after (see Kant, [1781/1787] 1999), nor of stating that consciousness is temporally extended, as Henri Bergson (1859–1941) stated (Bergson, [1889] 2007), nor of grasping the movement of retention and protention implicit in the apprehension of temporal objects (see Husserl, [1905] 1991), nor, finally, of merely asserting that being-in-the-world "is" time in its most intimate essence (see Heidegger, [1927] 1962). Rather, it is a turning of time upon itself that has no other foothold than the fact that it determines the *meaning* of subjective experience. We will see how Sigmund Freud's (1856–1939) concept of *Nachträglichkeit* (and its later translation as "*après-coup*") precisely affords this challenging explanation.

The conscious movement, through which subjectivity reaches out to experience in order to shape it, has nothing linear nor monodirectional about it, but is, as it were, representable as a multidimensional entity where the return to the Self is not a retreat, but rather the very result of the process – an impossible figure like those drawn by M.C. Escher. The fact that this result is an experience that is not only coherent but also as close as possible to the "facts" expresses a subjective work of *in-forming* experience, the meaning of which substantially governs any other moment of our living. Far from regarding this movement as a "distortion," we should instead refer to it as one of the fundamental "modes" of *generating coherence*, one that surpasses in internal structuring and experiential interconnectedness all other theoretical constructs of time.

Objective Versus Subjective Time: The "Ecstasies" of Temporality

According to Lehmann (1967), whereas "external time is objective, universal, and absolute . . . internal time is subjective, individual, and relative" (p. 798). The emotional coloring of experience determines whether time seems to flow quickly or slowly. When traumatized individuals experience a disruption of their temporal experience, objective time is lived as being "out of phase" when compared to inner time. As Meissner (2007) pointed out, "although my immediate experience can be measured and divided into the minutest fragments, my subjective experience is not of discrete points in time, but of a flow and continuity as present fades into the past" (p. 42). Furthermore, "immediate time perception is not a mathematical point but is the flow with extension in time" (Schilder, 1936, p. 539). For traumatized individuals, flashbacks and dissociation seem to stop time, so that everything seems to reoccur as it did in the past, where the world seems far away, untouchable. The timeless existence of depersonalization and derealization seems devoid of all life concerns. Ultimately, derealization and depersonalization, so common in traumatized individuals, point to a temporal perception that is unique and different from ordinary time sense: a temporality where present and eternity become equivalent (Williams, 2007).

According to Hartocollis (1986), there are two ways of experiencing time as a conscious and personal phenomenon: time as *duration* and time as *perspective*. The former develops before the notion of the latter, which is the feeling that objects exist in a temporal continuum and that specifically characterizes the adult mind. Time as duration is linked to the achievement of object constancy and the capacity to identify oneself as separate from objects. By contrast, time as perspective requires the capacity to remember and wait, along with the feeling of frustration for object-oriented needs and wishes. Freud (1915) wrote that memories are constituted in the present out of repressed material, even though the unconscious mind represents their timeless substratum. Hartocollis (1986) elaborated that the traumatized individual perceives anxiety and depression as painful affects in the present, regardless of when the trauma actually occurred. When the ego feels inadequate to cope with a threat lying in the future, anxiety emerges; when threat is perceived as situated in the past, the resulting affect is depression. In both cases, the sense of time becomes of primary importance when the Self feels threatened, whether by past (experienced) or future (expected) trauma.

Under the heading of dissociation and trauma lies the breaking up of the unifying thread of temporality. As Husserl ([1905] 1991) had already pointed out, there is no such thing as a present "now," but every now is, as it were, "thick," because it contains both the immediate past and future, that is, it consists of "protention" to the future, "presentation" of the present, and "retention" of the past altogether. In this view, inner time consciousness and consciousness *tout court* are directly related to the temporality of sensation. Consciousness produces a sensitive impression that differs from itself *without* differing (Lévinas, [1974] 1981), because it has just passed and is about to come. According to Heidegger ([1927] 1962), past, present, and future are the *ecstasies* of temporality (from the Greek word ἔκστασις [*ekstasis*], meaning "standing outside"). Past, present, and future each "stand outside" or transcend itself pointing toward the other two and forming an indissoluble unity where the three moments are unified in a "present continuous."

Now, this ecstatical unity of temporality is disrupted by the experience of emotional trauma, whereby the individual gets trapped in a timeless experience (Stolorow, 2007). When the individual experiences trauma, all duration seems to collapse into one single event. The disruption of the temporal unity of the Self implies that the traumatized individual's world becomes incommensurable with the reality of others. If temporality is the grounding structure of the *Dasein* ("being-there") – the human being's most authentic existential status (Heidegger, [1927] 1962), then trauma disrupts the entire individual's universe. Furthermore, if the ecstatic unity of temporality is what unifies experience, then the traumatized subject becomes fragmented into pieces that are then hard to bring back together. In this sense, by altering the structure and unity of temporality, trauma disrupts at the same time the subject's understanding of his or her Self. The fragmentation of one's being-in-time can often go hand in hand with dissociation.

Heidegger ([1927] 1962) viewed temporality as the unity of the three "ecstasies" of temporality that define the *Dasein*: past (*Gewesenheit*), present (*Gegenwart*), and future (*Zukunft*). Aiming at understanding the essence of our authentic *being* in the present moment, Heidegger insisted that *Dasein* is one with time, and the true nature of the Self is characterized by the awareness of the limits of existence in time, that is, death. In *Being and Time* ([1927] 1962), as well as in the book *Kant and the Problem of Metaphysics* ([1929] 1990), Heidegger developed a notion that, according to Seeburger (2017), is very close to the contemporary concept of trauma. In particular, Heidegger's use of the term *Wesen* (which can be translated with "essence," associated with *an-wesen*, that is, *pre-sence*, and *ab-wesen*, that is, *ab-sence*) would point to the "wounding" of being by one's surroundings. Specifically, this wounding consists of the subject letting be hurt by the things that surround his or her authentic *Dasein*. The understanding of Being (*Seinsverständnis*), in this view, would always be a matter of ripping (*entreissen*) what is projected from out of forgottenness. This is exactly the traumatic nature of our "Being" as *Dasein*.

Because the latter is "thrown out" in the world and necessarily finite, this same finitude is traumatic itself, that is, human finitude *is* trauma.

What Heidegger ([1927] 1962) called "everydayness" is a sort of "numbing" from the traumaticity of life, that is, from the traumatic root of existence. Also, because facing trauma involves remembering and reinternalizing (*Wiedererinnerung*) what has been forgotten (the Being itself), this same remembering is traumatic in nature. Now, human beings are never isolated, but fundamentally embedded in their world. This involves being exposed to threatening life situations, including trauma. Now, trauma patients, more than other individuals, are asked to face threatening events and memories by accepting them as they are. The suddenness of a traumatic event may significantly alter an individual's life course: "the threat of death from the impact of trauma is often devastating to all affected by the unexpected event" (Ekeh, 2016, p. 173).

Heidegger ([1927] 1962) called "Care" (*Sorge*) the experience of being at service of another human being (or oneself), which signifies a way of being ahead of oneself in interacting with others. In fact, human beings are "thrown" in the world in a way that leaves them with no certainties about the future and their own existence. Human *thrownness* (*Geworfenheit*) signifies a situation where the individuals are exposed to different life situations regardless of whether or not they want to experience them. For instance, the experience of one's death is anxiety – provoking precisely because nothing can be known about it. The awareness of death is linked to the limitedness of possibilities concerning human existence. Death forces human beings to realize that they are susceptible to it without the possibility to gain mastery over it. The constant threat of death sets human beings in a position of fear and anxiety.

When faced with the inevitable, traumatized persons become aware of their *finitude*. Healing from trauma is rooted in "*Care.*" According to Heidegger ([1927] 1962), when individuals are "thrown" into a traumatic situation, they become aware of human finitude, that is, of being *human*. The first step toward "authenticity," which is fundamental to a healthy life, is the ability to live in the "here and now," which in turn develops into the ability to imagine a possible future for oneself. Of note, even in the therapeutic setting, it is a matter of understanding the whole individual *as such*, and not only as a "trauma patient."

In his analysis of anxiety, Freud (1926) made an important distinction between *traumatic anxiety*, that is, a state of "psychical helplessness" (p. 166), and *signal anxiety*, which is meant to anticipate the danger of traumatization by repeating it "in a weakened version" (p. 167). Stolorow (2011) found it helpful to picture a "continuum of anxiety" (p. 36), of which traumatic anxiety and signal anxiety represent the two opposite poles. In this view, emotional trauma produces an affective state that is very similar to what Heidegger ([1927] 1962) characterized as the main feature of anxiety, where the traumatized person is plunged into a form of authentic "Being-toward-death" (*Sein-zum-Tode*). The key to unlocking the meaning of trauma would rely on what Stolorow (2007) called "the absolutisms of everyday life" (p. 16), which is very close to what Heidegger used to call "they" (*Man*).

A massive deconstruction of the "absolutism of everyday life" (Stolorow, 2007) exposes the traumatized individual's existence to an unpredictable world, where no safety can be assured. For the person who endured trauma, the world becomes shattered, as the unifying thread of temporality is broken. Trauma individualizes human beings, but in a way that brings them only an excruciating solitude. This is also what happens if one embraces his or her Being-toward-death in all its authenticity, in what Heidegger ([1927] 1962) also called "anticipation" (p. 349). "Being-toward-death is essentially anxiety" (Heidegger, [1927] 1962, p. 310), where the meaning of everyday life collapses. The concept of anxiety, Being-toward-death, and trauma are thus connected precisely when trauma frees the individual's authentic possibilities as a human being. A non-evasive recognition of one's finitude can occur only if one does not escape his or her very nature, but rather finds a *relational home* for it (Stolorow, 2011), in which he or she can be held.

Stolorow (2007) did not view trauma as an instinctual flooding of a Cartesian container, but rather as an experience of "unbearable affect" (p. 3), which can be grasped only within the relational system in which it is embedded. In this sense, trauma is itself constituted in an intersubjective context where severe emotional pain cannot find a relational context in which it can be held. Threatening painful experiences are not traumatic in and for themselves: *pain is not pathology* (Stolorow, 2007). It is rather the absence of a "relational home" to the person's painful emotional reaction that becomes a source of a traumatic experience. When a holding context is missing, in which painful affect can become integrated, traumatized individuals dissociate self-threatening emotions from their overall experience. As a result, a split between mind and body occurs, which lies at the core of emotional trauma, where the development of the capacity for affect tolerance and the ability to use emotions as guiding signals are also impaired.

Structure of the Book

Chapter 1 presents the historical origins of trauma, touching on phenomenology, psychiatry, and neuroscience. Although originally referring to a physical injury, the word "trauma" later came to indicate the psychic wounding stemming from a sudden, emotional, and unmanageable shock. Person-specific, developmental, event-specific, and post-traumatic variables all play a crucial role in the onset of post-traumatic psychopathology. Just like the phenomenological conceptions of trauma, the various editions of the *DSM* have also witnessed radical changes across the years. Finally, several cognitive neuroscientific theories have been put forward to explain PTSD symptomatology, analyzing its neuro-biological and neurophysiological bases. Traumatic psychopathology can ultimately offer a clinical model of post-traumatic stress disorder (PTSD) that contributes to a deep understanding of the consciousness of time.

Chapter 2 moves from Janet's theory of the intertwining between trauma and dissociation, and also analyzes Freud's concept of *Nachträglichkeit*, crucially involved in the psychoanalytical understanding of the temporal dimensions of trauma. Freud's case of Emma shows how *Nachträglich-keit* is the mechanism through which what occurs at a further moment in time can produce a traumatic explosion through a retroactive investment at the time of the original shock. *Nachträglichkeit* refers to the process through which traumatic psychopathology is constituted, in a temporal dimension that has nothing linear nor monodirectional, but resembles a prismatic, multidirectional temporal figure like those depicted by Escher. The original event remains an "asemantic" mnestic trace that is not nar-ratively organized, until a process of "*après-coup*" (the common French translation of *Nachträglichkeit*) emerges and bestows a meaning on it.

Chapter 3 deals with the timelessness of the unconscious mind, which has long been debated in both phenomenology and psychoanalysis. The temporal tension between lived time and timelessness is one of the core features of human existence. According to Freud, our unconscious mind has no temporal limitations whatsoever, no existence but outside time, and no conception of death. More contemporary theories focus instead on the multidimensional features of the temporality of human uncon-scious existence. "Chronestesia," our conscious representation of time, is achieved at late stages in human development, and seems to be produced within the dialectic between need and wish-fulfillment. Traumatic psy-chopathology is associated with a sense of timelessness, where conscious-ness becomes stuck in an eternal compulsion to repeat, leaving no room for the past to be processed, nor for future plans to be conceived.

Chapter 4 analyzes the dimension of "desynchronization" with the Otherness as one of the temporal hallmarks of traumatic psychopathol-ogy. The temporal synthesis of "retention" and "protention" produces the "intentional arc" that underlies human experience. Because trauma cannot be integrated into the dialectic movement of the individual's narrative, it tends to remain verbally ineffable. The traumatized person tends to live in a world of "alienation," with no integration between the temporal dimen-sions of past, present, and future. The lack of temporal structure, which characterizes traumatic experiences, points to the original co-dependency between our psychic life and our being-in-time. Ultimately, the very nature of trauma produces a disruption of its temporally perceived dimension.

Chapter 5 deals primarily with dissociation, that is, the disruption of the ordinary integration of consciousness and memory. In traumatized individuals, autobiographical memories show specific types of disruption, and can produce traumatic flashbacks, namely, memory fragments encoded in more primitive brain regions than the ones subserving the storage of ordinary autobiographical memories. Experiencing flashbacks amounts to "reliving" the traumatic event, rather than just "remembering" it. The so-called "speechless terror," which goes hand in hand with the inhibition of Broca's area, hinders the subject's capacity to use verbal language to communicate, thus impairing the encoding of conscious semantic memory. Dissociating amounts to "losing time," and involves a disruption of a coherent sense of Self in time. Ultimately, trauma seems to suspend time sense by producing temporal fragmentation, which seems to reinstate or preserve a sense of agency over the traumatic episode.

Chapter 6 focuses on the effects that trauma produces on the subjective organization of memory. Psychological trauma leads to altered memory functioning, expressed in distorted recall of events. To experience temporal continuity, the Self must be able to construct a narrative where the "here and now" is dynamically related with past and future horizons. A stable sense of identity emerges when the individual perceives the "here and now" as an integral part of a temporal continuum. Trauma hinders the continuity of the sense of Self in time, as traumatic memories are not integrated within the structure of the subject's narrative memory. Trauma breaks the experience of time, as it shatters the person's sense of Self. Experimental affective and cognitive neuroscience confirmed that trauma can be regarded as a "disorder of memory," whereby the intersubjectively constituted world turns into a world of alienation.

Chapter 7 tackles the problem as to whether a single or multiple mechanisms exist in the brain, which would represent the neural basis of human temporal perception. Traumatic stress consists of a biological, psychological, and social shocking experience. Chronic adversities produce lasting scars in the brain, especially when endured during early developmental stages. PTSD is also associated with inflammation of the immune system, which renders trauma patients more prone to psychological and physical pathology. Stress is particularly damaging when it is unpredictable, as it becomes associated with a sense of helplessness and hopelessness. Fear conditioning, emotional circuits, memory consolidation, epigenetics, and genetic factors are all involved in the etiology of PTSD symptomatology. The brain of PTSD patients seems to lose the ability to integrate experience into a unified whole. At the core of trauma resolution lies the reestablishment of the processes of psychic and neural integration and self-organization.

Chapter 8 refers to the dialectical intertwining between *Chronos* and *Kairos*. *Kairos* points to the trauma patient's tentative efforts to create a "kairotic" space as a defense against *Chronos*. Trauma patients build their experience upon a "denial of time," which is intrinsic to resistance to change and transformation. Trauma results in a sense of "extended time," whereby a shifting back and forth between outer perception and self-awareness occurs. Trauma patients seem to lack a sense of temporal identity. They live in a universe devoid of object relations, and feel "alone in eternity." Human feelings about time and timelessness may be either constructive or destructive, depending on their relationship to the pleasure principle (*Eros*) and the death drive (*Thanatos*), respectively. Finding an adaptive dialectic between these two poles is the scope and goal of human existence.

Notes

1. Augustinus, *Confessions*, Bk. 11, Sec. 14, p. 26.
2. In this regard, it is also noteworthy to recall Martin Heidegger's (1889–1976) statement about thinking: "To philosophize means to begin to think. We must always become beginners again. . . . To begin means: every time to think every thought as though it were being thought for the first time" (Heidegger, [1927] 1962, p. 54).
3. Curiously, Eagleman (2008) classified the so-called temporal distortions in terms of succession, order, and duration, similarly to the categories that Immanuel Kant (1724–1804) used to describe the temporal sequence of the objectified "I" (*Ich*) (Kant, [1781/1787] 1999).
4. In physics, Isaac Newton's (1643–1727) absolute time had already been overcome, thanks to the discovery of irreversible processes in thermodynamics, and the so-called arrow of time had already proved to be an arbitrary construction. Einstein, arguing the dependence of time intervals on the reference system, and the new perspectives put forward by quantum mechanics, completed the revolution that determined the obsolescence of the previous conception of time.

References

American Psychiatric Association. (2013). *Diagnostic and statistical manual of mental disorders* (5th ed.). Washington, DC: Author.

Arlow, J. A. (1986). Psychoanalysis and time. *Journal of the American Psychoanalytic Association, 34*(3), 507–528.

Augustinus, A. (397–398) 1972. *Confessions*. Menston, Yorkshire: Scholar Press.

Bergson, H. (1889) 2007. *Time and free will: An essay on the immediate data of consciousness*. London: Routledge.

Brena, G. L. (2009). Per una rilettura degli esperimenti di Libet. In G. L. Brena (Ed.), *Neuroscienze e libertà* (pp. 67–82). Padova: CLEUP.

Buonomano, D. (2018). *Your brain is a time machine: The neuroscience and physics of time*. S.l.: W. W. Norton.

Chiereghin, F. (2008). La coscienza: un ritardato mentale? *Verifiche, 37*, 283–316.

Chiereghin, F. (2011). Paradoxes of the notion of antedating. A philosophical critique to Libet's theory of the relationships between neural activity and awareness of sensory stimuli. *Journal of Consciousness Studies, 18*(3–4), 24–43.

Csordas. T. J. (2012). Psychoanalysis and phenomenology. *Ethos, 40*(1), 54–74.

D'Agostino, A., Mancini, M., & Rossi Monti, M. (2019). Phenomenology in psychoanalysis: Still an open debate? *Psychopathology*, *52*, 104–109.

Eagleman, D. M. (2008). Human time perception and its illusions. *Current Opinion in Neurobiology*, *18*(2), 131–136.

Ekeh, A. (2016). Being-in-the-world of the trauma patient: A Heideggerian perspective. *Journal of Trauma Nursing*, *23*(3), 173–176.

Freud, S. (1915). The unconscious. In J. Strachey (Ed.), *The standard edition of the complete psychological works of Sigmund Freud* (Vol. 14, pp. 159–215). London: Hogarth Press.

Freud, S. (1926). Inhibitions, symptoms, and anxiety. In J. Strachey (Ed.), *The standard edition of the complete psychological works of Sigmund Freud* (Vol. 20, pp. 77–175). London: Hogarth Press.

Frewen, P., & Lanius, R. A. (2015). *Healing the traumatized self*. London and New York: W. W. Norton.

Fuchs, T. (2018). *Ecology of the brain: The phenomenology and biology of the embodied mind*. Oxford: Oxford University Press.

Hartocollis, P. (1986). *Time and timelessness or the varieties of temporal experience: A psychoanalytic inquiry*. Madison, CT: International University Press.

Heidegger, M. (1927) 1962. *Being and time*. New York: Harper and Row.

Heidegger, M. (1929) 1990. *Kant and the problem of metaphysics*. Bloomington: Indiana University Press.

Hinton, L. (2015). Temporality and the torments of time. *Journal of Analytical Psychology*, *60*(3), 353–370.

Husserl, E. (1905) 1991. *On the phenomenology of the consciousness of internal time*. The Hague: Nijhoff.

Jaques, E. (1998). *The form of time*. Arlington, VA: Cason Hall & Co.

Kant, I. (1781/1787) 1999. *Critique of pure reason*. Cambridge: Cambridge University Press.

Knöll, J., Morrone, M. C., & Bremmer, F. (2013). Spatio-temporal topography of saccadic overestimation of time. *Vision Research*, *83*, 56–65.

Lehmann, H. E. (1967). Time and psychopathology. *Annals of the New York Academy of Sciences*, *138*(2), 798–821.

Leoni, F. (2019). Phenomenological psychopathology and psychoanalysis. In G. Stanghellini, M. Broome, A. Raballo, A. V. Fernandez, P. Fusar-Poli, & R. Rosfort (Eds.), *The Oxford handbook of phenomenological psychopathology*. Oxford University Press.

Lévinas, E. (1974) 1981. *Otherwise than being or beyond essence*. Nijhoff: The Hague.

Libet, B. (1999). Do we have free will? In B. Libet, A. Freeman, & K. Sutherland (Eds.), *The volitional brain* (pp. 47–57). Exeter, UK: Imprint Academic.

Libet, B. (2004). *Mind time: The temporal factor in consciousness*. Cambridge, MA: Harvard University Press.

Libet, B. (2007). The neural time factor in conscious and unconscious events. In G. R. Bock & J. Marsh (Eds.), *Experimental and theoretical studies of consciousness: Novartis Foundation Symposia Ciba Foundation Symposium 174* (pp. 123–146), Chichester, England: John Wiley & Sons.

Libet, B., Feinstein, E. W., & Pearl, B. (1979). Subjective referral of the timing for a cognitive sensory experience. *Brain*, *102*, 193–224.

Libet, B., Gleason, C. A., Wright, E. W., & Pearl, D. K. (1983). Time of conscious intention to act in relation to onset of cerebral activity (readiness-potential). *Brain*, 106(3), 623–642.

Loewald, H. W. (1962). Superego and time. *International Journal of Psychoanalysis*, 43, 264–268.

Mann, J. (1982). *Time-limited psychotherapy*. Cambridge, MA: Harvard University Press.

McLean, C. L., Klest, B., & Freyd, J. J. (2007). Dissociation and cognitive distortion: Functional and effective similarities. *PsycEXTRA Dataset*.

Meissner, W. W. (2007). *Time, self and psychoanalysis*. Plymouth: Jason Aronson.

Mezzalira, S. (2018a). Distorsioni temporali e coscienza dell'azione intenzionale. *Rivista Internazionale di Filosofia e Psicologia*, 9(1), 14–32.

Mezzalira, S. (2018b). Distorsioni temporali e continuità dell'esperienza percettiva. Aspetti fisiologici e considerazioni fenomenologiche. *Verifiche*, 47(1–2), 213–241.

Mezzalira, S. (2019). *Neuroscienze e fenomenologia. Il caso dei "neuroni specchio."* Padua: Padua University Press.

Ornstein, R. E. (1997). *On the experience of time*. Boulder, CO: Westview Press.

Schilder, P. (1936). Psychopathology of time. *The Journal of Nervous and Mental Disease*, 83(5), 530–546.

Seeburger, F. (2017). Seeing nature whole in fragments. In J. Coleman (Ed.), *Seeing and being seen: Aesthetics and environmental philosophy*. Hamilton Books.

Selzer, M. (1997). Wound culture: Trauma in the pathological public sphere. *University of Sussex Library*, 80, 3–26.

Stolorow, R. (2007). *Trauma and human existence*. New York: The Analytic Press.

Stolorow, R. (2011). *World, affectivity, trauma*. New York: Routledge.

Stolorow, R. D., & Atwood, G. E. (1984). Psychoanalytic phenomenology: Toward a science of human experience. *Psychoanalytic Inquiry*, 4(1), 87–105.

Van der Hart, O., Nijenhuis, E., Steele, K., & Brown, D. (2004). Trauma-related dissociation: Conceptual clarity lost and found. *Australian and New Zealand Journal of Psychiatry*, 38(11–12), 906–914.

Whitrow, G. J. (1980). *The natural philosophy of time*. Oxford: Clarendon Press.

Williams, P. (2007). Making time: Killing time. In R. J. Perelberg (Ed.), *Time and memory* (pp. 47–64). London: Karnac Books.

Chapter 1

Time and the Nature of Psychological Trauma

This chapter presents the historical origins of trauma, touching on phenomenology, psychiatry, and neuroscience. Although originally referring to a physical injury, the word "trauma" later came to indicate the psychic wounding stemming from a sudden, emotional, and unmanageable shock. Person-specific, developmental, event-specific, and post-traumatic variables all play a crucial role in the onset of post-traumatic psychopathology. Just like the phenomenological conceptions of trauma, the various editions of the *DSM* have also witnessed radical changes across the years. Finally, several cognitive neuroscientific theories have been put forward to explain post-traumatic stress disorder (PTSD) symptomatology, analyzing its neurobiological and neurophysiological bases. Traumatic psychopathology can ultimately offer a clinical model of PTSD that contributes to a deep understanding of the consciousness of time.

What Is Psychological Trauma?

The term "trauma" is the modern translation of the Greek word τραῦμα, which stands for "wound" or "injury" (Mattox et al., 2013). In the medical lexicon, this notion does not refer to a psychological stress, but to an alteration of the anatomical and functional state of the organism produced by the action of a physical agent capable of causing damage to the integrity of the person (Branchini, 2013). It was not until the end of the nineteenth century that the Jewish-German psychiatrist Hermann Oppenheim (1858–1919) provided the first theory of a traumatic neurosis resulting from distortions of nervous system activity following a strong emotional shock (Oppenheim, [1889] 1992; see also Holdorff, 2011). As Leys (2000) pointed out, the term "trauma" acquired a more psychological meaning when it was employed by several turn-of-the-century figures to describe "the wounding of the mind brought about by sudden, unexpected, emotional shock" (p. 4). Therefore, although originally referring to a physical injury, later on the word came to indicate "the psychic wounding that can potentially follow a traumatic episode" (Dass-Brailsford, 2007, p. 3).

DOI: 10.4324/9781003230601-2

Regardless of its source, psychological trauma is often unexpected, as the person is unprepared to face it, and there is nothing the individual can do to prevent it from happening. What accounts for the traumaticity of an event is something that is not predictable, that is, how the individual *experiences* the event, rather than the event *itself*. Even though stress and trauma are commonly regarded as *states*, a better conceptualization, proposed by Payne et al. (2004), regarded them as *events*, that is, as dynamic processes linked to various physiological and psychological responses that can differ in their expression. In fact, stress is determined not by a situation that is given in the environment, but by the individual's reaction to it. That is, there is no physiological state that defines (traumatic) stress as such. Not only do high levels of physiological arousal accompany stress, but the latter is also perceived as threatening and as something to be avoided. It seems that (traumatic) stress depends on whether an organism perceives to be in control of the surrounding situation (Kim & Diamond, 2002). It is likely that factors such as the severity of the event, the individual's personal history, the meaning of the event for the person, the coping skills held by the subject, and the reactions of his or her support system all play a role in developing PTSD (Ozer & Weiss, 2004).

Trauma literature is in agreement that most coping occurs within the first weeks and months following the traumatic event (Shalev, 2002). Tuval-Mashiach et al. (2004) also argued that there are two coping mechanisms, which seem to play a crucial role in the early phases following trauma: narrative and cognitive mechanisms, which function in an interactive fashion and parallel each other. However, even though exposure to traumatic stress is a necessary condition to develop PTSD, the majority of trauma-exposed individuals do not develop the syndrome (Kessler et al., 1995). This is why examining the typical effects of the stressor alone cannot identify PTSD pathogenesis. PTSD seems to involve a failure of mechanisms associated with recovery and restitution of physiological homeostasis, perhaps resulting from subjective predisposition (Yehuda & McFarlane, 1995). According to Yehuda and LeDoux (2007), PTSD develops along with a failure to recover from traumatic stress: "the clinical syndrome of PTSD may describe several biological phenotypes (e.g., some characterized by exaggerated responses, some by inadequate recovery mechanisms) that reflect individual variation originating from pretraumatic risk factors" (p. 19). In fact, individual differences, related to genetic and epigenetic factors in behavioral and brain responses to stress, are supposed to play a crucial role for a rational understanding of PTSD onset and symptomatology.

Through the dynamic creation of a narrative, there seem to be three factors correlated with a positive outcome of PTSD treatment: (1) continuity and coherence; (2) the creation of meaning; and (3) self-evaluation, which is correlated to control, feeling guilty or responsible, and being active or passive (Cicchetti, 2016). On the other hand, there are many factors that contribute to causing PTSD: (1) *person-specific* variables (research has shown that a gene-controlling serotonin transport may play a key role in developing PTSD); (2) *developmental* variables, which refer to events that occurred early in life and can make the individual more vulnerable to developing PTSD; (3) *event-specific* variables, including environmental factors leading to an increased likelihood of developing PTSD; (4) *post-traumatic* variables, which are just as important as predicting or preventing PTSD from developing (Sears & Chard, 2016). In this view, a lack of social support also appears to be among the most critical variables for facilitating PTSD development. Conversely, positive social support seems to help prevent PTSD onset or reduce the severity and duration of the symptoms.

Phenomenology of Trauma

Several theories have been put forward to explain the nature of trauma. In what Stanghellini (2009) called "trauma-break-in," trauma is thought of as something that breaks the subject's boundaries as a foreign body and remains trapped in it. The idea that trauma is something external that penetrates the individual, however, clashes with the dialectic manifested by the relationship between the individual and the surroundings. Instead of being thought of as a set of effective barriers, subjective life can indeed be conceptualized in terms of a "conversation" between inner and outer world (Stanghellini, 2009).

According to the notion of trauma as "mortification (of desire)", alternatively, it is an element of the internal world that contrasts with reality. In this view, more than looking like a "fact" in the outer world, trauma is supposed to let something in the internal world *emerge* and rub against reality. It is in this sense that trauma can be thought of as the mortification of a desire. Here, what is at play is not just a break-in from outside inward, but the *relationship* between inside and outside. Accordingly, trauma is something that *there is not*, more than something that properly "is." Trauma is something lacking, that is, an element of the outside world that does not find acceptance in the inner world of the subject.

A further characteristic of trauma is its *repetitiveness*, as traumatized individuals tend to endlessly (unknowingly and unintentionally) repeat their trauma. This paradigm, known as "trauma-repetitiveness," points to a process of rewriting past situations in the light of new experiences, thus providing the key to a semantic interpretation. The individuals' responsibility when repeating their trauma is only apparent. In fact, they cannot do otherwise, and their hope to overcome the trauma by constantly repeating it proves to be illusory, as this same hope lacks the awareness of the trauma as such. On the contrary, this repetition acquires the nuance of a *repetition compulsion*, without the awareness of the traumatic nature of the original event – above all of its *meaning*. Stanghellini

(2009) called it a *"repetition without reminiscence"* (p. 246), which becomes mechanical and automatic, that is, stereotypical, and leaves no room for the elaboration of the original trauma.

Now, "the [traumatic] symptom is a wordless presentation of an unnamable dilemma" (Wright, 1976, p. 98). This phenomenon can be interpreted in two ways. First, one might think that the so-called death instinct is the strategy through which the individual tends (or tries) to reduce the triggers associated with the traumatic occurrence. Or, second, one might think that "internal working models" (relational patterns acquired during early social interactions, which are repeated later in life) are installed in the re-presentation of the trauma like a self-fulfilling prophecy. The concept of trauma as "emergence of sense" has therefore the merit of clarifying the relationship between time and trauma as well as its meaning (Stanghellini, 2009).

Typically, we tend to bestow meaning on events based on our past experience. In contrast, trauma has the character of the novelty, of the *"first-timeness"* (Straus, 1982): trauma is the *"radical alterity"* (Stanghellini, 2009, p. 247). The novelty does not connote the traumatic event itself, but rather the *sense* we give it. Trauma takes shape as something radically different from what is already known, and is therefore comparable to no previous experience. Trauma is "the Thing" (*la Chose*, in French) as Jacques Lacan (1901–1981) used to say. "The Thing" is what the subject traces unconsciously and emotionally, but whose meaning the person does not grasp at the conscious level, namely, an unnamed object. "The Thing" is that "something" that lies at the core of experience, and grounds the process of *Nachträglichkeit* (Boothby, 2001).

Lacan used to call "ex-timacy" (*ex-timité*) the peculiar characteristic of trauma as opposed to what is most intimate within the subject, that is, the Self. In the notion of "trauma-Otherness," an experience is traumatic if it is not translatable into a meaningful discourse, if it is left without a word, if it cannot be told and therefore intersubjectively shared. Fonagy and Target (2006) spoke in this regard of a defect of "mentalization," that is, an inability to reflect on experience. On the one hand, a mentalization defect hinders the elaboration of the trauma; on the other hand, the trauma induces dissociative dynamics that hampers mentalization processes. Trauma, (absence of) mentalization, and dissociation would therefore be intertwined in a vicious circle. Ultimately, mentalization is of crucial importance in allowing traumatized individuals to achieve greater perspective on the trauma through reflection upon personal and intersubjective states of mind (Allen & Fonagy, 2006).

According to the so-called "mimetic" interpretation of trauma, the stressor can deconstruct the individual's cognitive and perceptual apparatus, rendering it unable to recall the traumatic event (Leys, 2000). According to an "antimimetic" perspective, on the contrary, individuals tend to distance themselves from the traumatic event *by deviating* from it and by viewing it as if it were "outside." Therefore, the mnestic trace of the trauma is not integrated into conscious memory, as trauma cannot be assimilated as a mnestic trace open to intentional retrieval. In the first instance, the individual is too close to the trauma to process it; in the second instance, the person is so far from it to the point that he or she dissociates from it. Either way, the traumatic event remains a "foreign body" impossible to integrate into one's own life story, and the traumatic event does not find room in the subject's narrative identity. Trauma can therefore be thought of as the opposite of narration, which refers instead to the Otherness as to that *quid novi* to be assimilated within the individual's experience. Naming the traumatic event as something "other" is an essential condition to the generation of one's identity narrative; however, if the event cannot be narrated, it will be established *as* trauma.

Trauma can thus be regarded as the radically "Other" when compared to the individual's life story – something that bears no "sense" in the subject's experiential horizon. Trauma occurs in the intersubjective dimension when we do not know how to find a "relational home" for the event (Stolorow, 2007). Traumatized individuals do not know how to contextualize the traumatic event in their self-narrative. "Contextualizing" the trauma means to give it a *meaning* and a *sense* in the framework of one's self narrative. In this view, a traumatic event becomes traumatic precisely because of its ability to be like "a key in a lock." Only with the right key one can penetrate the trauma and let it be organically integrated into a whole narrative. The *specificity* of the traumatic experience consists here of the intertwining between the traumatic event and the subject's personality structure.

Trauma tends to be widespread and to repeat itself in a play that does not allow the individual to situate it in the past. Trauma has the feature of the *present continuous*. In the self-re-creation of the trauma, the individual is placed in front of the inability to act otherwise. Yet trauma can also be seen as a moment of truth, as an opportunity for individuals to break away and grasp themselves in the traumatic occurrence as if it was a mirror. In the concept of "trauma-revelation," the focus goes on what is most intimate in the person. In this perspective, the revelation is traumatic not as pathogenic, but as *epiphanic*. Moving from the ex-timity, individuals can reach a state of intimity with themselves, successfully knowing their experience from within. As "revelation," trauma places individuals in front of themselves and thereby allows them to be capable to know themselves more deeply, shedding light on the never expressed potential of their Self (Stanghellini, 2009).

PTSD in the Various Editions of the *DSM*

Trauma has been present among human beings at least as far back as our earliest recorded history (Sears & Chard, 2016). Yet the concept of PTSD was not acknowledged until, in 1980, it was included in the third edition of the *DSM* (APA, 1980). PTSD has been controversial since its introduction as a psychiatric disorder in the *DSM-III* (Pai et al., 2017). The diagnosis was based on the assumption that a limited set of traumatic events (defined in Criterion A: the "stressor criterion") is causally associated with a distinct clinical syndrome (Criteria B through D: the "symptom criteria"). This inclusion was largely due to the growing awareness of the high rates of traumatic stress exhibited by soldiers of the Vietnam War that had a significant impact on the lives of those who experienced the combat. The diagnostic criteria for PTSD underwent significant changes over time, until the release of the *DSM-5* (APA, 2013).

The *DSM-III* (APA, 1980) explicitly adopted a restrictive approach to the stressor, according to which the fact that an event precedes the emergence of PTSD symptoms does not suffice for it to qualify as a traumatic event. This assumption has been retained despite the great changes the various editions of the *DSM* have gone through (APA, 1987, 1994, 2000, 2013). As a result, the cases when a full PTSD picture emerges in the aftermath of an event that does not meet Criterion A (referred to as "non-Criterion A" events, or minor stressors) are to be classified as Adjustment Disorder (AD) rather than PTSD (APA, 1987, p. 249). The *DSM* implies that the traumatogenic potential of an event can be deduced a priori by considering the peculiarities of the situation, whereas in AD a subjective vulnerability is considered to be more prominent (Bistoen et al., 2014).

PTSD has a variable course and can be acute or chronic, and also varies according to whether it is intentionally perpetrated or not (Santiago et al., 2013). Pai et al. (2017) noted that not all stressful events involve trauma. In the *DSM-5* definition of PTSD, stressful events not involving an immediate threat to life, physical injury, or sexual violation are not considered traumatic. The *DSM-5* has, in fact, clarified and narrowed the types of events that qualify as "traumatic." Non-immediate, non-catastrophic life-threatening illnesses, such as terminal cancer, no longer qualify as trauma. Ultimately, trauma is necessary, but not sufficient for consideration of PTSD without a qualifying exposure to that trauma. As Pai et al. (2017) pointed out, significant changes to the diagnostic criteria from the *DSM-IV-TR* (APA, 2000) to the *DSM-5* (APA, 2013) include (a) the relocation of PTSD from anxiety disorders category to a new diagnostic category named "Trauma and Stressor-related Disorders"; (b) the elimination of the subjective component from the definition of trauma; (c) the tightening of the definitions of trauma and exposure to it; (d) the increase and rearrangement of the symptoms criteria; and (e) changes in additional criteria and specifiers.

As opposed to the previous editions, the *DSM-5* provides a more detailed description of what constitutes a traumatic event: for the individual to meet Criterion A, the person must have directly experienced and/or witnessed actual or threatened death, serious injury, or sexual violation (APA, 2013). Criterion A is not only the most fundamental part of the nosology of PTSD, but also its most controversial aspect (Friedman, 2013). A further major change is the addition of a new cluster of symptoms involving negative alterations in cognition and mood, which capture negative beliefs such as self-blame, guilt, and shame. It is now specified that each symptom must be specifically identified as being associated with the traumatic event. A final change in the *DSM-5* is the addition of a new PTSD subtype that accounts for prominent dissociative symptoms: depersonalization and/or derealization (APA, 2013).

Therefore, it seems that Criterion A is neither a sufficient nor a necessary condition for developing a full syndrome of PTSD. Conversely, a variety of non-Criterion A events have been reported to produce the full clinical picture of PTSD. Therefore, considerable debate exists as to whether or not non-Criterion A events should be accepted as traumatic stressors (Hooff et al., 2009). Little is known about what distinguishes delayed versus immediate onset forms of the disorder. Ehlers and Clark (2000) proposed that delayed onset of PTSD may develop in some people due to a subsequent event, which gives the original event a more threatening meaning. The most substantial conceptual change in the *DSM-5* for PTSD seems to be the removal of the disorder from the anxiety disorders category. The rationale for this is that research has shown that PTSD involves multiple emotions (e.g., guilt, shame, and anger) that lie outside of the fear/anxiety spectrum (Resick & Miller, 2009), thus providing evidence against the inclusion of PTSD within the anxiety disorders.

Furthermore, the *DSM-IV-TR* (APA, 2000) provided three qualifying exposure types for PTSD: direct personal exposure, witnessing of others experiencing trauma, and indirect exposure through trauma experience of a family member or other close associate. The *DSM-5* has retained all three types of exposure from the *DSM-IV/TR*, now listed in the *DSM-5* as A1–A3. A fourth exposure type (A4) has been added: repeated or extreme exposure to aversive details of a traumatic event. Each symptom must be anchored to the traumatic event through a temporal and/or contextual relationship (North et al., 2009). According to the *DSM-5* (APA, 2013), in order to qualify, the symptoms must begin (symptom criteria B and C) or worsen (symptom criteria D and E) after the traumatic event. In fact, however, even though the symptoms must be linked to a traumatic event, this linking does not imply causality or etiology. Hence, "the diagnostic criteria for PTSD are actually descriptive and agnostic toward etiology and therefore consistent with the generally descriptive and agnostic approach to defining psychiatric disorders in the American diagnostic system" (Pai et al., 2017, p. 4).

PTSD Theories in Cognitive Neuroscience

Among the vast array of theoretical models of psychopathology, several cognitive neuroscientific theories – mono- or multi-representational – have been put forward to explain PTSD symptomatology (Dalgleish, 2004). For instance, schema-based theories move from the premise that we tend to filter reality through a mentally preexisting knowledge of the Self, others, and the world, subserving the task of organizing experience at different levels of abstraction (Fiske & Linville, 1980). Similarly, associative network theories are based on a single feature of mental representations as a way of explaining different aspects of psychopathology, PTSD included. More specifically, these theories try to connect different representations in order to provide a general account of how disparate pieces of information can be brought together and give rise to a specific affect (see, among others, Foa et al., 1989).

Foa et al. (1989) built back upon a previous theory put forward by Foa and Kozak (1986), and applied it to the case of PTSD. Their theory, also known as the fear network account of emotional processing in PTSD, aims at explaining how trauma-related information is emotionally processed. This network would essentially represent a mnestic trace of the trauma, where the reexperiencing of the stressful situation is thought to be the result of the activation of the fear network. When applied to PTSD, this network is assumed to be disarmed by prolonged exposure to the feared stimuli in a therapeutic or familiar support context. Of note, in this case, fear extinction is not produced by an "un-learning" process, but rather by a "re-learning" process. Foa and Riggs (1993) elaborated that traumatic memories are less coherent compared to other autobiographical memories precisely because the information processing becomes disrupted at the time of the trauma. The traumatized individuals' biases in attention, perception, and memory would therefore be the consequence of extreme emotions experienced at the time of the trauma, which would lead to disorganized mnestic traces of it. For instance, disorganized narratives have been proven to be correlated with increased trauma-related anxiety in individuals that have been subject to rape (Foa et al., 1995).

Other theories include more than one representation format to explain psychopathology, PTSD symptomatology included (Dalgleish, 2004). For instance, Brewin et al.'s (1996) "dual representation theory" involves two types of representations that mirror the subject's experience of the trauma. On the one hand, the so-called "verbally accessible memory" (VAM) can not only be deliberately retrieved and modified, but it is also contextualized in the person's autobiography. On the other hand, the so-called "situationally accessible memory" (SAM) cannot be deliberately accessed or edited by the individual; moreover, it is not contextualized, and becomes activated when the triggers of the original event come to the forefront (Brewin et al., 1996).

Ehlers and Clark (2000) proposed a cognitive model aimed at providing a theoretical structure to ground a new cognitive-behavioral treatment for PTSD individuals. In traumatized subjects, past experiences tend to activate a sense of threat about present and future. Based on this model, the main elements playing a part in the "current threat" experienced by these persons consist of the individual differences in appraising the trauma and in the type of memory-based representation process, which can be modified according to its more or less successful integration with other events stored in the long-term memory.

The so-called SPAARS (Schematic, Propositional, Analogue, and Associative Representational Systems) model, originally formulated as an account of ordinary emotional experiences that could have been applied to psychopathology, is comprised of four levels of mental representation: a schematic representational level, propositional representations, an analogical representational system, and associative representations (Dalgleish, 1999). In this view, emotions are regarded as organizing elements associated with specific activation or inhibition patterns across different levels of representation. As Dalgleish (2004) stated, in this model, "the function of emotion modes is to rapidly reconfigure the components of the system to address the circumstances that originally led to the generation of the emotion" (p. 249). As to PTSD, the theory regards traumatic events as stressful occurrences capable of triggering feelings such as fear, helplessness, and horror, as the individual's survival is experienced as threatened. Furthermore, information about the event would be encoded in parallel as propositional, analogical, and schematic representations, distributing trauma memories across different representational systems rather than in one single place. Finally, PTSD symptomatology is supposed to be produced along with repeated appraisal of the threatening features of trauma-related representations.

Emotional awareness refers to the ability to be consciously aware of one's own and others' emotions. It involves the capacity to reflect upon internal affective experience and enables self-reflection and regulation of affective states (Lanius et al., 2011). The development of emotional awareness is negatively affected by early adverse experiences, such as chronic neglect or physical and emotional abuse, which may result in a sense of helplessness. In the attempt of disconnecting from extreme emotions, which become out of control, abused or neglected children can also become disengaged from their inner emotional experience. As a matter of fact, individuals suffering from PTSD are often unaware of their own emotional states and can hardly verbalize their subjective experience. PTSD patients often experience affective disturbances in relation to themselves and others. Emotion dysregulation in PTSD seems to be associated with two different pathways (Lanius et al., 2010). On the one hand, emotion dysregulation results from fear conditioning through stress sensitization and kindling, where symptoms progressively increase over time as a consequence of ongoing stimulation. On the other hand, the other pathway refers to the crucial role played by the early childhood environment. Childhood neglect or abuse can nega- tively influence adequate development of emotional and arousal regulatory neural systems, resulting in emotion dysregulation and diminished ability to regulate physiological arousal in the face of threatening situations.

Socio-emotional processing and self-referential processing are two fundamental concepts in social cognitive neuroscience. Social emotions refer to metacognitive processes and require the capacity to consider the relevance of the stimuli for the Self and others (Lanius et al., 2011). Of note, PTSD subjects' brains show altered responses in areas involved in higher-order social cognition, that is, mentalization and theory of mind. Self-referential processing, which is mediated by cortical midline struc- tures, is also impaired in traumatized individuals, and is also supposed to be associated with the so-called default mode network, one of the main intrinsic or resting state networks in the brain. The default mode network becomes activated when we engage in stimulus-independent thought, and grounds future information processing; it also becomes activated in relation to autobiographic memory recall, theory of mind tasks, and prospection, that is, thinking about the future (Buckner et al., 2008). Bluhm et al. (2009) demonstrated that individuals suffering from chronic PTSD due to prolonged childhood abuse significantly showed reduced resting state connectivity within the default mode network. Notably, these results point to the conclusion that traumatic psychopathology "may offer a clini- cal model for understanding how the brain differentiates past from present, thus contributing to the neuroscientific study of the consciousness of time" (Frewen & Lanius, 2015, p. 97).

PTSD Versus Complex PTSD

The *DSM-5* (APA, 2013) does not recognize the diagnosis of complex PTSD, as does instead the *Psychodynamic Diagnostic Manual* (*PDM-2*: Lingiardi & McWilliams, 2017). Mucci et al. (2018) distinguished between traumati- zation due to a natural catastrophe from trauma occurring within human relationships, especially within the early caregiver–infant dyad. Further- more, the authors made a distinction between different levels of inter- personal trauma, which can involve a severe lack of attunement between child and caregiver (early relational trauma) or severe neglect, maltreat- ment, and abuse, which result in distortions of reality, inability to regulate one's inner emotional life, and self-harm or harmful behaviors toward others. Further, traumatic identification with the aggressor implies that the abused child remain psychically intertwined with the aggressor. Finally, transgenerational trauma involves a chain of secrecy and violence that the persons involved tend not to talk about. Also, early adverse experiences profoundly impact the individuals' stress responsiveness, rendering them more vulnerable to psychiatric disorders later in life (Mucci et al., 2018).

Complex PTSD was first described by Herman (1992) as a syndrome observed in survivors of prolonged and repeated trauma. The 11th revision to the World Health Organization (WHO) International Classification of Diseases (ICD-11) identified complex PTSD as a new condition (Karatzias et al., 2019). The ICD-11 diagnosis of complex PTSD is comprised of six symptom clusters, three of which are shared with PTSD (i.e., reexperiencing, avoidance, and sense of threat), and three additional symptom clusters involving affect dysregulation, negative self-concept, and relational difficulties (Brewin et al., 2017). Even though it partly overlaps with typical PTSD (Resick et al., 2012), complex PTSD is in fact supposed to require a slightly different type of treatment – for example, augmented cognitive-behavioral therapy (Bryant, 2010) – when compared to typical PTSD. As Cloitre et al. (2013) argued, "the different symptom profiles that describe PTSD and complex PTSD are associated with different subgroups of individuals, different levels of impairment, and different risk factors (trauma history)" (p. 10).

Complex PTSD extends beyond the typical PTSD symptomatology because of dysregulation in three psychobiological domains: emotion processing, self-organization, and relational functioning (Ford, 2015). Complex traumatic stressors represent "a subset of the larger universe of traumatic stressors that have as their unique trademark a *compromise of the individual's self-development and psychophysiological integrity*" (Ford, 2009, p. 22). In this view, what distinguishes complex trauma from all other forms of psychological trauma is, on the one hand, the timing of its occurrence (typically, the developmental period during which self-identity and self-regulation are consolidated), and, on the other hand, its very nature (the disruption of the individual's attachment system caused by acts of relational betrayal). This is also why complex trauma is often referred to as "relational trauma," and occurs most often in crucial developmental periods, such as infancy or childhood (Copeland et al., 2007).

Lanius et al. (2011) examined the role of social cognitive and affective neuroscience in order to better understand the psychology and neurobiology of complex trauma, and to find effective types of treatment for it. As opposed to PTSD, which tends to follow single traumatic incidents, complex trauma is thus regarded as a repeated interpersonal traumatic stress, taking place during crucial developmental moments and involving a disruption of emotional regulation. Terr (1991) divided childhood trauma into two basic types: Type I and Type II.

> Type I trauma includes full, detailed memories, "omens," and misperceptions. Type II trauma includes denial and numbing, self-hypnosis and dissociation, and rage. Crossover conditions often occur after

sudden, shocking deaths or accidents that leave children handi-
capped. In these instances, characteristics of both type I and type II
childhood traumas exist side by side.

(p. 10)

The betrayal component of complex trauma can be related to amnesia as
an adaptive response to physical or psychological abuse (Freyd, 1994).
Ultimately, because complex trauma affects self-integrity, self-regulation,
and attachment security, it not only compromises physical survival, but
has to do more closely with the development and survival of the Self.

References

Allen, J. G., & Fonagy, P. (2006). *Handbook of mentalization-based treatment*.
Chichester, West Sussex, UK: Wiley.

American Psychiatric Association. (1980). *Diagnostic and statistical manual of mental disorders* (3rd ed.). Washington, DC: Author.

American Psychiatric Association. (1987). *Diagnostic and statistical manual of mental disorders* (3rd ed.-tr). Washington, DC: Author.

American Psychiatric Association. (1994). *Diagnostic and statistical manual of mental disorders* (4th ed.). Washington, DC: Author.

American Psychiatric Association. (2000). *Diagnostic and statistical manual of mental disorders* (4th ed.-tr). Washington, DC: Author.

American Psychiatric Association. (2013). *Diagnostic and statistical manual of mental disorders* (5th ed.). Washington, DC: Author.

Bistoen, G., Vanheule, S., & Craps, S. (2014). *Nachträglichkeit*: A Freudian perspective on delayed traumatic reactions. *Theory & Psychology*, *24*(5), 668–687.

Bluhm, R. L., Williamson, P. C., Osuch, E. A., Frewen, P. A., Stevens, T. K., Boksman, K., Neufeld, R. W., Théberge, J., & Lanius, R. A. (2009). Alterations in
default network connectivity in post-traumatic stress disorder related to early-
life trauma. *Journal of Psychiatry and Neuroscience*, *34*, 187–194.

Boothby, R. (2001). *Freud as philosopher: Metapsychology after Lacan*. New
York: Routledge.

Branchini, R. (2013). *Trauma studies*: prospettive e problemi. *LEA – Lingue e
letterature d'Oriente e d'Occidente*, *2*, 389–402.

Brewin, C. R., Cloitre, M., Hyland, P., Shevlin, M., Maercker, A., Bryant, R.
A., Humayun, A., Jones, L. M., Kagee, A., Rousseau, C., Somasundaram, D.,
Suzuki, Y., Wessely, S., van Ommeren, M., & Reed, G. M. (2017). A review of
current evidence regarding the ICD-11 proposals for diagnosing PTSD and
complex PTSD. *Clinical Psychology Review*, *58*, 1–15.

Brewin, C. R., Dalgleish, T., & Joseph, S. (1996). A dual representation theory of
posttraumatic stress disorder. *Psychological Review*, *103*, 670–686.

Bryant, R. A. (2010). The complexity of complex PTSD. *American Journal of
Psychiatry*, *167*(8), 879–881.

Buckner, R. L., Andrews-Hanna, J. R., & Schacter, D. L. (2008). The brain's
default network: Anatomy, function, and relevance to disease. *Annals of the
New York Academy of Science*, *1124*, 1–38.

Cicchetti, D. (2016). *Developmental psychopathology: Developmental neuroscience*. Hoboken, NJ: John Wiley & Sons, Inc.

Cloitre, M., Garvert, D. W., Brewin, C. R., Bryant, R. A., & Maercker, A. (2013). Evidence for proposed ICD-11 PTSD and complex PTSD: A latent profile analysis. *European Journal of Psychotraumatology, 4*, 1–13.

Copeland, W. E., Keeler, G., Angold, A., & Costello, E. J. (2007). Traumatic events and post-traumatic stress in childhood. *Archives of General Psychiatry, 64*, 577–584.

Dalgleish, T. (1999). Cognitive theories of PTSD. In W. Yule (Ed.), *Post-traumatic stress disorders: Concepts and therapy* (pp. 193–220). Chichester, UK: Wiley.

Dalgleish, T. (2004). Cognitive approaches to posttraumatic stress disorder: The evolution of multirepresentational theorizing. *Psychological Bulletin, 130*, 228–260.

Dass-Brailsford, P. (2007). *A practical approach to trauma: Empowering interventions*. London: Sage Publications.

Ehlers, A., & Clark, D. (2000). A cognitive model of posttraumatic stress disorder. *Behaviour Research and Therapy, 38*, 319–345.

Fiske, S. T., & Linville, P. W. (1980). What does the schema concept buy us? *Personality and Social Psychology Bulletin, 6*, 543–557.

Foa, E. B., & Kozak, M. J. (1986). Emotional processing of fear: Exposure to corrective information. *Psychological Bulletin, 99*, 20–35.

Foa, E. B., Molnar, C., & Cashman, L. (1995). Change in rape narratives during exposure therapy for PTSD. *Journal of Traumatic Stress, 8*, 675–690.

Foa, E. B., & Riggs, D. S. (1993). Posttraumatic stress disorder in rape victims. In J. Oldham, M. B. Riba, & A. Tasman (Eds.), *American psychiatric press review of psychiatry* (Vol. 12, pp. 273–303). Washington, DC: American Psychiatric Press.

Foa, E. B., Steketee, G., & Rothbaum, B. O. (1989). Behavioral/cognitive conceptualization of post-traumatic stress disorder. *Behavior Therapy, 20*, 155–176.

Fonagy, P., & Target, M. (2006). *Psychoanalytic theories: Perspectives from developmental psychopathology*. London: Whurr.

Ford, J. D. (2009). Understanding psychological trauma and posttraumatic stress disorder (PTSD). In J. D. Ford, D. J. Grasso, J. D. Elhai, & C. A. Courtois (Eds.), *Posttraumatic stress disorder* (pp. 1–30). Oxford: Academic Press.

Ford, J. D. (2015). Complex PTSD: Research directions for nosology/assessment, treatment, and public health. *European Journal of Psychotraumatology, 6*, 1–6.

Frewen, P., & Lanius, R. A. (2015). *Healing the traumatized self*. London and New York: W. W. Norton.

Freyd, J. (1994). Betrayal trauma: Traumatic amnesia as an adaptive response to childhood abuse. *Ethics & Behavior, 4*(4), 307–329.

Friedman, M. J. (2013). Finalizing PTSD in DSM-5: Getting here from there and where to go next. *Journal of Traumatic Stress, 26*(5), 548–556.

Herman, J. L. (1992). Complex PTSD: A syndrome in survivors of prolonged and repeated trauma. *Journal of Traumatic Stress, 5*, 377–391.

Holdorff, B. (2011). The fight for 'traumatic neurosis', 1889–1916: Hermann Oppenheim and his opponents in Berlin. *History of Psychiatry, 88*(4), 465–476.

Hooff, M. V., Mcfarlane, A. C., Baur, J., Abraham, M., & Barnes, D. J. (2009). The stressor Criterion-A1 and PTSD: A matter of opinion? *Journal of Anxiety Disorders, 23*(1), 77–86.

Karatzias, T., Murphy, P., Cloitre, M., Bisson, J., Roberts, N., Shevlin, M., Hyland, P., Maercker, A., Ben-Ezra, M., Coventry, P., Mason-Roberts, S., Bradley, A., & Hutton, P. (2019). Psychological interventions for ICD-11 complex PTSD symptoms: Systematic review and meta-analysis. *Psychological Medicine, 49*(11), 1761–1775.

Kessler, R. C., Sonnega, A., Bromet, E., Hughes, M., & Nelson, C. B. (1995). Posttraumatic stress disorder in the national comorbidity survey. *Archives of General Psychiatry, 52*, 1048–1060.

Kim, J. J., & Diamond, D. M. (2002). The stressed hippocampus, synaptic plasticity and lost memories. *Nature Reviews Neuroscience, 3*, 453–462.

Lanius, R. A., Bluhm, R. L., & Frewen, P. A. (2011). How understanding the neurobiology of complex post-traumatic stress disorder can inform clinical practice: A social cognitive and affective neuroscience approach. *Acta Psychiatrica Scandinavica, 124*, 331–348.

Lanius, R. A., Frewen, P. A., Vermetten, E., & Yehuda, R. (2010). Fear conditioning and early life vulnerabilities: Two distinct pathways of emotional dysregulation and brain dysfunction in PTSD. *European Journal of Psychotraumatology, 1*, 5467–5477.

Leys, R. (2000). *Trauma: A genealogy*. Chicago: University of Chicago Press.

Lingiardi, V., & McWilliams, N. (2017). *Psychodynamic diagnostic manual: PDM-2*. New York & London: The Guilford Press.

Mattox, K. L., Moore, E. E., & Feliciano, D. V. (2013). *Trauma*. New York: McGraw Hill.

Mucci, C., Scalabrini, A., & Northoff, G. (2018). Traumatogenic disturbances: PTSD, complex PTSD and trauma-related disorders. In H. Boeker, P. Hartwich, & G. Northoff (Eds.), *Neuropsychodynamic psychiatry*. Cham: Springer.

North, C. S., Suris, A. M., Davis, M., Smith, R. P. (2009). Toward validation of the diagnosis of posttraumatic stress disorder. *American Journal of Psychiatry, 166*, 34–41.

Oppenheim, H. (1889) 1892. *Die traumatischen Neurosen, nach den in der Nervenklinik der Charité in den 8 Jahren 1883–1891 gesammelten Beobachtungen*. Hirschwald.

Ozer, E. J., & Weiss, D. S. (2004). Who develops posttraumatic stress disorder? *Current Directions in Psychological Science, 13*(4), 169–172.

Pai, A., Suris, A., & North, C. (2017). Posttraumatic stress disorder in the DSM-5: Controversy, change, and conceptual considerations. *Behavioral Sciences, 7*(1), 1–7.

Payne, J. D., Nadel, L., Britton, W. B., & Jacobs, W. J. (2004). The biopsychology of trauma and memory. In D. Reisberg & P. Hertel (Eds.), *Memory and emotion* (pp. 76–128). Oxford: Oxford University Press.

Resick, P. A., Bovin, M. J., Calloway, A. L., Dick, A. M., King, M. W., Mitchell, K. S., Suvak, M. K., Wells, S. Y., Stirman, S. W., & Wolf, E. J. (2012). A critical evaluation of the complex PTSD literature: Implications for DSM-5. *Journal of Traumatic Stress, 25*, 241–251.

Resick, P. A., & Miller, M. W. (2009). Posttraumatic stress disorder: Anxiety or traumatic stress disorder? *Journal of Traumatic Stress, 22*, 384–390.

Santiago, P. N., Ursano, R. J., Gray, C. L., Pynoos, R. S., Spiegel, D., Lewis-Fernandez, R., & Fullerton, C. S. (2013). A systematic review of PTSD prevalence and trajectories in DSM-5 defined trauma exposed populations: Intentional and non-intentional traumatic events. *PLoS ONE, 8*(4), e59236.

Sears, R. W., & Chard, K. M. (2016). *Mindfulness-based cognitive therapy for posttraumatic stress disorder.* Chichester, West Sussex, UK: Wiley Blackwell.

Shalev, A. Y. (2002). Acute stress reactions in adults. *Biological Psychiatry, 51*(7), 532–543.

Stanghellini, G. (2009). Trauma. In G. Stanghellini & M. Rossi Monti (Eds.), *Psicologia del patologico: Una prospettiva fenomenologico-dinamica* (pp. 235–262). Milano: Raffaello Cortina.

Stolorow, R. (2007). *Trauma and human existence.* New York: The Analytic Press.

Straus, E. W. (1982). *Man, time, and world: Two contributions to anthropological psychology.* Pittsburgh: Duquesne University Press.

Terr, L. C. (1991). Childhood traumas: An outline and overview. *American Journal of Psychiatry, 148,* 10–20.

Tuval-Mashiach, R., Freedman, S., Bargai, N., Boker, R., Hadar, H., & Shalev, A. Y. (2004). Coping with trauma: Narrative and cognitive perspectives. *Psychiatry: Interpersonal and Biological Processes, 67*(3), 280–293.

Wright, K. J. (1976). Metaphor and symptom: A study of integration and its failure. *International Journal of Psychoanalysis, 3,* 98–106.

Yehuda, R., & LeDoux, J. (2007). Response variation following trauma: A translational neuroscience approach to understanding PTSD. *Neuron, 56*(1), 19–32.

Yehuda, R., & McFarlane, A. C. (1995). Conflict between current knowledge about posttraumatic stress disorder and its original conceptual basis. *American Journal of Psychiatry, 152,* 1705–1713.

Chapter 2

The Concept of *Nachträglichkeit* and the Traumatic Disruption of Linear Time

This chapter moves from Janet's theory of the intertwining between trauma and dissociation, and also analyzes Freud's concept of *Nachträglichkeit*, crucially involved in the psychoanalytical understanding of the temporal dimensions of trauma. Freud's case of Emma shows how *Nachträglichkeit* is the mechanism through which what occurs at a further moment in time can produce a traumatic explosion through a retroactive investment at the time of the original shock. *Nachträglichkeit* refers to the process through which traumatic psychopathology is constituted, in a temporal dimension that has nothing linear nor monodirectional, but resembles a prismatic, multidirectional temporal figure like those depicted by Escher. The original event remains an "asemantic" mnestic trace that is not narratively organized, until a process of "*après-coup*" (the common French translation of *Nachträglichkeit*) emerges and bestows a meaning on it.

Janet's Theory of Trauma and Dissociation and Freud's Concept of Trauma

Pierre Janet (1859–1947) was a central figure in the development of the psychological notion of trauma, which he understood as the cause of psychiatric pathology. Originally, "it was Janet that made the connection between dissociative psychopathology and traumatic experiences" (Putnam, 1989, p. 416). According to Janet ([1889] 2005, 1919), trauma was at the origin of dissociation. Traumatic memory, which the subject cannot comprehend, would contribute to the creation of a system of fixed subconscious ideas (accessible only by hypnosis) that would crucially influence the traumatized person's behavior. In this view, trauma patients would remain unconsciously attached to their trauma, thus arresting the development of their personality at the time of the traumatic occurrence. Janet assigned a central role to environmental trauma arising in the course of affective and cognitive development, which exerts a fragmenting and disorganizing effect on the individual's psyche, and prevents the person from recording a mnestic trace of the event. Traumatic memories,

DOI: 10.4324/9781003230601-3

if repeated during development, or if particularly intense, can then be excluded from the flow of consciousness, and form dissociated secondary personalities (Lingiardi & Mucci, 2014).

In Janet's theory of trauma and dissociation, only a part of the interaction between organism and environment enters consciousness. In adaptive situations, environmental information is automatically integrated on the basis of preexisting knowledge schemas, and integration of memory fragments is the basis of healthy personality. However, when traumatic experiences are not related to preexisting memory systems, they are separated from consciousness, thus becoming pathological fragments of the Self that influence the individual's behavior and mental functioning by weakening and fragmenting it. Of note, this kind of memory cannot be transformed into a coherent narrative. Traumatic memories are split from awareness, and yet continue inevitably to intrude as terrifying perceptions, feelings, or somatic experiences (Van der Kolk, 2007).

Freud (1920) described trauma in terms of a sudden laceration of the "protective shield" of the ego, due to a frightful and sudden experience that the person is not prepared to face. He already thought of trauma as related to the individual's helplessness and unreadiness to face it (Perelberg, 2015). This goes along with an excessive amount of excitation that is not open to representability. The excess of psychic energy caused by strong emotion lies at the core of the removal of the event. Because it is not integrated into consciousness, trauma cannot be remembered verbally; however, its unconscious registration remains stuck in the form of a compulsion to repeat. In this sense, repetition might be "a substitute for memory" (Green, 2007, p. 16), which also affects the person's attachment patterns. This is also why, according to Liotti (2004), trauma, dissociation, and attachment disorganization constitute three aspects of a single psychopathological process.

In their *Studies on Hysteria*, Breuer and Freud (1895) had already embraced the idea of trauma as a consequence of the removal of infantile seduction episodes, advancing the hypothesis of a repression caused not much by a concrete experience of the event, but rather by a later and more conscious *interpretation* of it. The notion of *Nachträglichkeit*, exhibited for the first time in the *Project for a Scientific Psychology* (1895), highlighted the fundamental role of the psychic latency period in the definition of an event as traumatic. Bistoen et al. (2014) argued that the Freudian concept of *Nachträglichkeit* can provide interesting perspectives on both traumatic reactions following non-Criterion A events and delayed-onset of PTSD. Accordingly, it was the fact that "less severe stressors" can cause intense long-term distress that urged Freud to think of the mechanism of *Nachträglichkeit*.

A proper translation of the term *Nachträglichkeit* does not exist in English, yet it might be rendered as "deferred action,"[1] "afterwardsness," "retroactive temporality," "belatedness," "latency," or "retrospective attribution"

(Strachey, 1934), as well as with the French word "*après-coup*" (Lacan, [1953–1954] 2013). These translations of the original Freudian term have long been debated (Eickhoff, 2006). Laplanche and Pontalis ([1967] 1973) drew attention to the fact that the expressions "afterwards," "afterwardsness," and "*après-coup*" are translations open to interpretations that resemble the original meaning of *Nachträglichkeit* (Balsamo, 2009). As Eickhoff (2006) pointed out, "*Nachträglichkeit* provides the memory, not the event, with traumatic significance and signifies a circular complementarity of both directions of time" (p. 1453). Multiple temporal vectors (e.g., retroactivity and after-effect) seem thus to be united in the substantive form coined by Freud. The past is not simply remembered, but *constituted*, that is, *formed* in the "here and now." As a result, it will only become what it will always have been in the future, that is, a "future anterior" (Lacan, 1981).

Freud believed that hysterical symptoms were caused by a psychic trauma that followed an earlier traumatic event. The notion of *Nachträglichkeit* implies that the initial event only exerts its full pathogenic power at a later developmental stage, when it is revived by a subsequent encounter. *Nachträglichkeit* refers to the process through which traumatic psychopathology is constituted, and involves (at least) *two* etiological moments rather than one. Therefore, it is not the event *per se* that causes the traumatic symptoms, but the way in which the individual perceives it and reacts to it. Ultimately, memory can "cause" trauma in a way that actual experience may not (Mather & Marsden, 2004).

The Case of Emma and *Nachträglichkeit*

Freud's case of Emma (Freud, 1895) shows how the experience of trauma is intrinsically bounded by memory processes. Emma Eckstein was a Viennese woman who sought out Freud's help when she was 27. She was subject to a compulsion that did not allow her go into shops alone. As Freud (1895) stated, once

> she went into a shop to buy something, saw the two shop-assistants (one of whom she can remember) laughing together, and ran away in some kind of *affect of fright*. In connection with this, she was led to recall that the two of them were laughing at her clothes and that one of them had pleased her sexually.
>
> (p. 353)

Further investigation revealed a second memory that was chronologically prior to the first:

> [O]n two occasions when she was a child of eight she had gone into a small shop to buy some sweets, and the shopkeeper had grabbed her

genitals through her clothes. In spite of the first experience she had gone there a second time; after the second time she stopped away.

(p. 354)

Freud (1895) concluded that the laughing of the shop assistant in the second encounter had unconsciously activated the grin of the shopkeeper who touched Emma in the first place. This reviving of the older scene produced a *sexual release* that was transformed into *anxiety*. Curiously, the only element of the older scene that reached Emma's consciousness was her clothing. The assault in its very nature was thus replaced by a "symbol" (Neyraut, 1997). In this case, according to Freud, one is faced with a case of a memory producing an affect that did not arise as an experience, because the developmental change brought about later on had made possible a different understanding of Emma's memory. The astonishing idea that Freud (1895) put forward is that "a memory is repressed which has only become a trauma by *deferred action* [*nachträglich*]" (p. 356). This scenario changes the commonly understood relationship between trauma and memory in such a way that one might conclude that the memory of the sexual assault *becomes* traumatic because of a change that occurs only during later developmental periods, that is, only as a "re-transcription of memorial content" (Mather & Marsden, 2004, p. 210).

Because of its relation to temporality and causal relationships, Blum (1996) proposed that *Nachträglichkeit* can be regarded "as an unrecognized precursor of the contemporary concept of developmental transformation" (p. 1155). However, more than considering, as Blum (1996) argued, that "deferred action then occurred when an unconscious memory of seduction was revived and altered after puberty" (p. 1152), *Nachträglichkeit* points to the fact that the original wound is *created* only in the form of the *après-coup*, that is, it is *constituted* in consciousness *as* trauma. Therefore, the so-called primal event is such only in conjunction with another event, and becomes an "event" only in this connection. The further event might be regarded as the "*agent provocateur*" of the traumaticity of the original occurrence (Bistoen et al., 2014). Indeed, the case of Emma points to the necessity of thinking of

> (a) two distinct etiological moments in time, (b) separated by a delay or time lag, (c) in which the first scene initially remains without consequence, (d) but is transformed by the subsequent one, and (e) becoming traumatic in a retroactive fashion.
>
> (p. 674)

The moment of the original event, as classically understood, chronologically precedes the traumatic symptoms, and can only be identified *retrospectively*. Freud's (1895) capital discovery is that the psychopathological power of the latter scene derives from a former experience that did not become consciously traumatic until the latter episode occurred. As Bistoen et al. (2014) pointed out, in the symbolic realization of the trauma, *it is the memory that becomes traumatic, not the event itself.* In this sense, *Nachträglichkeit* can be regarded as a mechanism that alters the subjective experience of the past, and results in a modification of the present (Friedman et al., 2011). Notably, this is why "deferred action" is not the most appropriate translation of *Nachträglichkeit*, because it conveys a sense of linearity of the temporal unfolding of experience. Our conception of time in terms of a monodimensional duration (that of succession and diachrony) is thus destroyed. As opposed to the ordinary understanding of the temporal unfolding of consciousness, Freud's notion of *Nachträglichkeit* posits that what occurs at a later time becomes "explosive" only through a retroactive investment of the original moment.

Nachträglichkeit presupposes that the effects of a potentially traumatic event need to wait for a further event to become manifest. The belated onset of traumatic psychopathology does not occur at random, but seems to be *logically determined* (Bistoen et al., 2014). Certain traumatic occurrences may wait for a long time before encountering another event that is actually reminiscent of them, bringing them to the forefront. Although *Nachträglichkeit* posits that trauma is constituted in (at least) two different moments, it is not entirely correct to say that the further episode triggers an earlier latent trauma that has already been suffered. It is only at a later time that the initial event is *rendered* traumatic, wounding the subject for the very first time. The notion of *Nachträglichkeit* suggests that the traumatic event elicits the *constitution* of a traumatic memory, rather than reviving an old wound that was *already* constituted.

The issue remains as to why the revival of the memory of the first scene produces traumatic psychopathology, when the experience, itself, did not. The concept of *Nachträglichkeit* helps to formulate an answer. According to Freud, the first experience was somehow "missed" by the subject, and belatedly experienced by a subject who had undergone significant changes in terms of developmental (sexual) achievements. In other words, the first experience was not lived *as such* when it occurred in the first place. Caruth (1995) contended that the traumatogenic potential of this kind of stress is situated neither in the first event nor in the second one, but in the *gap* between the two. This is why the initial absence of signification does not directly lead to psychopathology; instead, it is its belated understanding that triggers traumatic symptomatology. The original distressing event cannot be understood because the subject lacks the symbolic means for it. The event, however, leaves behind a mnestic trace, but this remains "mute," as it is not yet associated with other elements that can confer meaning to it (Caruth, 1995).

It is only in the concatenation of a *signifying chain* that an element can receive temporal signification. The first experience is retained in a very specific fashion, because it is not accessible for conscious recollection. As long as the second scene cannot be signified and associated with further elements, it cannot be subjectively lived; that is to say, it remains "a-subjective." Due to the failure to give a meaning to the event and to realize what has just happened, the subject is confined "outside" the event, which remains an "unclaimed experience," to use Caruth's (1996) words. Indeed, the event can be said not to be experienced subjectively at the time of its "objective" occurrence, as if the initial experience opened up a "question" to which only a second event can provide an "answer" (Lacan, [1957] 2006).

As time passes, the person acquires the keys to unlock the enigma of the original scene, which results in the realization of the initial scene. Here, "realization" refers to the fact that the new experience is what makes possible to understand the elements that the subject had missed in the initial experience. It is only at the time of the further experience that the trauma begins to be lived as a new subjective experience. Therefore, as it were, both *experiences happen simultaneously* when the trauma is eventually signified. It is at this moment, the moment of *realization*, that the memory of the original event becomes traumatic.

It is now clear why the traumatized person does not carry a wound that waits to be rendered explicit. On the contrary, the subject *becomes* wounded only at the moment of its symbolic realization, that is, when the wound acquires *significance*. What matters here is not the past as such, but the way it is experienced in the "here and now," when the subject is finally able to bestow meaning on it after a further event has rendered the initial scene meaningful. To conclude, the initial absence of meaning, that is, the event as not yet understood in its meaning, is "distressing" but not "traumatic" in nature (Bistoen et al., 2014). Only at a later time the subjective experience of the event does begin. In this view, trauma may be conceptualized as a failure to "close" or to "finish" the event. The truth about the original event, which is constituted at a later stage, is not reconcilable with the views of the Self and the world as previously constituted. It is an "unbearable truth," something that cannot be born to reality (Bistoen et al., 2014).

As to Emma's experience, Stanghellini (2009) regarded the original encounter as "traumatic," the latter as "traumatogenic." The case of Emma seems to point to a condition where what is received into memory is a collection of bodily, non-verbal, and implicit experiences specifically lacking a semantic connotation, which will be taken on when a second event *will make* the first event *actual*. Only *in retrospect*, then, the original event can be defined *as* traumatic. The sense of trauma is the result, as it were, of a "deferred" binding between the original incident, which remains with no semantic explicit inscription, and a further event that would not be traumatic in and of itself, but is traumatogenic because it draws from the first event and aids in writing its meaning.

The original occurrence remains an "asemantic" mnestic trace that is not narratively organized. It is an encounter that will not be integrated into a coherent narrative until a further event allows the former to *become present*, allowing the person to grasp its semantic connotation digging in the horizon of meanings available in his or her world. It is as if the further event "write a caption" (Stanghellini, 2009, p. 244) below the image of the original one. The traumatic occurrence is not simply placed in a remote time. The traumaticity of the first event remains somehow hidden until a further event makes its entry on the stage, giving it a sense and a meaning. To use Emmanuel Lévinas's (1906–1995) words, trauma is the result of a "rebellious diachrony" (Lévinas, [1974] 1981), meaning that the temporality of trauma is not linear (past to present, present to future). In traumatic situations, it is this present situation that gives sense to a past that would be otherwise compelled to remain latent in its traumaticity (Swain, 1985).

Wo Es war, soll Ich werden: The Fate of Subjectivity

Freud seemed to entrust not only the means but also the scope of analysis to the famous sentence "*wo Es war, soll Ich werden*," whose structure contains a double opposition, that is, "*Es/Ich*" and "*war/werden*." Here, as Perrella (2015) pointed out, the neutral subject ought to be replaced with the real subject, identified as *Ich*. The ego, in this case, is assumed as the subject of the feedback that recognizes itself *as* itself. *Ich werden* should therefore be understood in the sense of a process of *becoming oneself*, and this becoming is assigned to the ego as an ethical task – *soll*, that is, "should" in the ethical sense (Perrella, 2015, p. 161). Therefore, where there was *Es*, the indeterminate subject must establish the determining subject (*Ich*). The reality of the ego lies precisely in its becoming, which is a temporal process in nature: "I must (*Ich soll*) become I (*Ich werden*)." The ego (the subject in its temporal becoming) is here assumed in its fundamental duality, that is, as the subject of the task and as the object of becoming. The ego must separate itself from itself, recognizing the split within it, in order to become – to produce – itself where there was the *Es*. In producing itself in the place of "having been," the ego assumes upon itself the ethical task of becoming (becoming primarily itself), that is, becoming what it has already been – in Nietzsche's words, to "become what one is."

The relevance of the Freudian sentence lies in the temporal structure that characterizes it, that is, between the "*war*" of a being that no longer is, and a "*soll werden*" of the Self that becomes itself. This is a way of conceiving time that is radically different from the one that character-izes the classical reasoning laws, supported by the principle of sufficient reason (or principle of causality). As a result, it is no longer possible to think of time as isomorphic to the concept of causality, that is, as absolute, linear, and monodirectional. In traumatic experience, the time spent between the initial event and the event through which the subject interprets the original occurrence as traumatic does not exist from the historical or biographical point of view, that is, it is a "null time" (Per-rella, 2015).

Trauma is considered contemporary to the event that re-presents it, over and over again. Now, time, as such, divides the subject (Lacan, [1973] 2004). Indeed, the subject at the time of the original event is not the same as the subject at the time of the traumatogenic explosion. However, in trauma, the subject at the second time keeps on feeling as the subject of the first time. This experience is based on the unconscious responses of the subject to the traumatogenic event – and the unconscious mind, as Freud wanted, is out of time. In the symbolic realization of the trauma, the arrow of time ceases to be identified with the univocal and monodirectional causality of the reasoning principle. Instead, the future becomes linked to the past, which is such only as a *retroaction* (or acting backward) of the present. Without the consideration of time as an area of subjective redetermination of the past, that is, without the possibility of making the past a "future anterior" (Lacan, 1981), the phenomenon of trauma remains with no explanation.

Memory might be thought of as the projection of the free invention of a past produced by subjectivity. Memory does not contain a mere sum of traces, but is rather a moment of the subjective act that is represented as a movement in time. The past is never determined once and for all, but is always exposed to redetermination by means of subjective acts of life. That is to say, the past never remains identical, but is *produced* together with the present as a feedback or retroaction of the latter on the for-mer. Past, present, and future are the three "hypostases" of time, without which time could not be given, just as space could not be given without the three dimensions of width, height, and depth.

The concept of delayed gratification is supposed to play a crucial role in psychic functioning and growth of the Self (Singer, 1955). The child's capacity to delay gratification tends to increase with age (Atance & Jack-son, 2009). In psychoanalytic thinking, the frustration generated by the absence of the desired object is supposed to go hand in hand with the sense of time, that is, with the child's ability to anticipate the return of the object. Accordingly, the inability to wait for the absent needed object results in a sense of *timelessness*. In contrast with the instantaneous wish-fulfillment and the immediate gratification of unwanted emotions stands the traumatized individual's capacity to tolerate unwanted feelings until the capacity to stay with previously intolerable emotional states emerges. Along with this process, a notion of development is produced, as the latter is associated with the resignification of life events. By tolerating time passing, the individual becomes able to hold opposed emotional states, where experience is not fragmented but rather unified in a coherent narrative (Omer & Alon, 1997).

Traumatic experiences are based on a *contrast of temporalities* (Sabbadini, 1989a, 1989b), which brings about two distinct elements, repetition and irreversibility, that is, time as inevitably leading to loss and death. Hatred, one of the most common emotions that trauma patients deal with, grows along with the suppression of retroactive time. Yet this same suppression is associated with resignification, because "retroactive resignification *is* developmental progression" (Birksted-Breen, 2003, p. 1509). Therefore, the forward movement goes along with the backward movement; similarly, the movement of going back necessitates the movement of moving forward. For the traumatized individual, the temporal progression is disrupted, as there is no longer room for a past that can be processed, nor for a future entailing hope. The past becomes a mere collection of instants and the future is eradicated, as the individual is unable to formulate prospective plans. When associative elements of time are disrupted, isolation comes to the forefront. What is severed is especially the relationship between past and future, that is, the connection between the temporal dimensions of human existence. Instead of using therapy as an opportunity for emotional growth, trauma patients become stuck in time, which seems then to stop. The resignification and the forward movement, which accompany the disruption of linear time, are hindered, so the entire person's life is disaggregated into separated moments (Birksted-Breen, 2003).

Time is intimately connected to the wholeness of the person's biography, and to the forward movement of resignification of past through the "here and now." The disruption of this binding process amounts to a temporal disruption. This corresponds to the "shattered time" (Green, 2002, p. 1) that characterizes dreams, where everything appears as happening in the present moment. The emphasis on *Nachträglichkeit* reintroduces the concept of temporality by unifying disparate elements, both retrospective and progressive, into a coherent narrative. Ultimately, it is not by dismantling the development of meaning that patients can fight off their trauma, but rather by finding a meaning that brings together all traumatic temporal dimensions.

It is now clear why charting the characteristics of the (traumatic) situation itself cannot predict its subjective outcome. On the contrary, it is rather the focus on subjectivity as a whole (and as embedded in its environment) that allows for an understanding of why an event *becomes* traumatic for the person. The concept of *Nachträglichkeit* offers valuable means to understand why the impact of a situation on the subject cannot be predicted a priori, but is always unique and based on the particular interaction between the person and his or her environment. Furthermore, the subjective impact of a situation is never given once and for all, but is subject to subsequent alterations through the ascription of new meanings to it. In other words, the traumatic resignification constituted in further moments in time is not the ultimate signification, but is subject to modification through the addition of new, subsequent elements in the subject's personal narrative. Trauma can thus be understood as an element that shatters the person's understanding of others, the world, and his or her Self.

Nachträglichkeit and the "après-coup"

Nachträglichkeit points to the fact that a traumatic event is always constituted by an event *and* a subject, and can never be understood in isolation. Understanding traumatic reactions requires examining where the traumatic situation is situated in the person's life, and how it affects the individual's knowledge and expectations about others, the world, and him- or herself. The demand that traumatic suffering be validated as "real" raises ontological questions that cannot be answered looking at external "facts" only. As Bistoen et al. (2014) put it, "trauma confronts us with the unimaginable and the uncontrollable. . . . The Real is never where it is expected, and the place where it does arise is of a highly subjective and singular determination" (p. 682).

In Freud's works, the term *Nachträglichkeit* rarely (if ever) involves a retroactive power of the unconscious mind, as it is in the case of the French *après-coup* (Laplanche & Pontalis, [1967] 1973).[2] In its French translation as "*après-coup*," which has become extremely common in psychoanalytical literature, the concept of *Nachträglichkeit* appears as a two-faced herm, which constitutes itself as a moment that is simultaneously traumatic ("*coup*") *and* transforming, through a meaning that appears later ("*après*"). The *après-coup* exhibits the role of psychic latency in the definition of the traumaticity of an event, and refers to the atemporality of the Freudian unconscious mind, which ignores contradiction (André, 2008). The *après-coup* condenses in a single braid two movements apparently excluded in ordinary logic, that is, the simultaneity of past and present – and vice versa. Moreover, the *après-coup* refers to the retranscription of a content that was previously not cathected in its symbolic significance. It unifies the sedimentation of a mnestic trace, on the one hand, and a re-elaboration mechanism on the other.

André (2008) spoke in this regard of a "retrospective ascription of meaning in the sense of looking back *a posteriori* as a moment of reorganization of personal meanings in the light of later events" (p. 496). According to Birksted-Breen (2003), the reason why Freud used the same term to refer to progressive and retrospective time is precisely that there is no clear demarcation between the two, because the two temporalities (developmental and *après-coup*), while seemingly so different, in fact go together. According to Benvenuto (2018), the *après-coup* is "one of the symptoms of psychoanalysis, a point in which it reveals itself and at the same time suffers itself" (p. 72). The *après-coup* repeats *and* transforms at the same time. This is why it is different from the pure repetition compulsion, where the psyche is victim of a self-destruction. Gostecnik (1997) regarded repetition as

> a method for achieving a new solution to an old problem. In other words, the reincarnation and reactivation of the old, archaic experience in a new environment and different interrelational matrix can be conceptualized as *Chronos*; the time of prolonged suffering before the "appointed time" of salvation as *Kairos*.[3]
>
> (p. 57)

The *après-coup* generates a "*coup*" that does not exist without the "*après.*" In fact, there is no "*après*" without a "*coup*", and there is no "*coup*" without "*après.*" In this view, the violence of the trauma and the openness to its sense and meaning go hand in hand. The paradox of the *après-coup* is that at the beginning there is an "after," as in the well-known rhetoric figure of the *hysteron proteron*, where what comes "later" actually comes "before." In fact, the *après-coup* is "a moment of truth" (André, 2008, p. 477), a "passage" from trauma to significance, from repetition to reminiscence, from silence to narration. Only in a further moment what is not thinkable is realized (retrospectively) in a two-faced process, where perception and representation feature as the main characters (Mangini, 2015). In this perspective, every mnestic trace is constituted through a process of *après-coup*, which is an anti-traumatic psychic mechanism through which the *sense* of an event confers causal power to a preceding occurrence (André, 2008).

Human thinking does not proceed by juxtaposition of levels but, on the contrary, continually seeks to find dynamic points of integration between different ways of looking at phenomena. In fact, it is precisely from these points of intersection that a new understanding can stem, giving rise to a meaning that always arises in the form of *après-coup* (Scoppola, 2011). According to Sandler (1994), it is crucial that the psychoanalyst give absolute priority to the understanding, and possibly interpreting, what happens at the moment of analysis. In this sense, psychoanalysis is based on the "here and now." On the other hand, however, working on the "here and now" involves a more complex temporality, based on the Freudian notion of *Nachträglichkeit*. In fact, the "here and now" makes sense only inasmuch as it contemplates the ambiguity of the multiple directions of temporality. When psychoanalysis emphasizes that only the present is knowable, one must nonetheless acknowledge that the present stands in a complex relationship with the actual past. In the analytic session, a past is given new meaning through a retrospective attribution, that is, through a process of *après-coup* (Birksted-Breen, 2003). As Benvenuto stated in 1989 in his conversation with Laplanche in Paris, "*[a]nalysis then is not so much the reminiscing reconstruction of a web of past traumas, but instead a sort of education towards new languages for relations.*"

Notes

1. For a critique of this translation, see Sodré (1997).
2. There are three usages of the term *après-coup*. The first one means just "later." The second one implies a movement from past to future ("deferred action"), that is, something is deposited in the individual but becomes active only at a later time. The third meaning implies that something is somehow perceived, but it only takes on meaning "retrospectively."
3. For the distinction between core "repetition" and "repetition compulsion," see Holowchak and Lavin (2015).

References

André, J. (2008). L'après-coup nella teoria e nella clinica. *Psicoterapia e Scienze Umane, 42*(4), 471–498.

Atance, C. M., & Jackson, L. K. (2009). The development and coherence of future-oriented behaviors during the preschool years. *Journal of Experimental Child Psychology, 102*, 379–391.

Balsamo, M. (2009). *Forme dell'après-coup*. Roma-Milano: Franco Angeli.

Benvenuto, S. (1989). Après Coup. Retroactive Memory. A Conversation with Jean-Bertrand Pontalis. 13 October 1989, Paris. *European Journal of Psychoanalysis*.

Benvenuto, S. (2018). The après-coup, après coup. *Language and Psychoanalysis, 7*(2), 72–87.

Birksted-Breen, D. (2003). Time and the après-coup. *International Journal of Psychoanalysis, 84*(6), 1501–1515.

Bistoen, G., Vanheule, S., & Craps, S. (2014). *Nachträglichkeit*: A Freudian perspective on delayed traumatic reactions. *Theory & Psychology, 24*(5), 668–687.

Blum, H. P. (1996). Seduction trauma: Representation, deferred action, and pathogenic development. *Journal of the American Psychoanalytic Association, 44*(4), 1147–1164.

Breuer, J., & Freud, S. (1895). Studies on hysteria. In J. Strachey (Ed.), *The standard edition of the complete psychological works of Sigmund Freud* (Vol. 2). London: Hogarth Press.

Caruth, C. (1995). *Trauma: Explorations in memory*. Baltimore: Johns Hopkins University Press.

Caruth, C. (1996). *Unclaimed experience: Trauma, narrative, and history*. Baltimore: Johns Hopkins University Press.

Eickhoff, F. (2006). On *Nachträglichkeit*: The modernity of an old concept. *The International Journal of Psychoanalysis, 87*(6), 1453–1469.

Freud. S. (1895). Project for a scientific psychology. In J. Strachey (Ed.), *The standard edition of the complete psychological works of Sigmund Freud* (Vol. 1, pp. 283–397). London: Hogarth Press.

Freud, S. (1920). Beyond the pleasure principle. In J. Strachey (Ed.), *The standard edition of the complete psychological works of Sigmund Freud* (Vol. 18, pp. 7–64). London: Hogarth Press.

Friedman, M., Resick, P., Bryant, R., & Brewin, C. (2011). Considering PTSD for DSM-5. *Depression and Anxiety, 28,* 750–769.

Gostecnik, C. (1997). Chronos versus kairos in psychotherapy. *American Journal of Pastoral Counseling, 1*(1), 49–60.

Green, A. (2002). *Time in psychoanalysis: Some contradictory aspects.* London: Free Association Books.

Green, A. (2007). The construction of heterochrony. In R. J. Perelberg (Ed.), *Time and memory* (pp. 1–21). London: Karnac Books.

Holowchak, M. A., & Lavin, M. (2015). Beyond the death drive: The future of "repetition" and "compulsion to repeat" in psychopathology. *Psychoanalytic Psychology, 32*(4), 645–668.

Janet, P. (1919). *Les medications psychologiques: Etudes historiques, psychologiques et cliniques sur les methodes de la psychotherapie.* Paris: Felix Alcan.

Janet, P. (1889) 2005. *L'automatisme psychologique: Essai de psychologie expérimentale sur les formes inférieures de lactivité humaine.* Paris: L. Harmattan.

Lacan, J. (1981). *The language of the self: The function of language in psychoanalysis.* Baltimore: Johns Hopkins University Press.

Lacan, J. (1973) 2004. *The four fundamental concepts of psycho-analysis.* London: Karnac Books.

Lacan, J. (1957) 2006. The instance of the letter in the unconscious or reason since Freud. In B. Fink (Ed.), *Ecrits: The first complete edition in English* (pp. 412–442). New York: W. W. Norton.

Lacan, J. (1953–1954) 2013. *Seminar: Book I. Freud's papers on technique.* New York: W. W. Norton.

Laplanche, J., & Pontalis, J.-B. (1967) 1973. *The language of psychoanalysis.* London: Hogarth Press.

Lévinas, E. (1974) 1981. *Otherwise than being or beyond essence.* Nijhoff: The Hague.

Lingiardi, V., & Mucci, C. (2014). Da Janet a Bromberg, passando per Ferenczi. *Psichiatria e Psicoterapia, 33*(1), 41–62.

Liotti, G. (2004). Trauma, dissociation, and disorganized attachment: Three strands of a single braid. *Psychotherapy: Theory, Research, Practice, Training, 41*(4), 472–486.

Mangini, E. (2015). *Elementi dell'esperienza psicoanalitica: Pulsione, immagine, parola poetica.* Milano: Cortina Edizioni.

Mather, R., & Marsden, J. (2004). Trauma and temporality. *Theory & Psychology, 14*(2), 205–219.

Neyraut, M. (1997). *Les raisons de l'irrationnel.* France: Presses Universitaires de France.

Omer, A., & Alon, A. (1997). *Constructing therapeutic narratives.* New York: Jason Aronson.

Perelberg, R. J. (2015). On excess, trauma and helplessness: Repetitions and transformations. *International Journal of Psycho-Analysis*, 96(6), 1453–1476.

Perrella, E. (2015). *Il tempo etico. La ragione freudiana* (Vol. I). Ariccia: Aracne.

Putnam, F. W. (1989). Pierre Janet and modern views of dissociation. *Journal of traumatic stress*, 2, 413–429.

Sabbadini, A. (1989a). Boundaries of timelessness. Some thoughts about the temporal dimension of the psychoanalytic space. *International Journal of Psycho-Analysis*, 70, 305–313.

Sabbadini, A. (1989b). How the infant develops a sense of time. *British Journal of Psychotherapy*, 5(4), 475–484.

Sandler, J. (1994). Fantasy, defense, and the representational world. *Infant Mental Health Journal*, 15, 26–35.

Scoppola, L. (2011). *La parola non trovata. Mente, corpo, istituzione.* Milano: Franco Angeli Editore.

Singer, J. L. (1955). Delayed gratification and ego development: Implications for clinical and experimental research. *Journal of Consulting Psychology*, 19(4), 259–266.

Sodré, I. (1997). Insight et après-coup. *Revue française de psychanalyse*, 61(3), 1255.

Stanghellini, G. (2009). Trauma. In G. Stanghellini & M. Rossi Monti (Eds.), *Psicologia del patologico: Una prospettiva fenomenologico-dinamica* (pp. 235–262). Milano: Raffaello Cortina.

Strachey, J. (1934). The nature of the therapeutic action of psycho-analysis. *International Journal of Psychoanalysis*, 15, 127–159.

Swain, G. (1985). De la marque de l'événement à la rencontre interieure. Images populaires et conceptions savantesen psychopathologie. In J. Guyotat & P. Fedida (Eds.), *Evenement et psychopathologie*. Villeurbanne: SIMEP.

Van der Kolk, B. A. (2007). The history of trauma in psychiatry. In M. J. Friedman, T. M. Keane, & P. A. Resick (Eds.), *Handbook of PTSD: Science in practice* (pp. 19–36). New York: The Guilford Press.

Chapter 3

Time, Trauma, and the Unconscious Mind

This chapter deals with the timelessness of the unconscious mind, which has long been debated in both phenomenology and psychoanalysis. The temporal tension between lived time and timelessness is one of the core features of human existence. According to Freud, our unconscious mind has no temporal limitations whatsoever, no existence but outside time, and no conception of death. More contemporary theories focus instead on the multidimensional features of the temporality of human unconscious existence. "Chronestesia," our conscious representation of time, is achieved at late stages in human development, and seems to be produced within the dialectic between need and wish-fulfillment. Traumatic psychopathology is associated with a sense of timelessness, where consciousness becomes stuck in an eternal compulsion to repeat, leaving no room for the past to be processed, nor for future plans to be conceived.

Timelessness and the Unconscious Mind

The unconscious dimension of the human mind has long been a matter of debate in the dialogue between phenomenology and psychoanalysis (Legrand & Trigg, 2017). According to Freud (1915), the unconscious mind is timeless: "the processes of the system Ucs [Unconscious] are *timeless*, i.e., they are not ordered temporally, are not altered by the passage of time; they have no reference to time at all" (p. 187). The unconscious mind "seems to occupy a quantum universe in which all time is simultaneous and consequently reversible" (Roberts, 2003, p. 206). The parallelism between time and consciousness allowed Bonaparte (1940) to conclude that when consciousness awakens, then time arises as well. The consequence of the aforementioned parallelism is that time and its properties are to be found in consciousness rather than outside the individual. According to Bonaparte (1940), there are several interpretations of Freud's statement that the unconscious mind is timeless. First, it might mean that the unconscious mind has no "knowledge" of time. Yet this seems more like a truism, because the unconscious mind knows nothing

DOI: 10.4324/9781003230601-4

about any concept, not to speak of the concept of time. Second, the statement might imply that the unconscious mind, although unaffected by time, is not subject to its jurisdiction. In this view, human unconscious mind might in fact bear temporal properties that are different from those of conscious awareness. Like the world submersed by the ashes of the Vesuvius, the unconscious mind might keep track of events in a unique fashion, that is, as an underground world where nothing remains the same. But even this explanation encounters a problem: on the one hand, our primitive and instinctual heritage seems to remain unchanged over time; on the other hand, these same impulses might undergo some modifications. A final meaning to be taken into account as to Freud's statement that the unconscious mind is timelessness is that the latter might fail to "perceive" time, that is, cannot have any notice of it whatsoever. As in our dreams, past and present seem intertwined, and traces of past events are intermingled with actual situations. If development is a lifelong process, then subjective time sense can be understood as an "amalgam of past temporal conceptualizations, current developmental themes, and environmental influences" (Colarusso, 1998, p. 113).

Von Franz (1966) pointed out that human impulses, wishes, perception, and thoughts can be unconscious, but this does not justify the reification of something as "the" Unconscious. However, it ought to be observed that unconscious (i.e., forgotten) contents can undergo specific transformations during their underground existence. Therefore, the unconscious mind seems to be a "psychism sui generis" (Von Franz, 1966, p. 219), which is likely to work differently from our conscious mind. This kind of psychism, which we call "the" Unconscious, also surfaces in awakened states by interrupting the continuity of conscious mental operations, and during sleep in the form of dreams. During dreams, the regularity and discernibility of time becomes confused, and it is only afterward, in awakened states, that the individual can place events in a temporal order. Because unconscious processes contain no notion of time as succession or duration, only analysis and interpretation make them to a continuum (Von Franz, 1966).

Saying that the unconscious mind is timeless means therefore that it has no temporal limitations whatsoever, no existence but outside time, and no conception of death. This property of the unconscious mind is consistent with its characteristic of being a "realm of pure wish-fulfillment" (Gifford, 1980, p. 133), from which negation and contradiction are ruled out. Timelessness is manifested not only in dreams, but also in specific conditions like falling in love with someone (Bonaparte, 1940), as the lover's emotional state resembles the unity of mother and infant. The denial of time passing is intrinsic to resistance to change, and also to development. Research conducted by Gifford (1960) showed that babies gradually adapt to a 24-hour day–night periodicity, when a sense of rhythm takes place as a part of the earliest development of ego functioning. This adaptation is mediated by the relationship with the mother, which might also underlie the early development of the ability to differentiate present from future. Piaget ([1927] 2007) used to think that only humans are able to conceptualize time and, more specifically, future dimensions. Indeed, only at about 12 years of age does the child show the capacity to form abstract concepts of time. Time sense is possibly the last skill human beings acquire throughout their (phylogenetical and ontogenetical) development.

Time, Existence, and Ego Development

Infants live in time before being aware of what time actually is (Droit-Volet et al., 2007). According to Piaget ([1937] 1954), along with the development of sensorimotor activity, a feeling of "efficacy" develops, which refers to the children's ability to realize that their action is effective in getting them what they want. What is then established is the conscious awareness of activity as a way to set up a causal relationship between the child's desires and their fulfillment. As a result, the child becomes aware of a sort of primitive object constancy, which is the precursor of the experience of duration and represents the most elementary sense of time, that is, what Tulving (2002) called "chronestesia."

The concept of time also emerges from "primary narcissism," that is, the immediate discharge of the infant's needs and the equally immediate satisfaction of them (Abraham, 1976). Here, the present is repetitive and undifferentiated, and begins to differentiate as the infant starts *waiting* for its needs to be satisfied. In other words, the initial lack of differentiation between mother and child is reflected in the infant's perception of time as omnipresent. Developmentally, when the ego and the non-ego start differentiating, the concept of time also arises (Bonaparte, 1940). The intrusion of time occurs when the fusion between mother and child is disrupted. The substance of time becomes then founded in the frustration due to the mother's intermittent availability. Therefore, "the present tense is the one in which wishes are represented as fulfilled" (Freud, 1900, p. 535). Only after two years of life the child becomes able to understand what is "not now," that is, "soon" or "later" (Arlow, 1986). Children of this age experience time in terms of how long it takes to perform a specific action. Gradually, children are able to transpose temporal properties to objects instead of their own needs. At the age of five or six, children learn that a single time continuum exists separately from individual actions. The awareness of time as such develops as do children's attention and short-term memory capacities, along with the slow maturation of the prefrontal cortex.

According to Piaget (1966), "time appears as a relationship" (p. 214). The notion of time seems to be comprised of two different concepts: succession (temporal order) and duration (temporal length). In this view, three logical operations characterize the developing child: the ordering of events, the classification of durations, and the measurement of time. The third operation implies coordination between the first two. It is indeed the third operation that allows the child to start counting. At the age of eight, children start counting time on their own, but it is not until the age of ten that children start counting time regularly and with no input from adults (Piaget, 1966). On the basis of the maturation of this ability, Cohen (1966) proposed that "subjective time" (time as it is perceived by the individual) parallels "objective time" (the ticking of the clock). As a result, a model of the mechanism for measuring time is generated, which resembles a biological "internal clock." It seems that the emergence of the concept of time in children results from the interaction between the child's private rhythmic experiences and the rhythm of external forces (Mann, 1982). As to the temporal dimensions of the child's development, a sense of past, present, and future stems from a hunger-feeding satisfaction sequence, which requires an adequate mother–child relationship. Indeed, "the awareness of time arises when the pleasurable, in other words 'timeless' satiation of the infant is interrupted by the first 'need' through the feeling of hunger. Thus, the first feeling of hunger writes the first diagram of time" (Orgel, 1965, p. 103).

Time represents realistic "necessity" (Harnik, 1925). The infant's ego is not sufficiently developed to conceptualize a sense of time, but it nonetheless has enough awareness of the external world to register a primitive relationship between frustration and satisfaction, and therefore a sense of *"the time it takes to move from one state to the other"* (Colarusso, 1979, p. 245). This is why the sense of time is inescapably associated with early nurturing and emotional processing associated with it. However, it is not until a sense of the Self as a unified whole emerges that the concept of time can be formulated (Seton, 1974). Interference with early time adaptation might lead to behavioral disturbances later in life (Meerloo, 1966). The wish of "killing time" is associated with a disavowal of the need for the object (Williams, 2007). Overall, the development of a sense of reality rests upon the perceived sequence of the person's life events, and the later acquisition of real time sense is linked to past experiences. It is in this sense that time represents the "reality principle," where finite time is the "father," and infinite time, or immortality, is the "mother" (Arlow, 1986): Father Time is "the master of life and death" (p. 524).

The same struggle against time is repeated as the superego develops. In other words, the struggle against time is represented by the struggle against the superego demands. The past continues to exist in the unconscious mind of an individual at every moment of his or her life. In turn, time, as well as its unconscious meaning, constantly accompanies the here and now of an individual, that is, the conglomerate of past, present, and future that shape human temporality. As a result, if one can eliminate the sense of time, then one can get rid of death. As Bonaparte (1940) noted, life is marked by a double attitude toward time. On the one hand, individuals are overwhelmed by the infinite time governing the outside world. On the other hand, individuals are likewise overwhelmed by the finitude of their limited existence of the short life span they must accept.

The temporal tension between lived time and timelessness is one of the core features of human existence (Loewald, 1972). Individuals struggle to hold the temporal dimensions with a large view, but they continually suffer because of the transience of their temporal existence. This suffering is often reflected in human fascination with time, which sheds light on one of the deepest mysteries of human existence. Time is constantly out of control, because it allows growth and development and yet it restricts human life. Human beings unsuccessfully attempt to transcend time. Torres (2007) elaborated on the idea that time has always eluded the human willingness to know it, classify it, and impose boundaries on it. The author stressed the manifold of temporal expressions, which can be understood as (a) objective, (b) body-related, and (c) intrapsychic or mental. A further articulation of the notion of time is then based on the concept of change: change implies time, and time involves change, and both are related to the identity of human beings.

Now, the very notion of "identity" rests upon the concept of a continuum of past into present, that is, on the awareness that the continuity of subjectivity is based on the flowing of past experiences into present events. Time lies at the core of identity and our relationship with objects. Torres (2007) also introduced the concept of "renunciation" in order to explain the human progress toward the achievement of mental maturity. In this view, there would be an "unavoidable renunciation" (p. 249) that each individual must suffer at some point in life, which consists of accepting that it is necessary to forever leave something behind, that time goes by, and the past can no longer be grasped in its actuality. As to traumatized individuals, they face a double impossibility: consciously returning to the past on the one hand, and controlling the future on the other hand. As a result, renouncing persistence in time is associated with the acceptance of an end of time, which, in turn, is linked with remaining in contact with the present reality.

Time, Eternity, and Traumatic Fragmentation

According to Freud (1923), "death is an abstract concept with a negative content for which no unconscious correlative can be found" (p. 58). The wish to slow down time, to stay perpetually young, and to eliminate the awareness of change are all linked to the most fundamental existential dread – the fear of death, which is intrinsically associated with the concept of time (Hartocollis, 1986). In this view, human beings are prone to escape the trap of time in order to run away from (the idea of) death. The awareness of death as "not being" (Hartocollis, 1986, p. 207) elicits what the existentialist Danish philosopher Søren Kierkegaard (1813–1855) represented as the feeling of "dread."[1] About a century before Borges's famous proclamation, "Time is the substance I am made of," Kierkegaard ([1844] 1944) stated that the human being "is a synthesis of psyche and body, but he is also a *synthesis of the temporal and the eternal*" (p. 149), and further contended,

> precisely because every moment, as well as the sum of the moments, is a process (a passing by), no moment is a present, and accordingly there is in time neither present, nor past, nor future. . . . If it is claimed that this division can be maintained, it is because the moment is *spatialized*, but thereby the infinite succession comes to a halt, it is because representation is introduced that allows time to be represented instead of being thought.
>
> (pp. 149–150)

In this view, however, the present is not a concept that can be associated with time, unless one regards it as something infinitely *lacking* content, as something that is endlessly vanishing. No matter how quickly it may disappear, the present is "posited," and this process gives rise to the categories of past and future. On the contrary, as Kierkegaard ([1844] 1944) argued, when being thought, "the eternal is the present in terms of annulled succession (time is the succession that passes by)" (p. 150). In the eternal there is no difference between past and future. Time is, then, infinite succession, and life in time has no present. The moment is only an abstraction from the eternal. The present is the eternal, the eternal is the present, and the present is full of meaning. This is why "the moment is not a determination of time, because the determination of time is that it 'passes by'" (p. 150) – and the moment does not. When one determines time as present, the latter has already gone, and is thus time past. Indeed, the Latin term *momentum* (stemming from *movere*: "to move") expresses the merely vanishing. It is in the moment that "time and eternity touch each other, and with this the concept of *temporality* is posited, whereby time constantly intersects eternity and eternity constantly pervades time" (Kierkegaard, 2000, p. 152).

As to the symbolic meaning of temporality, human experience oscillates between being dragged by one's past and being attracted by what comes from ahead. Loewald (1972) opined that there are two poles of temporal experience, both exceptional and rare: at one extreme lies the experience of eternity; on the opposite pole, the experience of traumatic fragmentation. By "eternity," Loewald (1972) meant a state where the flow of time is suspended, a *nunc stans*, a state where there is no division between past, present, and future, no remembering, no wish, no anticipation, but "merely the absorption in being, or in that what is" (p. 405). In psychiatric psychopathology, this characterizes the heights of manic episodes, the depths of depression, and the states of bliss or despair, when all temporal dimensions are disrupted, and what is left is only the "now."

Traumatic fragmentation, by contrast, is a state where the temporal dimensions are left in bits and pieces, and no longer bear any meaning. The temporal continuum and the intertwining between past, present, and future disintegrate, so that each instant stands by itself, with no connection with the others. Whereas in the experience of eternity all temporal dimensions vanish into a unified "now," in traumatic fragmentation time is annihilated in the disconnection between instants. Accordingly, the experience of eternity seems to be of "two kinds: timeless and timeful" (Hartocollis, 1986, p. 211). The former is proper to blissful and mystical experiences, which resemble those of love and the states of consciousness characterized by the possession of the loved object. The latter characterizes instead pain and anguish, in the eternal present where neither past nor future are meaningful, and where the present feels like eternity. The most significant rebellion against time amounts to a rebellion against death – the "epitome of narcissistic mortification" (Arlow, 1986, p. 525). Death is the end of the ego, the extinction of the Self, the final breath of consciousness. As to the need to escape the end of life, Mainemelis (2002) opined that the creative process is a movement generated to transcend spiritual death. Creativity is, in this view, a quest for immortality, a way to experience the ultimate limit of human beings, and an attempt to defy the experience of death. An evolving vision of the future characterizes the creator in what Bergson ([1907] 1911, [1934] 1946) called the subject's existential *unfolding* in time.

The awareness of death emerges progressively throughout human development. The child becomes aware that life has an end at about ten years of age, and "the certainty of the end is the greatest narcissistic injury an individual can suffer" (Torres, 2007, pp. 249–250). In this view, true maturity involves the acceptance of the end of life as the end of self-awareness. The final "renunciation" is renunciation to life, to the fulfillment of one's wishes, and ultimately to the openness of one's experience of the future. If something can only exist within the individual's life, that is, within time, then death lies, just like love, "outside time."

Trauma as Absence of (Temporal) Meaning

Lyotard (1984) defined the postmodern condition in terms of the "paradox of the future anterior" (p. 81). In this view, the temporal logic underlying postmodernism illuminates some features of a contemporary psychological condition that similarly problematizes our conception of presence, that is, PTSD. When some aspects of the traumatic situation remain inaccessible to present consciousness, their failure to become conscious is unconsciously manifested in a series of symbolic symptoms that cannot be explained by human reason. In this regard, PTSD (like postmodern temporality) seems to challenge the idea that coherent self-consciousness is the necessary condition of human experience. PTSD, as the experience of inner temporal fragmentation, seems to occupy the far end of a *continuum* that is commonly regarded as our "ordinary" experience. The association between a traumatic event and PTSD symptomatology is still unclear, and is rendered even more complicated by the existence of other diagnostic classifications (Mather & Marsden, 2004): "the sense in which traumata can be said to be 'present' creates almost as many difficulties as their point of origination. It is this doublet of causality and presence that perhaps necessitates a reorientation of the analyses of PTSD" (p. 207).

As we have seen, trauma disrupts the common idea of a linear temporality, which goes from past to present and from present to future. As in the case of Emma (Freud, 1895), it may be that the patient's symptoms precede his or her discovery of a particular event or memory that contributed to triggering them. That is to say, time can mainly flow from current psychological states back to the triggering event. In this inversion of the relationship between the traumatic event and the related stressful symptoms, trauma points to a radical reconceptualization of the concept of time: life is *lived* forward, but can be *understood* only retrospectively. In PTSD, the connection between the traumatic event and the subsequent symptomatology can only be represented in terms of *absence*, that is, in terms of the failure to integrate the event into a coherent life narrative. This points to the (negative) definition of trauma as something that has failed to present itself at the time of its occurring, and that can be activated only through subsequent symptoms that are somehow its by-product.

As previously discussed, *Nachträglichkeit* describes a temporal relation between (at least) two events that are different in nature, the former being a shocking situation of such traumatic intensity that the subject is unable to properly "experience" it, the latter being a possibly and relatively trivial event, only tangentially linked to the first, that catalyzes a response of disproportionate affective charge, only explicable by reference to the first event. In this sense, "the paradox of *Nachträglichkeit* is that the first event is only *experienced* after the second event even though the latter is not chronologically prior" (Mather & Marsden, 2004, p. 211). The original event is never present to consciousness as a temporal moment of self-narrative until its symbolic realization is produced. Otherwise said, the first event appears to be *engendered* by the second event, ripping off the linear and monodirectional conception of time. We can think of trauma as a "gap" in memory, an unconscious "absence" that the individual is not capable of making conscious until a further event comes about and brings the traumatic event to conscious awareness. This further event seems to "generate" the first as a primary event, because it is only *after* the further event that the first becomes the "primal scene." In a sense, "it is in the repetition (symptomatic acting out) of *what did not take place* that the enigma of PTSD resides" (Mather & Marsden, 2004, p. 212).

The French philosopher Jacques Derrida (1930–2004) was also strongly influenced by both Husserl's original phenomenology of time (Coate, 2017) and Freud's conception of psychic temporality (Hamrit, 2008). Derrida regarded time as something that can only be thought of from a present perspective (Shain, 2019): "'time' has always designated a movement conceived in terms of the present, and can mean nothing else" (Derrida, 1973, p. 68). Freud's temporality would be brought back to the "auto-affective structure of time," as described by Husserl ([1905] 1991) and Heidegger ([1929] 1990) (see Giovannangeli, 2001). Derrida's (1973, 1978) concept of *différance* was coined to express the idea that "differing" and "deferring" are mutually reinforcing terms. In fact, the process of differing would be also one of deferring the original moment, and would thus never be present itself. In this view, the present is always transcended toward a horizon that must recede in order to make a "presence" possible. In fact, it is only through processes of differing and deferring that something can be signified. Moreover, a signified concept is never present in itself, but is inscribed in a set of differences from which it derives its meaning. This is why the original moment of presence can never occur, as it can only be re-presented through a process of difference and deference.

As to the relationship between "retention" and "representation," Derrida ([1967] 2011) argued:

> [T]heir common root, the possibility of repetition in its most general form, the trace in the most universal sense, is a possibility that not only must inhabit the pure actuality of the now, but also must constitute it by means of the very movement of the *différance* that the possibility inserts into the pure actuality of the now.
>
> (p. 58; see also Lamy-Rested & Cross, 2017)

Based on the concept of *Nachträglichkeit*, Van der Kolk (1996) translated Derrida's idea in terms of a past existing only as a mnestic trace that remains in a process of erasing traces, whose affective significance cannot be assimilated into a coherent narrative. Now, these traces are not "signs" in any lexical sense. It is as if the ego discovered "too late" what it needed to know in the first place, and used pathological defenses (e.g., repression) in order to protect itself from further pain. The initial scene, as in the case of Emma, is not "buried" in memory, because its experience has never been present to consciousness. It is in a process of "recollection" that the initial scene becomes traumatic in memory, whereas the traumatic response testifies to an experience that cannot be articulated nor called to presence.

As to traumatic psychopathology, the question is how an experience that has *never* been present to consciousness may have indeed a belated effect. How can a diagnosis of PTSD be secured when there is no traumatic "event" as a guarantor of the presence of the condition? The premise is that an event that has never been lived through is *dissociated* from consciousness and is thus "forgotten." PTSD patients often claim that they initially "remembered" the trauma only in the form of somatosensory flashback experiences. Traumatic memories are initially stored as a set of sensory fragments that cannot be linguistically translated, and a narrative of the trauma comes about only later on. Trauma is not initially narratively organized, and seems to serve no communicative function. As individuals remember more and more elements of the trauma, they become able to construct a narrative that can "explain" what happened to them. Even after acquiring a personal narrative for the trauma, however, the individual is normally still haunted by flashbacks that come in the form of sensory perceptions and affective states.

Van der Kolk (1996) thought of PTSD as a set of "signs" that do not "communicate." PTSD patients are compelled to develop a narrative in order to conceptualize their trauma as a "play of difference," where

> an absence (the sensory fragments, which are not yet present) becomes presence (narrative), but presence still inflected with absence (an incomplete construction that "explains" a story), which becomes a personal narrative (fully present self-identity) but remains still ultimately threatened by the negative power of continuing sensory fragmentation (dissociative memory).
>
> (Mather & Marsden, p. 217)

It is in this sense that the value of *différance* might be present in the form of *Nachträglichkeit*. A language for the trauma has to be invented, because what remains as a mnestic trace in the aftermath of the traumatic situation is not "language." This is why PTSD is always situated in the "future anterior" (Lacan, 1981), where the individual is called to invent a narrative frame for what *will have been* the truth (Agamben, 2008).

The Nonlinearity of Lived Time

As we have seen, psychic time is not linear. Future, past, and present must be engaged simultaneously, although not in the same way, in order to yield the sense of temporal fullness. Psychological trauma modifies the sense of time, which ceases to exist as continuous, meaningful, and subjectively experienced. Because the fullness of lived time is inaccessible, meaning is no longer rooted in our "being-in-the-world" (Heidegger, [1927] 1962), but is spread out over an abyss of "serial disintegration" (Lacan, [1955] 1993, p. 88). Because the disruption of the person's psychological well-being is reflected in his or her ability of estimating time, "the psychological states in which the reckoning with time is lost are the consequences of an unsuccessful incorporation of traumatic stimuli that are caused both by outside phenomena and by the actions of an individual's inner drives" (Denischik, 2015, p. 148).

The failure of the capacity to incorporate traumatic stimuli in one's temporal self-narrative produces psychological states in which the reckoning with time is disrupted. Psychic processes do not lie in a straightforward dimension of past, present, and future: In other words, psychic temporality has no one-way direction (past to present, present to future), but rather (according to *Nachträglichkeit*) what comes afterward might give new meaning to what came before, thus challenging the supposedly monodirectional arrow of time (Cournut, 1997). *Nachträglichkeit* implies that memory is a process of reconstruction to which the present gives ever new meanings to the other temporal dimensions. Experience is then an infinite progression of interpretation and reinterpretation.

There are many forms of time (Ornstein, 1997). Indeed, "there are not only many ways to measure time, but many times to be measured" (Meissner, 2007, p. vii). The experience of present, past, and future, but also of duration and simultaneity are just examples of these forms of temporal experience. For instance, the experience of the present seems more linked to short-term apperception, whereas lived duration appears associated with a sense of the past grasped by short-term memory. It is surely difficult not to conceive time in spatial terms, that is, as a linear arrow. However, as Maurice Merleau-Ponty (1908–1961) theorized, the living body is not a thing-among-other-things, as its structure is temporal in nature (Merleau-Ponty, [1942] 1963, [1945] 1962). The specific dimension of the living body is similar to that of the psyche, because it entails the potentiality of temporal finitude of human beings.

Consciousness cannot be separated from existential time (Scarfone, 2006). The relationship between unconscious timelessness and chronological time can be detected in several ways. For instance, in the presence of the repetition compulsion, redundant patterns keep coming back as if the individual had not learned from experience (Shapiro, 1985). This is also manifested by the eruption in the present of "untimely" mental contents belonging to other temporal dimensions (past or future) as well as in dreams, where the "*unpast*" – as Scarfone (2006, p. 811) called it – steps in from unconscious material. The transformation of timeless unconscious material into temporal conscious elements seems to rest primarily on language (Lacan, 1981). This is why psychic differentiation, one of the main goals of therapy, is made possible through speech acts, and "the synthesis of time can in turn be described in terms of differentiation" (Scarfone, 2006, p. 813). According to Merleau-Ponty ([1945] 1962), when time is at stake, "to be" and "to pass" are synonymous. In this view, an event does not cease to *be* when it becomes past: "time preserves what it has put into being at the very moment it expels it from being" (p. 480). From this perspective, the past continues to evolve as life moves forward; retranscription and recontextualization continually occur as time goes by – similarly to what is implied in Freud's concept of *Nachträglichkeit*.

The rejection of the temporal flowing brings about a paralyzing uncertainty (Scarfone, 2006). If Merleau-Ponty's ([1945] 1962) parallelism between being and passing is true, then the refusal of time (and death) amounts to a refusal of *being*. The disruption of psychic structures is not a consequence of time passing, and the wearing away of life does not amount to psychic disruption. On the contrary, by becoming conscious, human thoughts are propelled to generate new thinking. When regarded as temporal elements, human thoughts are better conceived of as transformative. Destruction might indeed be regarded as the preservation of something in a new form. In Freud's theory, the repetition compulsion, which has an "unbinding" effect in the human psyche, is associated with the death drive. The repetition compulsion keeps psychic elements stuck in their pristine form, devoid of any possibility to change: in repetition, time (and, therefore, being) is held captive to a motion that resists transformation, leaving no room for novelty and creativity.

When they are not inscribed in a time sequence, psychic processes tend to endlessly repeat, that is, to occur in an ever-present form. In this case, they become "*presentations* instead of re-presentations, *acts* instead of *thoughts*, or *phrases of affect* instead of *articulate phrases*" (Scarfone, 2006, p. 827). In this view, the therapeutic goal of psychoanalysis involves the articulation, translation, and transformation of actual time into a psychic representation. This amounts to transposing the "here and now" (the endless dimension of the unconscious mind) into the realm of conscious time. Therefore, "the repressed *does* carry a form of temporality," but a form of temporality that "evades *chronological* time" (Scarfone, 2006, p. 832). In other words, the repressed (unconscious) material lies outside of the temporal categories ruling the subject's conscious mind. The peculiar form of temporality proper of the unconscious mind is, as it were, *time with no memory*, that is, an endless series of "now."

López-Corvo (2013) proposed a significant distinction between "conceptual" and "preconceptual" trauma. Preconceptual trauma occurs mostly during the first year of life, when the infant lacks the ability to process (and give meaning to) external events; in turn, conceptual trauma occurs

when the mind, already existing at an adult stage, fails to process traumatic occurrences. According to López-Corvo (2013), there is a continuous
"*emotional entanglement*" (p. 289) between conceptual and preconceptual
traumas. The concept of "entanglement," borrowed from quantum physics, helps us to understand how, often, situations that occur at a mature
age become traumatic. They automatically trigger emotions that echo
similar "entangled" feelings from earlier, "preconceptual" occurrences. In
these instances, the hopelessness and helplessness experienced by the infant
returns unmodified in the adult's experience, *as if time had not elapsed.*

Although the adult mind can verbally symbolize events, the ego can
nonetheless become overwhelmed by a present shock, and start acting as
if the adult were replaced by an infant. In such circumstances, the adult
ego fails to tolerate the traumatic experience, and unconscious aspects
from preconceptual traumas take over automatically. Hence, the actual
situation that overwhelms the ego, along with the preconceptual trauma,
forms a dialectical twinship. In order to overcome this impasse, a change
in emotional experience must occur. As a result, the adult mind can learn
what unconditionality is, namely, being loved for who one is, rather than
for what one does. Through this process, the adult gains the perception
of being a unique, autonomous, and continually growing Self. This is
exactly what preconceptual trauma deprives the individual of, that is, the
ability to achieve a sense of selfhood, autonomy, uniqueness, and unconditionality. In this view, the continuous reiteration of the same, which
characterizes trauma, would be a symptom of the compulsive repetition
of preconceptual trauma (López-Corvo, 2013). Ultimately, as Gostecnik
(1997) pointed out, "the patient with preverbal traumatic experience
acts out instead of verbalizing the pain because the basic mechanism of
repression or suppression, which would enable him to deal with the affect
in a different way, is not yet developed" (p. 54).

Note

1. How to inhabit the timescale of our existence without suffering and how to
   fill the moment with eternity is what Kierkegaard explored in a portion of his
   work *The Concept of Anxiety* (1844), later included in the volume *The Essential Kierkegaard (2000).*

References

Abraham, G. (1976). The sense and concept of time in psychoanalysis. *Interna-
    tional Review of Psycho-Analysis*, *3*, 461–472.
Agamben, G. (2008). *Signatura rerum: Sul metodo*. Torino: Bollati Boringhieri.
Arlow, J. A. (1986). Psychoanalysis and time. *Journal of the American Psychoana-
    lytic Association*, *34*(3), 507–528.
Bergson, H. (1907) 1911. *Creative evolution*. New York: Holt.

Bergson, H. (1934) 1946. *The creative mind*. New York: Philosophical Library.

Bonaparte, M. (1940). Time and the unconscious. *International Journal of Psycho-Analysis*, *21*, 427–468.

Coate, M. (2017). On *Nachträglichkeit*, or a certain blindness of the "now": Time, self, and self-responsibility in Derrida's analyses of the Husserlian account of temporality. *Theoria and Praxis: International Journal of Interdisciplinary Thought*, *4*(1), 65–94.

Cohen, J. (1966). Subjective time. In J. T. Fraser (Ed.), *The voices of time* (pp. 257–278). New York: G. Braziller.

Colarusso, C. A. (1979). The development of time sense – From birth to object constancy. *International Journal of Psycho-Analysis*, *60*, 243–251.

Colarusso, C. A. (1998). A developmental line of time sense: In late adulthood and throughout the life cycle. *Psychoanalytic Study of The Child*, *53*, 113–140.

Cournut, L. J. (1997). Le sens de l'"après-coup." *Revue française de psychanalyse*, *61*(3), 1239–1246.

Denischik, M. (2015). Temporality in psychosis: Loss of lived time in an alien world. *The Humanistic Psychologist*, *43*(2), 148–159.

Derrida, J. (1973). *Speech and phenomena, and other essays on Husserl's theory of signs*. Evanston: Northwestern University Press.

Derrida, J. (1978). Cogito and the history of madness. In *Writing and difference*. London & New York: Routledge.

Derrida, J. (1967) 2011. *Voice and phenomenon: Introduction to the problem of the sign in Husserl's phenomenology*. Evanston, IL: Northwestern University Press.

Droit-Volet, S., Meck, W. H., & Penney, T. B. (2007). Sensory modality and time perception in children and adults. *Behavioural Processes*, *74*(2), 244–250.

Freud, S. (1895). Project for a scientific psychology. In J. Strachey (Ed.), *The standard edition of the complete psychological works of Sigmund Freud* (Vol. 1, pp. 283–397). London: Hogarth Press.

Freud, S. (1900). The interpretation of dreams. In J. Strachey (Ed.), *The standard edition of the complete psychological works of Sigmund Freud* (Vols. 4–5). London: Hogarth Press.

Freud, S. (1915). The unconscious. In J. Strachey (Ed.), *The standard edition of the complete psychological works of Sigmund Freud* (Vol. 14, pp. 159–215). London: Hogarth Press.

Freud, S. (1923). The ego and the id. In J. Strachey (Ed.), *The standard edition of the complete psychological works of Sigmund Freud* (Vol. 19, pp. 1–59). London: Hogarth Press.

Gifford, S. (1960). Sleep, time, and the early ego. *Journal of The American Psychoanalytic Association*, *8*, 5–42.

Gifford, S. (1980). The prisoner of time. *Annual of Psychoanalysis*, *8*, 131–154.

Giovannangeli, D. (2001). The delay of consciousness. In M. Meyer (Ed.), *Questioning Derrida: With his replies on philosophy*. London: Routledge.

Gostecnik, C. (1997). Chronos versus kairos in psychotherapy. *American Journal of Pastoral Counseling*, *1*(1), 49–60.

Hamrit, J. (2008). *Nachträglichkeit*. *PsyArt*, 1–5.

Harnik, S. (1925). Die triebhaft-affektiven Momente im Zeitgefhl. *Imago*, *11*, 32–57.

Hartocollis, P. (1986). *Time and timelessness or the varieties of temporal experience: A psychoanalytic inquiry.* Madison, CT: International University Press.

Heidegger, M. (1927) 1962. *Being and time.* New York: Harper and Row.

Heidegger, M. (1929) 1990. *Kant and the problem of metaphysics.* Bloomington: Indiana University Press.

Husserl, E. (1905) 1991. *On the phenomenology of the consciousness of internal time.* The Hague: Nijhoff.

Kierkegaard, S. (1844) 1944. *The concept of dread.* Princeton: Princeton University Press.

Kierkegaard, S. (2000). The moment and late writings. In H. V. Hong & E. H. Hong (Eds.), *The essential Kierkegaard.* Princeton, NJ: Princeton University Press.

Lacan, J. (1955) 1993. *The seminar of Jacques Lacan: The psychoses (book III, 1955–1956).* New York: W. W. Norton.

Lacan, J. (1981). *The language of the self: The function of language in psychoanalysis.* Baltimore: Johns Hopkins University Press.

Lamy-Rested, É., & Cross, D. (2017). Derrida between Freud and Husserl: Husserlian temporality and what remains of it . . . *CR: The New Centennial Review, 17*(1), 31–42.

Legrand, D., & Trigg, D. (Eds.). (2017). *Unconsciousness between phenomenology and psychoanalysis.* New York, NY: Springer.

Loewald, H. W. (1972). The experience of time. *The Psychoanalytic Study of the Child, 27*(1), 401–410.

López-Corvo, R. E. (2013). Time distortion between "conceptual" and "preconceptual" traumas. *The Psychoanalytic Review, 100*(2), 289–310.

Lyotard, J.-F. (1984). *The postmodern condition.* Manchester: Manchester University Press.

Mainemelis, C. (2002). Time and timelessness: Creativity in (and out of) the temporal dimension. *Creativity Research Journal, 14*(2), 227–238.

Mann, J. (1982). *Time-limited psychotherapy.* Cambridge, MA: Harvard University Press.

Mather, R., & Marsden, J. (2004). Trauma and temporality. *Theory & Psychology, 14*(2), 205–219.

Meerloo, J. A. M., (1966). The time sense in psychiatry. In J. T. Fraser (Ed.), *The voices of time* (pp. 235–252). New York: G. Braziller.

Meissner, W. W. (2007). *Time, self and psychoanalysis.* Plymouth: Jason Aronson.

Merleau-Ponty, M. (1945) 1962. *Phenomenology of perception.* London: Routledge & Kegan Paul.

Merleau-Ponty, M. (1942) 1963. *The structure of behavior.* Boston: Beacon Press.

Orgel, S. (1965). On time and timelessness. *Journal of the American Psychoanalytic Association, 13,* 102–121.

Ornstein, R. E. (1997). *On the experience of time.* Boulder, CO: Westview Press.

Piaget, J. (1937) 1954. *The construction of reality in the child.* New York: Basic Books.

Piaget, J. (1966). Time perception in children. In J. T. Fraser (Ed.), *The voices of time* (pp. 202–216). New York: G. Braziller.

Piaget, J. (1927) 2007. *The child's conception of time.* London: Routledge.

Roberts, J. (2003). Kairos, chronos and chaos. *Group Analysis*, *36*(2), 202–217.

Scarfone, D. (2006). A matter of time: Actual time and the production of the past. *Psychoanalytic Quarterly*, *75*(3), 807–834.

Seton, P. H. (1974). The psychotemporal adaptation of late adolescence. *Journal of the American Psychoanalytic Association*, *22*, 795–819.

Shain, R. (2019). Is there a trace of the future? Metaphysics and time in Derrida. *Comparative and Continental Philosophy*, *11*(1), 34–47.

Shapiro, R. B. (1985). Separation-individuation and the compulsion to repeat. Symposium on the 40th Anniversary of the William Alanson White Institute of Psychiatry, Psychoanalysis & Psychology: Psychoanalytic Controversies and the Interpersonal Tradition: What Cures: The Therapeutic Action of Psychoanalysis. *Contemporary Psychoanalysis*, *21*, 297–308.

Torres, M. A. (2007). The time dimension and its relationship to the analytic process. *International Forum of Psychoanalysis*, *16*(4), 247–253.

Tulving, E. (2002). Chronesthesia: Conscious awareness of subjective time. In D. T. Stuss & R. T. Knight (Eds.), *Principles of frontal lobe function* (pp. 311–325). New York: Oxford University Press.

Van der Kolk, B. A. (1996). Trauma and memory. In B. A Van der Kolk, A. C. McFarlane, & L. Weisaeth (Eds.), *Traumatic stress*. London: The Guilford Press.

Von Franz, M.-L. (1966). Time and synchronicity in analytic psychology. In J. T. Fraser (Ed.), *The voices of time* (pp. 218–232). New York: G. Braziller.

Williams, P. (2007). Making time: Killing time. In R. J. Perelberg (Ed.), *Time and memory* (pp. 47–64). London: Karnac Books.

Chapter 4

Trauma, Time, and Psychopathology

This chapter analyzes the dimension of "desynchronization" with the Otherness as one of the temporal hallmarks of traumatic psychopathology. The temporal synthesis of "retention" and "protention" produces the "intentional arc" that underlies human experience. Because trauma cannot be integrated into the dialectic movement of the individual's narrative, it tends to remain verbally ineffable. The traumatized person tends to live in a world of "alienation," with no integration between the temporal dimensions of past, present, and future. The lack of temporal structure, which characterizes traumatic experiences, points to the original co-dependency between our psychic life and our being-in-time. Ultimately, the very nature of trauma produces a disruption of its temporally perceived dimension.

Temporal Desynchronization and Psychopathology

Trauma, like mental illness, not only interrupts the continuity of ordinary life, but can also trigger a radical change in perceived temporality, even to the point of disrupting the experience of the Self in time. On the one hand, human beings are limited by the surrounding environment; on the other hand, self-reference, as a condition for the continuity of the Self in time, is not possible without a constant reference to the "Otherness" (Husserl, [1905] 1991). This points directly to the importance of temporality as *intersubjectively constituted*. Aiming at formulating the rationale for the temporality of psychopathology, Fuchs (2010) distinguished between implicit and explicit temporality, that is, between "temporality as pre-reflectively lived and temporality as consciously or reflectively experienced" (p. 3). Lived time coincides with the movement of life, a prereflective dimension that knows nothing of past nor future, and that lies at the core of everyday experience.

According to Fuchs (2010), implicit temporality requires two conditions. First, the basic continuity of consciousness, as opposed to a mere succession of instants, sets the ground for the connection of these moments in what Husserl ([1905] 1991) called *retention* of the past and

DOI: 10.4324/9781003230601-5

protention toward the future. This synthesis is operated automatically and unconsciously, and provides what Merleau-Ponty ([1945] 1962) called the "intentional arc" of directed activity. Now, the temporal continuity created by the synthesis of retention, presentation, and protention involves a prereflective self-awareness. The continuity of the Self in time is associated with the coherence of a basic sense of Self or "ipseity," as Merleau-Ponty ([1945] 1962) used to call it. The second condition for implicit temporality to become manifest is the basic energetic momentum of psychic life, which Fuchs (2010) called the "affective-conative momentum" or "conation" (p. 3). "Conation" is the foundation of spontaneity, whose disruption becomes manifested in pathologic states such as mania (when time seems to speed up) or depression (where time seems to slow down or even stop). Taken together, the syntheses of the temporal dimensions and conation form the intentional arc of attention, perception, and action, which are also the necessary conditions for the constitution of a coherent sense of Self in time (Noë, 2006).

The explicit experience of temporality is specifically produced when the subject's activity is interrupted by a "sudden" (Heidegger, [1927] 1962). Our perception of time is indeed generated through a disturbance of our lived experience, interrupting the routine of daily activities. Furthermore, the disruption of existential becoming is closely associated with negative emotions, such as displeasure or suffering. As opposed to implicit time, explicit temporality requires that the subject perform an active and conscious synthesis of retention and protention. This process requires a personal or narrative subject able to self-project into the future and to retain what has just passed. Finally, the emerging personal Self prompts the personal-historical or autobiographical time, which is always intersubjectively constituted through the synchronization with the activity of others. While implicit time is associated with synchronicity, explicit temporality is produced in a desynchronization with the Otherness, whereby time is experienced as a loss of synchronization. Ultimately, it is through these phases of desynchronization that explicit time emerges, that is, when the subject's temporality does not coincide with that of other individuals (Fuchs, 2010).

Trauma and Temporal Reality

According to Freud (1920), in order to overcome traumatic anxiety, the subject must be prepared to activate its defensive mechanisms in advance. However, when the traumatic shock occurs all of a sudden, the individual is not well equipped to face trauma effectively. "Terror" is then, according to Freud, the necessary condition for the absence of readiness to face anxiety. In other words, the suddenness of an unexpected trauma coincides with the onset of terror, because the individual was not anticipating the trauma through the onset of anxiety, and a defense against it can be built only "after the fact" (*nachträglich*). The retrospective buildup of anxiety can be accounted for only if trauma is regarded as a dynamic process rather than as a temporally fixed event. What was not available at the time of the trauma, namely, the individual's defense mechanisms, can become available only after the traumatic incident. That is to say, the retrospective buildup of anxiety is possible only retrospectively, in the form of the *après-coup*.

Most psychic events are unconscious and, insofar as trauma is concerned, "they are not ordered chronologically," because "time changes nothing in them," and therefore "one cannot apply to them the concept of time" (Freud, 1920, p. 60). In the unconscious mind, there is no linear sense of progression as in the conscious domain of our psyche. In order to master the traumaticity of an event, priority must be given to the intertwining between past and present. Indeed, the past features in the process of mastering the trauma only by means of an unconscious projection of the painful stressor. The temporal unfolding of memory is dominated by the projected past. In this view, the process of temporization is transformed because of an unresolved, traumatic stimulus that shocked the individual, but potentially remains to be mastered.

At the core of trauma is the void that threatens the individual's existence as a whole. When no activity or object can bestow a verbal expression on the traumatic occurrence, the possibility to express what has happened is inaccessible. Trauma remains ineffable, and yet it insists on the possibility to be expressed. But when the world cannot be told, this same world is made up in such a way as to conform to the ineffable, as traumatic loss of reality is not linguistically expressible. Its traumatizing character cannot be integrated into the dialectic movement of the coherent whole of the individual's narrative. The past ceases to be past. It is still there in the present, dominating the present and making a meaningful future impossible. When the rhythm of the temporal unfolding begins to fade, so do the necessary worldly relations (Denischik, 2015). In this view, the temporal nothingness arises from the *atemporal* absence of the regulating "play" of past, present, and future. For the traumatized individual, the disruption of the world's significance goes along with the disruption of its temporality, where the play of the temporal dimensions does not order, synthesize, nor integrate the moments into a temporal continuity. The traumatic dimension becomes, then, the reality of another world, and the non-time of trauma becomes the reality of what the individual *does not know* (at least until a further event makes sense of it). In both cases, the temporal rhythm of the individual's psychic life is disrupted under the pressure of a non-being, which does not allow the person to verbalize his or her own experience. In Denischik's (2015) words, "if existence unfolds in accord with the rules of temporal logic, then the atemporal nature of trauma . . . does not preclude that trauma from being both real and non-existent" (p. 154).

The co-dependency between human psychic life and its being-in-time is now evident. Modifications in psychic existence imply modifications in our temporal being-in-the-world, and vice versa. Trauma patients live in a world with *no temporal structure*, where the only activity is cogitation about the *nothingness* of the temporal dimension. They have no contact with the real world, and all their perceptions are distorted if compared with those of others. The transition from a traumatic state to a process in which the individual reflects on this state coincides with the transformation of traumatic non-time into the temporal understanding of lived experience. However, insofar as the individual is stuck in his or her traumatic state, the world remains flat, alien, radically other, because traumatic thoughts are not associated with a real event, but with a distorted perception of it. In both cases, the sense of time is entangled in a dialectic that does not leave room for a true reality, but remains stuck in the world of "alienation" (Denischik, 2015).

The very nature of subjectivity is thus put into doubt, and the vortex of nothingness makes existence uncertain. If the world ceases to exist, so does time. *The very nature of trauma produces a disruption of its temporal dimension.* Duration is no longer perceived as a true unfolding in time. Mental life undergoes a "*subduction in time*" (Minkowski, [1927] 1970, p. 294). If there is only a series of "now," then there is no unfolding in time, there is no longer a "present." It is as if the traumatized individual were stuck in a series of "snapshots" that do not open out onto authentic intersubjective existence. In other words, if the temporal unfolding of existence is based on the temporal unity of subjectivity, for the traumatized person there is no longer an egoic continuity in time. As Denischik (2015) argued, this dissipation of egoic continuity goes along with a state of "alienation" that the person enters without the possibility to escape from it. The world appears as radically other. Also, in this temporal dimension, the egoic identity becomes shattered, and perceived temporality disorganized, as egoic continuity is only preserved if the individual can be the spiraled center of his or her own past and present.

The abyss of trauma does not abide by the laws of the organizing principles of ordinary reality. Presence, absence, being, and world no longer carry a real meaning, as they are emptied of their deepest significance. The abyss of post-traumatic existence goes along with the person's resistance to experience the temporal unfolding as a lived dimension of a dynamically organized world. The traumatized individual becomes paralyzed in the immobility of an atemporal world, where individuals lose their own egoity. In other words, there is no longer an "I" with a past and a present unfolding in time, which are the only conditions for the individual to enter a "real" world of object relations.

Time and death are structurally intertwined, as they both refer to the boundaries of our existence and to the "circumscribed nature" (Lombardi, 2013, p. 691) of human beings. This is why working through mental growth, acceptance of one's limitations, and integration of mental functions are all crucial in the therapeutic process of trauma patients. Achieving a representation of death and time would thus foster the acquisition of spatiotemporal categories, including the distinction between past and present, internal and external, reality and illusion. In fact, time and death are inextricably interconnected. Because the body "forces the mind to face linear time" (Lombardi, 2013, p. 699), the perception of death, along with the anxiety that it brings about, can have the integrative function of unifying mind and body, or chronological time (*Chronos*) and lived time (*Kairos*).

Traumatic Disturbances in the Sense of Time

Disturbances in the sense of time and reality characterize in particular trauma-related disorders (Frewen & Lanius, 2015). Given that the sense of time is partly a function of the sense of reality, the space–time continuum is the background upon which individuals ground their experience of reality. Terr (1984) also hypothesized that trauma leads to temporal disturbances. The person's sense of time determines where an event is placed within one's self-narrative, and confusion in event placement is a symptom of trauma-related disturbances. For the traumatized individual, the sentence "time heals all wounds" does not make sense, because memories become frozen in time like the individual that experiences them. "Frozen time" and "dead time" have been regarded as two forms of psychopathology of temporality (Connolly, 2017). In this view, trauma generates a breakdown of the person's symbolic capacity, which is supposed to lead to the person's inability to think of death as a symbolic experience. "Frozen time" is associated with a refusal of *Chronos*, whereby the subject becomes stuck in a *timeless* reality. In turn, severe trauma produces a "death of time," which goes hand in hand with the loss of the dimension of *Kairos* (Connolly, 2017).

From a psychoanalytical point of view, the ego's function involves the organization and processing of the temporal features of experience (Modell, 1992). Accordingly, therapeutic change occurs when past, present, and future are realigned within the experience of a unified Self. The traumatized individual experiences memory difficulties in the aftermath of trauma because of a disordered perception of time and reality. In psychic life, past, present, and future are meaningful only within a linkage that brings them together. This nexus is not one of "succession," but one of "interaction" (Loewald, 1972, p. 407). They do not precede nor follow each other, but are intertwined and shape reciprocally in a framework that cannot be unraveled. The more the person is able to experience present perceptions (notwithstanding their intertwined relationship with memory and expectations), the less the past trauma and anxiety about the future can gain power over the experience of the "here and now."

Traumatic loss of the sense of Self is linked to the experience of depersonalization, which involves a perceived lack of being integrated into the Self's temporal unity and coherency. When traumatic experiences are reactivated, individuals do not feel as if they were living in the present, because the past is too overwhelming for them to experience time as developing. Upon reactivation of traumatic memories, the Self needs to face potential disintegration, that is, a fragmentation that hinders the Self in its capacity to maintain a sense of the temporal *dynamis*. The immersion in the traumatic reality is at times so intense that the person behaves as if he or she was reliving the trauma instead of just remembering it. This recollection not only hampers normal retrieval, leaving the subject without a sense of time, but also impedes the realization that trauma occurred in the past and is not part of the present. The realization that time has progressed is thus disrupted. Indeed, disturbances in the sense of time might be defensive mechanisms against overwhelming emotional states such as trauma (Van der Hart et al., 2005), and point to a crisis of the ego's object relations. This is why traumatic loss of control is often thought of as a loss of ego integration (Williams, 2007). In psychopathological conditions, time can indeed be perceived as threatening, or as a form of persecutory object. When time is experienced as a static entity, the sense of Self can dissociate from the world.

In traumatic situations, experience appears to stop because of a sort of "timeless warp" (Grinberg & Grinberg, 1981, p. 49). Trying to grasp the epistemological status of trauma with reference to time, Harris (2009) noted that during and after traumatic events, the individual lives in a state of "extended time," frozen in a moment that seems to precede the traumatic occurrence. The perception of the body as paralyzed mirrors the sense that time has frozen. Yet during and in the immediate aftermath of trauma, there is equally an inchoate fear of the near future, as if it had already happened: "fear is just memory in the future tense" (Winnicott, 1974, p. 104).

As Lacan (1981) stated,

> what is realized in my history is not the past definite of what was, since it is no more, or even the present perfect of what has been in what I am, but the future anterior of what I shall have been for what I am in the process of becoming.
>
> (p. 63)

Time is a constant reminder that the subject can never become self-identical, because the future anterior calls "into question the very foundations of subjective identity conceived in terms of an interiorizing memory," creating an *"anticipated belatedness* [of a] history always yet to come" (Lacan, 1981, p. 9). Here, we are faced with an *autopoietic* problem of identity, pertaining to how subjectivity must perpetually reproduce its identity in time by anticipating itself. Lacan ([1953–1954] 2013) remarked that, for Freud, the essence of analysis was

> the reintegration by the subject of his history right up to the furthermost perceptible limits, that is to say into a dimension that goes well beyond the limits of the individual. . . . History is not the past. History is the past in so far as it is historicized in the present – historicized in the present because it was lived in the past. . . . when all is said and done, it is less a matter of remembering than of rewriting history.
>
> (pp. 12–14)

The most dramatic reaction against time occurs in traumatic psychosis, where, as Freud (1915) had already stressed, trauma patients detach themselves from temporal reality and live in an inner *timeless* reality. In these circumstances, the sense of time dissolves and the past can only be experienced as occurring in the "here and now." In this view, "the present is controlled in order to predict the future: killing time permits survival to the next second, the next hour" (Williams, 2007, p. 57). In the face of traumatic shock, life becomes objectless, and pain overwhelmingly unbearable. The repetition compulsion fixates life in a temporality where nothing seems to change, where everything is "forever the same." This is a form of defense that trauma patients put into action to protect themselves from the dynamicity of time. In fact, "the existence of the repetition-compulsion implies that the past may be redone, if not undone" (Williams, 2007, p. 59). Ultimately, differences in the sense of time can be thought of as different ways in which intrapsychic structures can work to protect the person from further traumatization. More specifically, the ability to mourn separation from desired objects seems to be a necessary condition to form a Self that is capable of development, whereas structural and rigid defense mechanisms can indicate a progressive inability to tolerate separation from desired objects, reflecting disturbances in time sense.

Trauma, the Denial of Time, and the Origin of the Self

Inner time must be experienced and acknowledged to allow growth and development (Fink, 1993). Feeling one's own existence in time is an important developmental achievement. For traumatized individuals, however, the world is felt as *timeless*, that is, as a world where nothing changes: "an illusion of time standing still" (Bell, 2007, p. 66). Without time, psychic functioning becomes trapped in repetitive and compulsive processes, where individuals feel frozen and uncapable of further development. Difficulties in maintaining the awareness of a self-identity as a multidimensional *continuum* are what the psychopathological states related to the sense of *not feeling oneself* have in common (Sabbadini, 1989a, 1989b). These states include depersonalization, the sense of living in a dream, and the sense of being "double" (dissociative personality disorders seem here to represent the far end of the continuum).

From a genealogical point of view, Arlow (1984) agreed with Bonaparte (1940) that time is intertwined with the duration produced by the interval that divides need and gratification. The asynchrony between the child's needs and the mother's availability generates a sense of frustration. In this view, the origin of the human "rebellion" against the "tyranny" of time goes back to the infant's early development, when time begins to represent a "realistic necessity" (Arlow, 1984, p. 15). Indeed, disturbances in the sense of time might be regarded as specific types of affective states grounded in the unconscious material of our psyche. In fact, trauma stems from instinctual conflicts stored deep inside the unconscious mind, which bear a similarity with the failure of the infant's narcissistic omnipotence (Kohut, 1977). As a result, beyond the *Gestalt*-making function of the ego, there can be no time, because time does not pertain to the "actuality" of experience, but to the "ordering" of experience (Kurtz, 1988).

According to Meerloo (1948), the denial of time amounts to a rebellion against the denial of one's omnipotence and, by implication, of one's immortality. When the child's mind faces the denial of its omnipotence, ordinary temporal perception is compromised (Bergler & Róheim, 1946). Cohn (1957) contended that the repetitive rhythm of the compulsive personality resembles a time machine that keeps the notion of time away from conscious awareness. This would be a way to postpone the end of existence (death) by repressing time. The compulsive rhythm of the traumatized individual would also create a "regressive" time sense that would end up prevailing in the unconscious mind, whereas progressive time stems from the outward projection of this same temporality. Time, just like a mask reciting to the external world, is utilized as a defense against instincts, loss of identity, and being "one" with the mother (Dooley, 1941).

The human psyche has an essentially narrative structure (Carr, 1986). Telling a story about oneself is not only a mechanism through which the ego makes sense of its own life, but also a way through which identity takes shape (Sarbin, 1986). Not only does the psyche's narrative structure shape the individual's identity, but it also aids in constructing the landscape of what the individual presents to others. However, traumatic memories often lack the logical form present in non-traumatic narratives. By localizing the parts of the story that seem far from the construction of coherence and continuity, and by creating an alternative story as well, a richer construction of existence is rendered possible (Omer & Alon, 1997).

The ability to tell a coherent story after experiencing a traumatic event is also positively correlated with better recovery and coping (Gidron et al., 2002).

At birth, instincts, drives, and gratification are deeply intertwined. Narcissistic omnipotence rules the infants' life, where subject and object are inseparable and form an overarching whole. At these early stages of life, the infant is not able to distinguish past, present, and future. Sabbadini (1989a, 1989b) described this state as the "omnipresence" of the infant life – an all-embracing state of mind that seems to transcend time itself, ignoring past suffering and future anxiety. This kind of pervasive time seems indeed to relate to the timelessness of the unconscious mind, that is, an undifferentiated psychic dimension where time does not follow the laws of succession, duration, and irreversibility. In this view, the development of the child's sense of time is intertwined with the development of a sense of identity. In fact, in order to feel its temporal unity and continuity, subjectivity must have developed a sense of the temporal continuum. Conversely, a sense of past, present, and future is essential for the individual to feel "one." Very soon after birth, infants learn to postpone the fulfillment of their wishes and to face the frustration resulting from the temporal gap that is then produced.

As Bonaparte (1940) noted, when children learn to perceive external objects more and more accurately, they are better able to contextualize objects in the temporal framework of existence. However, infants retain for a long time their sense of time as an infinite duration, that is, time as timelessness. Therefore, the transition between a state of unity with the primary object of gratification and the subsequent stage of relative individuation (when the first awareness of one's self-identity begins to take shape) is thought to coincide with the birth of temporal awareness. In other words, the emergence of a sense of Self goes along with the achievement of a temporal awareness through the frustration due to the gap between need and gratification. This goes along with the substitution of the "pleasure principle" by the "reality principle," which is possible only when the infant is ready to give up its feeling of omnipotence.

Accepting the frustration produced in the delayed gratification of one's needs amounts to the establishment of a multidimensional sense of time. Early experiences are categorized and integrated in terms of pleasant or unpleasant affects. Colarusso (1979) also opined that the concept of time is intertwined with the dialectic between wish and gratification. Infants need and wait for the breast to fulfill their needs. However, the temporal delay between the child's needs and the mother's (more or less temporary) unavailability generates frustration. Time, then, begins to hinder the infant's sense of omnipotence. The sense of frustration also intensifies the link between time and reality. In this sense, the wish to go back and rewrite one's life story amounts to the willingness to reactualize in the present what has been unattainable in the past.

Of note, this process is also made possible by the establishment of a symbolic capacity that gives birth to verbal language (Arlow, 1984), through which the capacity for symbolization attains the goal of signifying the future as expectation and the past as memory. In fact, words are "time-binders" (Meerloo, 1966), because the relationship between time and language is mediated by a process of symbolization. If conscious awareness is mediated by self-awareness, such awareness is both given *and* limited by language. According to Freud (1930), the birth of the awareness of time is only possible when the differentiation between the Self and the external reality takes place, Gifford (1980) also stressed that our earliest awareness of external reality is experienced as related to the passage of time, which enforces adaptation to the 24-hour day–night rhythms.

From this point of view, how the caregiver manages the infant's temporal existence influence the latter's relation with time during subsequent developmental periods. To sum up, the infant experiences first (1) an original undifferentiated stage characterized by primary narcissism, where there is no distinction between subject and object, and time is experienced as omnipresent. This first condition turns then to (2) an intermediate stage of progressive separation between subject and object, which in turn leads to (3) a later stage, which eventually witnesses the development of the adult personality, and – provided that the individual does not experience unbearably negative affects, relations, or emotions – a sense of temporal continuity can begin to mark the existence of the Self (Sabbadini, 1989a, 1989b).

A central problem in conceptualizing subjective time is the persistence and identity of the Self as immersed in the flow of time (Meissner, 2007). In fact, understanding the nature of subjective time goes hand in hand with understanding its temporal continuity. The Self is both constant and inconstant, inasmuch as it allows for change to occur and, at the same time, remains the same despite the changes it goes through. The sense of temporal continuity seems fundamental in order for the Self to feel "one" over time. As Modell (1990) pointed out, "there is a core of the self that remains the same over time . . . yet the experience of self is also coterminous with an ever-changing flux of consciousness" (p. 1). Maintenance of temporal identity is based on a perspective on both past and future, which guarantees the continuity of the Self despite its temporal development. In this view, the most important contributing factors to the maintenance of the Self are, on the one hand, the spatiotemporal permanence of the unity of body and mind, and, on the other hand, the consolidation of self-representations over time.

Hägglund (2001) spoke of "timelessness" as an experience that can be either positive or negative. A positive experience of timelessness is produced when the Self is completely in contact with itself in the "here and now." This process is associated with the integration of the personality, a feeling of freedom, and a sense of being an integrated "whole." On the opposite end of the continuum, a negative experience of timelessness is linked to the fear of death and disintegration. From a psychoanalytical point of view, timelessness is originally thought of as the inseparable unity of the mother–child dyad, whereas "the passage of time symbolizes the period of separation" (Mann, 1982, p. 7). In this view, timelessness would reside in the unconscious mind of all individuals as a residual of this non-separateness. The state of timelessness described earlier corresponds to what infants experience in their fusion with the object of their needs. As we have seen, in fact, time is for the infant an eternal present (Bonaparte, 1940).

While objective time is perceived as a continuum of instants, subjective time is multifaceted and influenced by mood, emotions, thoughts, and even age (Colarusso, 1979). This is why the development of the sense of time is an essential ingredient in the development of the ability to tolerate frustration and the absence of wish-fulfilling objects. Furthermore, the development of time sense allows individuals to become aware of death as inescapable and omnipresent in human existence. The aforementioned intertwining of death and time points to the fact that, because existential time is primarily made up of the "here and now," human beings try to avoid time as a way to avoid destruction.

Time, Trauma, and Intersubjectivity

Most traumatic events occur in the context of intersubjective relationships (Van der Kolk, 2006), because trauma leads to significant reduction in the resourcefulness needed to navigate the world. In fact, developmental trauma originates in intersubjective contexts, and its core feature is the disruption of mutual regulation between the infant and the caregiver, which brings about a disorganized cognitive and emotional coping style (Duffy, 2012). Another consequence of developmental trauma is a narrowing of the range of the possible emotional landscapes that the person can experience. As a result, individuals exclude from their experience everything that threatens their stability in intersubjective contexts.

According to Stolorow (2007), emotional trauma occurs in the face of unbearable affect, which is constituted within an intersubjective context characterized by malattunement to the individual's emotional pain. What might be called the "intersubjective turn" in the history of psychoanalysis has been possible precisely because the "mind has been redefined from a set of predetermined structures emerging from inside an individual organism to transactional patterns and internal structures derived from an interactive, interpersonal field" (Mitchell, 1988, p. 17). Now, "lived time is the sequential progression of life; lived time is a sensing of one event after the other, and this sense of time is central to the embodied subject's dialectic relationship with the world" (Wyllie, 2005, p. 181). In this view, the dialectical relationship between the embodied individual and the surrounding world of objects generates the sense of lived time, which, in healthy subjects, is synchronized with the time of others.

Experiencing extremely intense suffering can dramatically alter the structure of subjective experience, thus closing the past and future dimensions to possible transformations. When the future is not experienced as a dynamic unfolding of possibilities, the individual lacks a dynamic view on his or her past as well, and both past and future, as it were, become "dead." When the feeling of experienced time is disrupted, the sense of time can speed up or slow down according to the person's cognitive and emotional state. Traumatized individuals experience past and future in an eternal pain, which comes unchanged from the past and is expected to remain unmodified in the future. The traumatized individual experiences ever-present suffering, which overwhelmingly takes over past and future: "all there is the immediate self-negating suffering of pain-here-now" (Wyllie, 2005, p. 176). As a result, the synthetic relationship between now-just-past, now-present, and now-yet-to-come is thus disrupted.

Traumatic psychopathology arises when intersubjective time is no longer part of the person's lived time (Kitamura & Kumar, 1982). In cases of severe trauma, time becomes *reversed*, because the person no longer moves toward the future; rather, the future moves toward the subject, who simply waits for it to become present. For the traumatized individual, the reversion of lived time goes along with a fixation on the past as an unchangeable dimension. The present becomes eternal repetition of the past, which lacks all possibilities for human openness to future dimensions (Fiorini & Canestri, 2009). Far from being created by an isolated mind, the concept of time is the result of early intersubjective experiences (Priel, 1997). In this view, the concept of time emerges from a self-with-other context, and represents the core of the differentiation between the Self and others.

The evolution of a sense of time is the result of a constant construction of meaning in intersubjective contexts. The sense of time is not only linked to the experience of pleasure and pain, but represents also a constitutive component of meaningful interpersonal exchanges. Priel (1997) contended that the failure of the infant's sense of omnipotence, regarded as the experience of "not having been *present*" (p. 439), results in the impossibility to experience the integration of past and present. In fact, "the dialectical movement between time and timelessness, between continuity and integration on one hand and discontinuity and disintegration on the other, constitutes the background of creative living" (p. 447). As Foehl (2020) pointed out, subject, world, and others are parts of the same emergent process.

References

Arlow, J. A. (1984). Disturbances of the sense of time – With special reference to the experience of timelessness. *Psychoanalytic Quarterly*, *53*, 13–37.

Bell, D. (2007). Existence in time: Development or catastrophe? In R. J. Perelberg (Ed.), *Time and memory* (pp. 65–102). London: Karnac Books.

Bergler, E., & Róheim, G. (1946). Psychology of time perception. *Psychoanalytic Quarterly*, *15*, 190–206.

Bonaparte, M. (1940). Time and the unconscious. *International Journal of Psycho-Analysis*, *21*, 427–468.

Carr, D. (1986). *Time, narrative, and history*. Bloomington: Indiana University Press.

Cohn, F. S. (1957). Time and the ego. *Psychoanalytic Quarterly*, *26*, 168–189.

Colarusso, C. A. (1979). The development of time sense – From birth to object constancy. *International Journal of Psycho-Analysis*, *60*, 243–251.

Connolly, A. (2017). Broken time. Disturbances of temporality in analysis. In A. Yiassemides (Ed.), *Time and the psyche: Jungian perspectives*. Routledge.

Denischik, M. (2015). Temporality in psychosis: Loss of lived time in an alien world. *The Humanistic Psychologist*, *43*(2), 148–159.

Dooley, L. (1941). The concept of time in defense of ego integrity. *Psychiatry*, *4*, 13–23.

Duffy, M. (2012). The body, trauma, and narrative approaches to healing. In A. Lock & T. Strong (Eds.), *Discursive perspectives in therapeutic practice*. Oxford: Oxford University Press.

Fink, K. (1993). The bi-logical perception of time. *International Journal of Psychoanalysis*, *74*, 303–312.

Fiorini, L. G., & Canestri, J. (2009). *The experience of time: Psychoanalytic perspectives*. London: Karnac Books.

Foehl, J. C. (2020). Lived depth: A phenomenology of psychoanalytic process and identity. *Psychoanalytic Inquiry*, *40*(2), 131–146.

Freud, S. (1915). The unconscious. In J. Strachey (Ed.), *The standard edition of the complete psychological works of Sigmund Freud* (vol. 14, pp. 159–215). London: Hogarth Press.

Freud, S. (1920). Beyond the pleasure principle. In J. Strachey (Ed.), *The standard edition of the complete psychological works of Sigmund Freud* (vol. 18, pp. 7–64). London: Hogarth Press.

Freud, S. (1930). Civilization and its discontents. In J. Strachey (Ed.), *The standard edition of the complete psychological works of Sigmund Freud* (vol. 21, pp. 64–145). London: Hogarth Press.

Frewen, P., & Lanius, R. A. (2015). *Healing the traumatized self*. London and New York: W. W. Norton.

Fuchs, T. (2010). Temporality and psychopathology. *Phenomenology and the Cognitive Sciences*, *12*(1), 75–104.

Gidron, Y., Duncan, E., Lazar, A., Biderman, A., Tandeter, H., & Shvartzman, P. (2002). Effects of guided written disclosure of stressful experiences on clinic visits and symptoms in frequent clinic attenders. *Family Practice*, *19*(2), 161–166.

Gifford, S. (1980). The prisoner of time. *Annual of Psychoanalysis*, *8*, 131–154.

Grinberg, L., & Grinberg, R. (1981). Modalities of object relationships in the psychoanalytic process. *Contemporary Psychoanalysis, 17*(2), 290–320.

Hägglund, T. (2001). Timelessness as a positive and negative experience. *Scandinavian Psychoanalytical Review, 24*(2), 83–92.

Harris, A. (2009). You must remember this. *Psychoanalytic Dialogues, 19*(1), 2–21.

Heidegger, M. (1927) 1962. *Being and time.* New York: Harper and Row.

Husserl, E. (1905) 1991. *On the phenomenology of the consciousness of internal time.* The Hague: Nijhoff.

Kitamura, T., & Kumar, R. (1982). Time passes slowly for patients with depressive state. *Acta Psychiatrica Scandinavica, 65*, 415–420.

Kohut, H. (1977). *The restoration of the self.* New York: International University Press.

Kurtz, S. A. (1988). The psychoanalysis of time. *Journal of the American Psychoanalytic Association, 36*(4), 985–1004.

Lacan, J. (1981). *The language of the self: The function of language in psychoanalysis.* Baltimore: Johns Hopkins University Press.

Lacan, J. (1953–1954) 2013. *Seminar: Book I. Freud's papers on technique.* New York: W. W. Norton.

Loewald, H. W. (1972). The experience of time. *The Psychoanalytic Study of the Child, 27*(1), 401–410.

Lombardi, R. (2013). Death, time, and psychosis. *Journal of The American Psychoanalytic Association, 61*(4), 691–726.

Mann, J. (1982). *Time-limited psychotherapy.* Cambridge, MA: Harvard University Press.

Meerloo, J. A. M. (1948). Father time. *Psychiatric Quarterly, 22*, 587–608.

Meerloo, J. A. M. (1966). The time sense in psychiatry. In J. T. Fraser (Ed.), *The voices of time* (pp. 235–252). New York: G. Braziller.

Meissner, W. W. (2007). *Time, self and psychoanalysis.* Plymouth: Jason Aronson.

Merleau-Ponty, M. (1945) 1962. *Phenomenology of perception.* London: Routledge & Kegan Paul.

Minkowski, E. (1927) 1970. *Lived time: Phenomenological and psychological studies.* Chicago, IL: Northwestern University Press.

Mitchell, S. A. (1988). *Relational concepts in psychoanalysis: An integration.* Cambridge & London: Harvard University Press.

Modell, A. H. (1990). *Other times, other realities: Toward a theory of psychoanalytic treatment.* Cambridge, MA: Harvard University Press.

Modell, A. H. (1992). The private self and private space. *Annual of Psychoanalysis, 20*, 1–14.

Noë, A. (2006). *Action in perception.* Cambridge, MA: The MIT Press.

Omer, A., & Alon, A. (1997). *Constructing therapeutic narratives.* New York: Jason Aronson.

Priel, B. (1997). Time and self: On the intersubjective construction of time. *Psychoanalytic Dialogues, 7*(4), 431–450.

Sabbadini, A. (1989a). Boundaries of timelessness. Some thoughts about the temporal dimension of the psychoanalytic space. *International Journal of Psycho-Analysis, 70*, 305–313.

Sabbadini, A. (1989b). How the infant develops a sense of time. *British Journal of Psychotherapy, 5*(4), 475–484.

Sarbin, T. R. (1986). *Narrative psychology. The storied nature of human conduct.* New York: Praeger.

Stolorow, R. (2007). *Trauma and human existence.* New York: The Analytic Press.

Terr, L. C. (1984). Time and trauma. *The Psychoanalytic Study of The Child, 39*(1), 633–665.

Van der Hart, O., Bolt, H., & Kolk, B. A. (2005). Memory fragmentation in dissociative identity disorder. *Journal of Trauma & Dissociation, 6*(1), 55–70.

Van der Kolk, B. A. (2006). Clinical implications of neuroscience research in PTSD. *Annals of the New York Academy of Sciences, 1071*(1), 277–293.

Williams, P. (2007). Making time: Killing time. In R. J. Perelberg (Ed.), *Time and memory* (pp. 47–64). London: Karnac Books.

Winnicott, D. W. (1974). Fear of breakdown. *International Review of Psychoanalysis, 1,* 103–107.

Wyllie, M. (2005). Lived time and psychopathology. *Philosophy, Psychiatry, & Psychology, 12*(3), 173–185.

Chapter 5

Dissociation and Traumatic Temporality

This chapter deals primarily with dissociation, that is, the disruption of the ordinary integration of consciousness and memory. In traumatized individuals, autobiographical memories show specific types of disruption, and can produce traumatic flashbacks, namely, memory fragments encoded in more primitive brain regions than the ones subserving the storage of ordinary autobiographical memories. Experiencing flashbacks amounts to "reliving" the traumatic event, rather than just "remembering" it. The so-called "speechless terror," which goes hand in hand with the inhibition of Broca's area, hinders the subject's capacity to use verbal language to communicate, thus impairing the encoding of conscious semantic memory. Dissociating amounts to "losing time," and involves a disruption of a coherent sense of self in time. Ultimately, trauma seems to suspend time sense by producing temporal fragmentation, which seems to reinstate or preserve a sense of agency over the traumatic episode.

The Origin of Dissociation

The term "dissociation" derives from a translation by William James (1842–1910) of the term *désagrégation*, first proposed by Janet ([1889] 2005) in the context of his studies on hysteria (see James, [1890] 1950). The word has been used for decades only with regard to the fragmentation pertaining to psychotic experiences. Originally, however, it referred to the concept of the human mind as naturally fragmented, such that the sense of a unified Self would be the result of a synthetic activity of the mind (Lapassade, 1996). The so-called Janetian "traumatic model" predicted that the individual's sense of unity in time is altered when faced with traumatic experiences, which produce dissociated mental states (Nemiah, 1998). The *DSM-5* (APA, 2013) defines dissociation as "a disruption and/or discontinuity in the normal integration of consciousness, memory, identity, emotion, perception, body representation, motor control, and behavior" (p. 291).

DOI: 10.4324/9781003230601-6

The phenomenological features of dissociation vary widely according to the different subjective experiences associated with it, but can include "depersonalization, derealization, emotional numbing, flashbacks of traumatic events, absorption, amnesia, voice-hearing, interruptions in awareness, and identity alteration" (Lanius, 2015, p. 1), which would all represent forms of trauma-related altered states of consciousness. Three main types of psychological dissociation can be distinguished (Van der Hart et al., 2004). In "primary" dissociation, the traumatic experience is processed in parts, rather than as an integrated whole. Here, traumatic experiences are isolated from the individual, rather than being separated from each other. "Secondary" dissociation involves the appraisal of events without the experience of their full emotional impact. In this second type of dissociation, a division can be witnessed as to the components of experience, that is, events are recalled, but lack their affective coloring. Finally, "tertiary" dissociation involves the development of separate identities, each containing emotional and cognitive material that is only partly, if not at all, available to others. This further type of dissociation involves the formation of distinct ego states.

Both Janet and Freud viewed dissociation as a "splitting of consciousness," even though their explanation of why dissociation occurs differed widely (Gullestad, 2005). The core concept in Janet's work is a narrowing of consciousness and a disintegration of the ordinarily operating synthesis of different cognitive processes. In contrast, Freud conceptualized dissociation as a dynamic defense, that is, a process of actively expelling painful thoughts and feelings from the psyche. As Gullestad (2005) pointed out, whereas Janet's view focused more on *deficit*, Freud based his theorization on *conflict*. Now, dissociative symptoms may be conceptualized not only from a descriptive psychopathological perspective, but also from an adaptational, process-oriented point of view. Accordingly, conflict and unconscious intention, as well as personal meaning, are equally essential conditions for a rational understanding of dissociation. From a developmental perspective, dissociation may be further conceptualized as a normative process through which the individual can regulate inner mental states in the face of outer threatening stimuli.

Today, the term "dissociation" has taken on a variety of meanings, ranging from avoidance of verbally articulating experience (Stern, 2017) to a type of defense that shrinks the world to a "narrow band of perceptual reality" (Bromberg, 2003, p. 561). As Stolorow (2011) pointed out, the latter conceptualization of dissociation is very close to Kohut's (1971) description of a "vertical split in the psyche" (p. 176). From a phenomenological perspective, defensive dissociation can be thought of as a sort of tunnel vision, a process of narrowing one's experiential horizon aimed at excluding unbearable emotions. Whereas Bromberg (2003) spoke of the "separateness of incompatible self-states" (p. 561), Stolorow (2011) emphasized also, and more broadly, the process of keeping apart incommensurable emotional worlds.

The experience of trauma hinders the person's sense of temporal continuity, or – to use Heidegger's ([1927] 1962) words – its "being-in-time." Traumatized individuals often learn to dissociate and compartmentalize threatening emotions (Stolorow, 2011). They can be high functioning in everyday life, and yet become inflexible in the presence of trauma-related stimuli. Trauma continues to affect the person at every level of his or her cognitive, emotional, and psychophysiological functioning. The traumatic situation is reenacted through body movements, breath, gestures, and perceptions. The experience of trauma freezes the subject's overall experience into an eternal present, confining the person to "the greatest burden" of Nietzsche's ([1883–1885] 2009) legacy, that is, an *eternal repetition of the same*. In traumatic experiences, the past ceases to be past and becomes present, whereas the future ceases to be future and becomes eternal repetition. But trauma also points to the limits of human existence. Indeed, "authentic temporality, insofar as it owns up to human finitude, is traumatic temporality" (Stolorow, 2011, p. 61).

Traumatic Flashbacks and "Speechless Terror"

During a flashback, PTSD patients are not able to create a storyline and relive the traumatic event as isolated sensory, emotional, and motoric imprints of the trauma (Foa et al., 1989). This process possibly occurs because in states of high arousal activation the central nervous system fails to synthesize the traumatic sensations into an integrated whole (Van der Kolk, 2000). In fact, traumatic memories are particularly disorganized in PTSD patients (Van der Kolk et al., 2001), so that the emotional processing involves organizing these memories (Foa & Riggs, 1993). In other words, failure to adequately process trauma-related information seems to underlie PTSD, and the degree of articulation of a narrative shortly after the trauma is associated with the severity of PTSD symptomatology (Amir et al., 1998).

The nature of traumatic flashbacks is quite different from memories of non-traumatic events, as the former are stored in more primitive brain regions and have less connection to cortical left hemisphere regions. This very nature of flashbacks results in mostly non-verbal somatic, sensory, and emotional symptomatology. Recalling a flashback amounts to experiencing a memory *as if* it was occurring in the "here and now." Flashbacks often occur spontaneously and cannot be controlled. They are usually more vivid than ordinary memories, and involve a disruption of temporal experience. Flashbacks are experienced as emotional and sensory fragments of the traumatic event, and as unchanging over time – as opposed to other kinds of memory, which tend to change upon recall. Trauma-related maladaptive responses are produced because trauma negatively impacts the individual's autobiographical memory, as shown by traumatic narratives.

Different cognitive models of PTSD agreed upon the fact that, in PTSD individuals, autobiographical memories show specific types of "disruption" (Stanghellini, 2009). These models hold that traumatic memories are dominated by sensory, perceptual, and emotional components that can be easily triggered by similar cues, and result in the intrusive and involuntary quality of trauma memories, which appear as fragmented and not organized into a coherent whole. Furthermore, experiencing flashbacks amounts to *reliving* the traumatic event, rather than just *remembering* it (Tulving, 2002):

> [F]lashbacks are differentiated from the normal recall of memories of past traumas by the fact that, when *remembering*, even if recall is intrusive and distressing, the past does not *become* the present. In contrast, *reexperiencing* (flashbacks) involves, by definition, the experience of a memory as if it is happening in the *present* tense.
>
> (Frewen & Lanius, 2015, p. 85)

Traumatic memories appear isolated from the rest of autobiographical memories. In trauma patients, they exhibit a lack of temporal organization when compared with other autobiographical memories. However, whether traumatic events lead to deficient or else enhanced memories is still a matter of debate (O'Kearney & Perrott, 2006). More specifically, while PTSD involves a disturbance in the temporal organization of trauma narratives, data addressing the fact that trauma narratives are fragmented still appear to be inconclusive. Decreased hippocampal activity is associated with the inability to localize events in time, resulting in the reexperiencing of traumatic events as if they were happening in the present moment. During flashbacks, the amygdala and the right hemisphere become more activated. Also, trauma can bring about the so-called "speechless terror," which hinders the person's capacity to use verbal language to communicate with others. Broca's area becomes inhibited, impairing the encoding of conscious semantic memory of the trauma. From an evolutionary point of view, it has been suggested that in threatening situations, nature would tell human beings to "shut up" in order to activate more effectively fight-or-flight responses to face danger (O'Kearney & Perrott, 2006).

Peritraumatic dissociation, that is, dissociation occurring during or in the immediate aftermath of a traumatic event, seems to be one of the most important predictors of PTSD (Ozer et al., 2003). In this view, dissociative encoding, that is, incomplete initial processing of the traumatic situation, would lead to PTSD symptomatology. More specifically, dissociation during or immediately after the traumatic episode prevents the individual from fully encoding the event, thus disrupting both memory storage and the ability to recall the event. Memory fragmentation goes hand in hand with abnormalities of sequence, coherence, and content of trauma narratives. Ultimately, dissociative encoding and lack of memory processing are the key mechanisms underlying the development of PTSD (Briere et al., 2005). At the core of dissociation stand memory disturbances, which lead to disorganized narrative recall and to frequent, involuntary memory intrusions.

From an empirical point of view, the link between dissociation and memory fragmentation has been disputed (Giesbrecht et al., 2008), as the former does not seem to be consistently and systematically associated with the latter. Bedard-Gilligan and Zoellner (2012) claimed that dissociation might not be a universally maladaptive strategy. In fact, dissociation occurs not only among trauma survivors, but also in well-adjusted persons. In this view, trauma-related dissociation may even be adaptive, as it would help individuals to protect themselves from encoding threatening memories and to possibly reduce psychophysiological arousal as well. Distress and arousal might equally affect memory fragmentation, which can be thought of as the epiphenomenon resulting from increased stress during trauma recalling. Accordingly, dissociation may serve as a mechanism of emotion regulation that helps individuals to avoid trauma-related thoughts, feelings, affect, and emotions (Bedard-Gilligan & Zoellner, 2012).

Dissociation and Traumatic Disruption of Time Sense

One of the most characterizing features of dissociation is time disruption (Sar & Rhoades, 2005). The most frequently reported dissociative symptoms are indeed time slowing down, speeding up, or even stopping. Furthermore, time disruption appears to be associated with memory impairment. In dissociation, a disconnection from the world results in extreme involvement with one's own inner world, rather than with the physical, tangible, concrete reality. When trauma patients experience a dissociative process, they are often unaware of the process starting, and only realize that they have phased out when they "come back" to the intersubjectively structured world of others. During this lapse of time, they are mentally disconnected from outer reality, focusing almost only on their inner world. The more trauma patients dissociate, the more is the time they essentially "miss." In this sense, dissociating amounts to "losing time" (Sar & Rhoades, 2005).

At times, dissociation points to a sense of time slowing down, as things seem to take much longer than expected to occur. Time dilation seems indeed to be a marker of some dissociative responses (Frewen & Lanius, 2015), as it is perceived as the only opportunity to face life-threatening situations. However, the persistence of an altered sense of time after the traumatic shock has passed can lead to personal and intersubjective maladaptive functioning. Emotional numbness has also been described in relation to the dimension of timelessness. In fact, "traumatized persons frequently appear fixated experientially at the time of the trauma; subjectively the experience may be something akin to a sense of timelessness, of being in an experiential vacuum or an abyss" (Frewen & Lanius, 2015, p. 80). In these occurrences, the person's subjective experience seems to stop or freeze at the time of the trauma, leaving no room for change and growth.

Therefore, trauma brings about temporal fragmentation, that is, different temporal perspectives and different experiences of duration. When psychological trauma is present, time sense is interrelated with the "stimulus barrier" or "protective shield" against overstimulation. This statement has been somehow criticized due to the observation that infants tend to seek stimuli, rather than avoid them (Shapiro & Stern, 1980). For this reason, Esman (1983) concluded that the "protective shield" functions more like a "filter" rather than as an impenetrable obstacle. The human perceptual apparatus seems indeed to function as a sieve against overstimulation, so perceptions become damaged in the process of being overrun (Terr, 1984). Furthermore, particularly severe trauma can be experienced or else remembered as foreshortened, whereas short-lived traumatic situations can be recalled and experienced as prolonged (Langer et al., 1961). On the one hand, experiencing a very extended trauma as shorter might serve as a mechanism of survival, that is, as a defense mechanism from hopelessness and helplessness. On the other hand, experiencing relatively brief traumatic occurrences in slow motion might serve the goal of perceiving the situation in more detail and, possibly, defending oneself from the aggressor and better face the threatening situation.

Trauma seems to suspend the sense of time in several ways: by condensing contiguous events into simultaneity; by skewing time, (e.g., when a traumatic event is misplaced to a time that precedes the trauma); by giving sense to events in retrospect; and by offering a sense of prediction (Stein, 1953). The brain is able to make instantaneous backward, retroactive adjustments, which might occur over longer time frames. Under shock, the retroactively adjusting brain can malfunction in relation to time sense. In these instances, warning stimuli that occurred long after the trauma can be mispositioned to a time preceding the shock. Omens are another example of temporal phenomena that characterize traumatic experience (Stein, 1953). Omens require that time be suspended, and that sequential ordering be rearranged with new significance. With an omen in place, individuals tend to perceive some form of control over the traumatic episode. Omens imply that past life events (especially those preceding the trauma) become charged with new meanings after the traumatic occurrence. Therefore, it seems that omens and premonitions following trauma represent attempts to gain belated mastery over uncontrollable situations (Stein, 1953), in the form of the *après-coup*.

Psychic temporal functioning offers coping mechanisms that constantly work to decrease external stress and internal anxiety. As time perception appears to be deeply vulnerable to stress, time disruption might be regarded as a traumatic symptom in clinical settings. Trauma patients seem to distort time as a way to reinstate a sense of control over the traumatic episode, that is, as a compromise to preserve their sense of agency. A main feature of PTSD and other trauma-related disorders is the alternation between the apparently opposite experiences of reliving the trauma and detaching from it, the latter involving little or even no awareness of the trauma itself. Nijenhuis et al. (2010) related these two processes to the emotional and functional systems controlling human bodily functions. They further associated traumatic reexperiencing with inborn and evolutionary derived defensive systems evoked by severe threat. As a complex system, our body tends to respond in ways involving adaptive functions, such as flight, fight, or freeze. In this view, detachment from trauma appears to be associated with different action systems, which control everyday life functions and are dedicated to the survival of the species. As distinct from repression, dissociation means the impossibility to create one's own experience in what might be called a "kairotic space":

> [K]airos is a relational phenomenon, and it has its effects on human life via the living history of the interpersonal field. It is through the medium of the field that the present retranscribes the past and the past shapes the present. And it is also through the field that, in dissociation, the past is denied its effect on the present, and the present is prevented from reshaping the past. To the extent that the field is frozen, it is our clinical intention to melt it; and in this process of addressing dissociation we melt time itself, allowing *kairos* to circulate freely once again.
>
> (Stern, 2017, pp. 505–506)

Trauma, Dissociation, and Personification

Dissociation has been described as a disruption of a coherent sense of Self, which goes hand in hand with symptoms such as numbing, derealization, depersonalization, and out-of-body experiences (Brewin & Holmes, 2003). Trauma-related memories tend to be experienced as fragmented and disjointed. Recalling these memories goes along with temporal disruption, insofar as the traumatic episode seems to be happening in the "here and now" and not in the past. Furthermore, the recalling of life-threatening situations seems to be unintentionally triggered by trauma-related cues. Severe threat may provoke a structural dissociation of the premorbid personality occurring between the individual's defensive system and the system underlying everyday life and the survival of the species. Brewin and Holmes (2003) described this form of dissociation as a process occurring between what they called "apparently normal personality" (ANP) and an "emotional personality" (EP). Whereas the EP constantly fails to create a meaningful narrative of the trauma, the ANP is associated with avoidance of traumatic memories, and possibly leads the individual to develop partial or even total amnesia. Both the ANP and EP are associated with a differential sense of Self, and display different psychobiological responses to traumatic memories (Brewin & Holmes, 2003). The EP is the manifestation of mental systems that involve traumatic memories (Nijenhuis et al., 2010). Traumatic memories represent those aspects of the threatening situations that are associated with different images of the body, and with a separate sense of Self as well. The EP ranges from the reexperiencing of unintegrated aspects of the trauma to dissociative parts of the personality, such as in dissociative identity disorder (DID). Whereas the narratively organized memory is verbal, social, and reconstructive in nature, traumatic memories are subjectively characterized by a sense of *timelessness*, that is, they tend to be experienced as something that cannot be changed (Baranger et al., 1988).

Upon reactivation of traumatic memories, access to other kinds of memories is obstructed. When the EP takes over the Self's temporal experience, a loss occurs as to the overall availability of memories for the ANP. Typically, the EP displays defensive motor behaviors, specifically in response to trauma-related stimuli. Also, the field of consciousness of the EP tends to be restricted to trauma-related triggers. While the EP can, in fact, synthesize and personify aspects of the trauma, it systematically fails to integrate current reality into a coherent narrative, leading the ANP to be eventually unable to adapt to present reality. In turn, the ANP is characterized by a loss of personification. This means that the ANP is unable to integrate traumatic memories within the psychic systems underlying memory. The EP constantly interferes with the ANP as traumatic memories, when reactivated, can overgrow consciousness itself. Ultimately, the ANP may become completely deactivated by the intrusions of the EP, resulting in amnesia of the traumatic event (Nijenhuis et al., 2010).

Now, mental health can be thought of in terms of the capacity for differentiation and integration (Janet, [1889] 2005, 1919). In this view, integration involves the constant implementation of mental actions into a coherent whole. First, a synthesis must be performed between internal and external events into new, meaningful mental processes. Second, a further synthesis ought to link experience and knowledge of events in their temporal unfolding. Adaptive behavior stems from the ability to create a meaningful experience in a synthesis of sensations, perceptions, thoughts, feelings, and emotions. Therefore, traumatized individuals can make sense of their experience only when they become able to synthesize their experience in coherent mental structures, which involve the organization of representations of internal and external events into a coherent narrative.

According to Brewin and Holmes (2003), integration has "personification" as its most salient component, that is, the mental action that relates synthesized pieces of psychic information to the person's general sense of Self. Personification refers to the act of relating a specific experience to the subject's overarching narrative. As previously noted, overwhelming events can interfere with this core functioning of personality. When traumatized individuals witness a failure in processes of personification, events that occur in their lives are not related to their sense of Self. In such circumstances, the synthesized material will be *noetic*, that is, pertaining to object-related experiences unrelated to the Self, but not *autonoetic*, that is, associated with experiences that are connected to the individual's sense of self-ownership (Brewin & Holmes, 2003). In fact, traumatized individuals feel that the experience actually occurred, and yet it is not part of their own biography. Accordingly, the corresponding memory will be semantic, but not episodic, because they will retain events without relating them to their Self, as they lack the capacity to reflect on experience.

According to Brewin and Holmes (2003), episodic memory involves a double kind of awareness, that is, awareness of the facts and awareness of the relatedness of these facts to one's own experience. As personification fails, so does the development of a coherent sense of Self over time. In order for personification processes to be successful, they must be based on the integration of the entire subject's life story. Non-traumatic events are typically integrated and synthesized into symbolic forms. However, traumatic experiences seem to remain relatively unintegrated and unavailable to the ordinary information processing systems. Severe threat modifies not only the individual's mental functioning, but also his or her ordinary bodily processes. Indeed, neurochemicals released during traumatic situations are highly concentrated in brain regions, such as the hippocampus and the prefrontal cortex, which subserve the execution of integrative mental actions that can interfere with the normal integration of experience. In this light, dissociation is a manifestation of acute integrative failure, that is, failure to synthesize and personify the traumatic episode (Brewin & Holmes, 2003).

Detachment and Compartmentalization in Dissociative Phenomena

Holmes et al. (2005) proposed to clarify the use of the term "dissociation" by splitting it into a dichotomy between two qualitatively different phenomena, which would also "differ as semidistinct psychological *processes*" (Frewen & Lanius, 2015, p. 6): "detachment" and "compartmentalization." "Detachment" would refer to an altered state of consciousness, characterized by a sense of separateness from specific aspects of experience, be it one's own body (as in out-of-body experiences), one's sense of Self (as in depersonalization), or the external world (as in derealization). These forms of detachment often occur together and possibly reflect a common neurobiological mechanism. Individuals experiencing detachment often report feeling "spaced out," "unreal," or in a "dreamlike state" (Holmes et al., 2005). During detachment, an absence or alteration of the person's emotional experience occurs.

In turn, the concept of "compartmentalization" encompasses dissociative amnesia and the neurological symptoms that characterize not only conversion disorders, but also other kinds of "somatoform dissociation." Compartmentalization refers to an inability to bring typically accessible information under the umbrella of conscious awareness. The actions that are no longer available to conscious control are said to be "compartmentalized." A significant feature of this phenomenon is that compartmentalized processes continue to work even when they are not available to intentional control, and are therefore prone to influence emotions, cognitions, and actions. This apparent disruption of functions is also a distinguishing feature of compartmentalization as opposed to detachment (Holmes et al., 2005).

Whereas compartmentalization refers to a lack of information within the cognitive system, detachment is associated with an experienced state of disconnection from the Self and the environment. As a result, treatment for compartmentalization may need to be aimed at acquiring the skills to reactivate and reintegrate compartmentalized components of the Self, whereas treatments for detachment ought to aim to prevent this condition from being triggered, or to terminate it once triggered. Ultimately, the paradigm delineated by Holmes et al. (2005) directly intends to help the individual to differentiate adequate treatment by distinguishing and selecting the most appropriate intervention for each specific person.

Some forms of dissociation are associated with conversion disorders, where the symptoms appear as linked directly to the individual's experience of his or her body. Growing evidence exists that points to the fact that trauma results in "somatoform dissociation" (Waller et al., 2001), in which the subject fails to adequately process somatic experience. Somatoform dissociation can become manifested as a "negative" somatic experience (e.g., as a lack of somatic experience, such as a disturbance of percep-tual skills or anesthesia), or as a "positive" somatic experience (e.g., as a heightened somatic state, such as pain or motor activity). More spe-cifically, somatoform dissociation seems to be directly proportional to the severity of reported trauma involving physical contact or injury, as opposed to other forms of dissociation linked to a wider range of non-contact trauma. In this view, somatoform dissociation can be defined as a set of adaptive psychophysiological responses to threat involving inescap-able physical injury, which lead to psychiatric disorders that might inter-fere with treatment of PTSD (Waller et al., 2001).

Depersonalization and derealization are common symptoms of anxiety disturbances, and are often acutely experienced during or in the after-math of traumatic events (Phillips et al., 2001). Furthermore, inhibitory mechanisms of detachment might be at work in the face of extreme emo-tional arousal. For instance, patients with a depersonalization disorder show reduced activation in brain regions associated with emotional expe-rience, and increased activation in areas linked to emotional regulation, which can produce a state of vigilant alertness, widened attentional focus, and apparent absence of emotions. This might be an adaptive strategy to maintain behavioral control over threatening situations.

Peritraumatic dissociation seems to be a risk factor for the experience of revictimization in trauma patients (Marx & Sloan, 2005). In fact, peritraumatic dissociation, as well as experiential avoidance, that is, the unwillingness to remain in contact with aversive personal experiences, are significantly related to PTSD symptomatology at baseline. Avoidance allows the individual to wall off the frequency and severity of trauma-related symptoms. However, it also results in the perpetuation of the same events that triggered the trauma-related symptomatology. In other words, trying to control internal events can lead to the loss of control over such events. In this view, psychological and behavioral difficulties are seen as the manifestation of the attempt to master psychic processes that are experienced as out of control. Thus, peritraumatic dissociation seems to overlap with avoidance processes, as they both serve as a tool to distance the individual from trauma-related triggers. In fact, somato-form dissociation can be regarded as the failure to fully integrate the somatic components of the traumatic experience (Waller et al., 2001). Trauma-related dissociation is maintained through deficits in integrative processes related to the Self and through pervasive avoidance as well.

Building back on Janet's theory of personality, Van der Hart et al. (2004) postulated that dissociation is a structural split of personality, which would be insufficiently able to integrate functions comprising the sense of Self. Based on Janet's and Freud's theory, the so-called "trau-matic model" (Nemiah, 1998, p. 18) stated that symptom reduction might entail a discharge of the traumatic effects of external events. In this view, the fusion of split parts of the personality into a coherent whole can be accomplished by removing the amnestic barriers between the alters, which can be achieved by reducing the intensity of anxiety. In turn, the so-called "structural model" (Nemiah, 1998, p. 21) emphasizes the presence of psychological conflicts between libidinal and aggressive drives on the one hand, and the defenses against their conscious emergence on the other. Trauma treatment aims at moderating the conflict between drives and defenses. When this step is achieved, the individual will be better able to let its drives become conscious without experiencing overwhelming anxiety.

According to Van der Kolk and van der Hart (1995), trauma has less to do with "repression," regarded in Freudian terms as an active refusal of a specific experience, than with "dissociation," through which the mind fails to organize an incomprehensible event as something that unfolds in a temporally structured narrative. Barnaby (2012) disputed both Freud's idea of traumatic repression of something that "has been there," and Van der Kolk and van der Hart's (1995) idea that dissociation is what primarily marks the traumaticity of an experience. Indeed,

> what if the experience of trauma registers an absence rather than a dislocated presence? What if the traumatic remnant is inaccessible precisely because it is *not stored* somewhere else in the mind? What if there is nothing to repress or what if there is nothing there to be transformed even into traumatic memory because there was no original experience to be remembered? Is it possible, then, to imagine that one could be traumatized precisely by what has not been experienced?
>
> (Barnaby, 2012, p. 120)

This seems to point to the notion of *Nachträglichkeit*, as it refers to the *constitution* of experience, rather than just a recall of it. In fact, what is constituted in the form of the *après-coup* is the mnestic trace of the original event, that is, the subjective experience of it. Furthermore, traumatic *Nachträglichkeit* would involve an ethical situation, because it is "inconceivable without a model of translation: that is, it presupposes that something is proffered by the other, and this is then afterwards retranslated and reinterpreted" (Laplanche, 1999, p. 265).

Phenomenology of Dissociation: The Four-Dimensional Model of the Traumatized Self

Presenting evidence of the dissociative subtype of PTSD, Lanius et al. (2010) distinguished it from non-dissociative types of PTSD. The former would be characterized by "overmodulation of affect, while the more common undermodulated type involves the predominance of reexperiencing and hyperarousal symptoms" (p. 640). This distinction has been suggested to be paramount in the assessment and treatment of PTSD individuals. In this view, reexperiencing and hyperarousal reactivity are regarded as manifestations of emotion dysregulation involving emotional undermodulation, mediated by failure in prefrontal inhibition of limbic brain areas. In contrast, the dissociative type of PTSD would be associated with emotion dysregulation involving emotional overmodulation, mediated by prefrontal inhibition of the same limbic brain regions (Lanius et al., 2010). Besides meeting full criteria for PTSD, the dissociative subtype of PTSD relates, as the term suggests, to dissociative symptoms (depersonalization or derealization) as responses to traumatic stimuli, which typically go along with emotional detachment (Schiavone et al., 2018).

Now, phenomenology has always stressed the subjective character of experience (e.g., Varela, 1996). In this sense, phenomenology refers to the investigation on "what it is like" (Nagel, 1974) to have certain experiences. Besides the *quantitative* features of experience, such as arousal or activation, span and extent of awareness, and sensory processes, phenomenology also recognizes more *qualitative* dimensions of conscious experience. In Thompson and Zahavi's (2007) framework, for instance, subjective experience can be classified according to four *qualitative* dimensions, that is, (1) temporality, (2) narrative, (3) embodiment, and (4) affect. Frewen and Lanius (2015) further referred to these constructs as (1) time, (2) thought, (3) body, and (4) emotions, respectively, and utilized them to describe traumatic psychopathology within the so-called "four-dimensional model" of trauma and dissociation:

> [T]he fundamental principle of the 4-D model for classifying trauma-related symptomatology is that the presenting symptoms of traumatized persons can be classified as either forms of normal waking consciousness (NWC) or trauma-related altered states of consciousness (TRASC) referring to the dimensions of time, thought, body, and emotion.
>
> (p. 28; see also Frewen & Lanius, 2014)

Therefore, the 4D model of dissociation is intended to provide a framework that brings together the phenomenological, neurobiological, and physiological features of trauma-related dissociation (Lanius, 2015).

As to the first dimension that characterizes the 4D model of trauma and dissociation, that is, *time*, Frewen and Lanius (2015) pointed out:

> [T]he consciousness of time also becomes altered during the experience of flashbacks, during which individuals report that the past (i.e., a memory), intrudes so fully on their present consciousness that

they lose experiential contact with their present environments; the traumatic memory is effectively experienced as though it were being *relived*.

(p. 37)

Narrative refers to the story-like organization of human consciousness, which is always *referential*, as it is always "about" something. This property of consciousness, also referred to as *intentionality*, can be directed inward (self-consciousness) or outward (exteroception). Also, consciousness is supposed to be always experienced from a "first-person" perspective, which refers to the person's ownership of thoughts, emotions, and actions, also referred to as *self-referential processing* (Northoff et al., 2006). Furthermore, consciousness is also *embodied* in the person's body, and *embedded* in the surrounding environment. Everything that occurs in our minds is deeply correlated with our body. As Damasio (1999) stated, "whatever happens in your mind happens in time and in space relative to the instant in time your body is in and to the region of space occupied by your body" (p. 145).

In the field of phenomenology, a distinction is commonly drawn between the two concepts of *Leib* and *Körper*, that is, between the "subjective or lived body" and the "physical or organic body," respectively. This double-faced expression of the body is so important that Fuchs (2018) proposed that possibly the hardest philosophical problem in Western thought, the so-called mind–body problem, might be reformulated in terms of the "*Leib-Körper* problem." In traumatic psychopathology, the conversion-like symptoms often reported by trauma patients have been regarded as "forms of *partial disembodiment*" (Frewen & Lanius, 2015, p. 40). Finally, phenomenology recognizes that consciousness has an emotional *valence* as well as an *arousal* dimension that covers a continuum of intensities. In this regard, traumatized individuals tend to experience both increased and decreased arousal, for example, feelings of fear, anxiety, guilt, and shame. Therefore, considering the phenomenological features of trauma seems to be crucial for trauma studies to have an impact also on consciousness studies, precisely because trauma might be seen as an extreme polarization of the common features of ordinary experience.

Dissociation and Attachment: Can Dissociation Be Adaptive?

Attachment can be regarded as

> a stable progression of cognitive, affective and behavioral styles that persist into adulthood, creating an interpersonal template that

underpins one's ability to relate to others, regulate emotion, mental-
ize (infer the mental state of others), and manage autonomic arousal
in order to cope with threatening feelings and situations.

(Dillon et al., 2014, p. 148)

Early disorganized attachment patterns involving traumatic experiences during infancy and childhood are predictive of later vulnerability
to dissociative reactions to trauma (Liotti, 2004). Disorganization of early
attachment is closely related to the collapse of the integrative functions
of consciousness that characterizes dissociative experiences. On this basis,
Liotti (2004) concluded that traumatic experiences, attachment patterns,
and dissociative experiences are "three threads woven into a single strand"
(p. 478). In fact, ongoing traumatization in infancy and childhood compromises the process of ego organization, and leads to an arrest of psychobiological processes. It seems that the severity of traumatization, as
well as disorganized attachment patterns, would lead to a more prominent
likelihood of dissociative symptoms in adolescence (Ogawa et al., 1997).
Indeed, "disordered attachment can be seen as a trauma in itself" (Dillon
et al., 2014, p. 148), and early lack of integration among different behavioral states is predictive of dissociated parts of the personality later on in
life.

The child's integrative capacity develops when cohesion among several behavioral states is promoted by secure attachment, which provides
physiological and psychological regulatory functions. Liotti (2004) also
stressed the link between attachment-related trauma and the tendency
toward dissociative mental operations during tasks involving autobiographical memories. Through continual enactment of trauma-related
memories, traumatized individuals create their world based on the traumatic event, and live in it in a dissociated way.

Bromberg (1998) defined dissociation in terms of a "normal hypnoid
capacity of the mind" (p. 561) that might even serve creative adaption. In
this perspective, dissociation is a mental *process* that can become a mental *structure*. It allows individuals to defend themselves from traumatic
stress by disconnecting the mind from stimuli that are too dangerous for
the maintenance of a normal sense of the Self. Therefore, dissociation
can serve the individual by retaining the protective layer afforded by the
separateness from stimuli that the individual is hardly able to deal with.
According to Simeon and Abugel (2006), dissociation can also represent
an adaptive mechanism that supports the overcoming of traumatic stress.
Dissociation works as a useful mechanism even after the traumatic event
has occurred, and would prevent the individual from "feeling too much,"
that is, to be too exposed to affective triggers of the trauma. According
to Gullestad (2005), this "positive" aspect of dissociation ought to be

acknowledged notwithstanding the contemporary focus of researchers on the disruptive character of it.

In order for the traumatic material to be symbolized, a link must be established between the experience of the event and the Self as the subject of that experience (Bromberg, 1998). This is why the more unsymbolized the affect, the more powerful the dissociative force that keeps different parts of the personality separated. In the face of imminent loss of selfhood, dissociation serves as a tool to unlink incompatible patterns of self-experience in the effort to preserve autonomy and the capacity to stay alive. The goal of psychotherapy, that is, the symbolic integration of trauma-related material into a coherent narrative, is achieved only when the affective memories of the trauma are linked to the sense of Self through the episodic memory, which serves as a major connective power between the Self and the traumatic experience. In this way, a shift from dissociation to a bearable conflict occurs, through a process in which different parts of the personality that have been kept apart can eventually be reconciled into a coherent whole, that is, within the subject as the conscious owner of his or her experience (Bromberg, 1998).

From a psychoanalytic perspective, what renders an event a traumatic stressor is the relationship between the agent and his or her perception of the situation. This means that trauma does not lie outside the individual's mind, but is rather grounded in the person's perception of the environment. In other words, attention needs to be drawn on the psychic elaboration of the traumatic situation, and also on the interpersonal linkage in which it occurs. As a defense mechanism, dissociation represents a reaction to the traumatic episode, that is, a chaotic flow of affects that the mind cannot regulate, a stream of thoughts that threatens the stability of the person and also his or her mental health (Bromberg, 1998). In this view, the intrapsychic conflict is experienced as unsustainable, and not just as unpleasant, because the discrepancy does not occur between discordant mental contents, but between alien aspects of the Self, that is, between states of the Self so discordant that they cannot coexist in a single state of consciousness without threatening to destabilize the temporal continuity of the Self.

Dissociation and trauma are therefore closely interconnected, especially if trauma occurs or is perpetrated within the individual's most significant relationships. When trauma represents an attack to the possibility of understanding the meaning of experience, the denial of such meaning provokes renunciation of one's sense of Self. This, in turn, creates a fragmentation and a void, which is filled only by the process that Sándor Ferenczi (1873–1933) called the "identification with the aggressor" (Ferenczi, [1932] 1995). In this view, the development of the child will then be characterized by dissociative processes and dynamics, in which the mind operates a division of the Self by organizing its parts as distinct personalities. The child would succeed to overcome the traumatic pain and survive such experience by means of a loss of consciousness and a splitting of personality. Ferenczi ([1933] 1955) also stated that external objects play a crucial role in structuring the psychic apparatus of the child. The two core concepts in this theorization are identificatory processes and the splitting of the ego. Ferenczi ascribed traumatic etiology to a "psychic violation" of the child by an adult due to a "confusion of tongues" between them, and to the adult's "disavowal" of the child's suffering.

> A trauma is produced in the child's psyche when these modalities of psychic invasion disqualify the child's thought and affect, denying it recognition, and this inevitably generates a split. The adult's language of passion unconsciously manipulates the eroticism of love and hate, clashing violently with the child's language of tenderness. This "misunderstanding" produces fear, disappointment and pain in the child, who had placed his trust in the adult.
>
> (Martín Cabré, 2008, p. 44)

When faced with the inability of defending itself from the aggressor, the child submits to the aggressor's desires, eventually identifying with the latter – "becoming" the aggressor (Frankel, 2002). Traumatic symptomatology is therefore closely linked to the adult's disavowal of feelings of guilt, which are then introjected by the child. In this instance, for the child, time ceases to exist, and past, present, and future become simultaneous. Extreme pain is unbearable, and the subject finds itself outside chronological, historical time, stuck within a present that is beyond history:

> [A]s opposed to the historical present that establishes presence and identity, in the traumatic present everything dissolves; there is no subject, nor is there opposition between subject and object. . . . Time is mummified, and the trauma acts like dead tissue, paralyzing the function of the *après-coup*.
>
> (Martín Cabré, 2008, p. 45)

References

American Psychiatric Association. (2013). *Diagnostic and statistical manual of mental disorders* (5th ed.). Washington, DC: Author.

Amir, N., Stafford, J., Freshman, M. S., & Foa, E. B. (1998). Relationship between trauma narratives and trauma pathology. *Journal of Traumatic Stress, 11*(2), 385–392.

Baranger, M., Baranger, W., & Mom, J. M. (1988). The infantile psychic trauma from us to Freud: Pure trauma, retroactivity and reconstruction. *The International Journal of Psycho-Analysis, 69*, 113.

Barnaby, A. (2012). Coming too late: Freud, belatedness, and existential trauma. *SubStance*, *41*(2), 119–138.

Bedard-Gilligan, M., & Zoellner, L. A. (2012). Dissociation and memory fragmentation in posttraumatic stress disorder: An evaluation of the dissociative encoding hypothesis. *Memory (Hove, England)*, *20*(3), 277–299.

Brewin, C. R., & Holmes, E. A. (2003). Psychological theories of posttraumatic stress disorder. *Clinical Psychology Review*, *23*(3), 339–376.

Briere, J., Scott, C., & Weathers, F. (2005). Peritraumatic and persistent dissociation in the presumed etiology of PTSD. *American Journal of Psychiatry*, *162*(12), 2295–2301.

Bromberg, P. M. (1998). *Standing in the spaces: Essays on clinical process, trauma, and dissociation*. Hillsdale, NJ, and London: The Analytic Press.

Bromberg, P. M. (2003). Something wicked this way comes: Trauma, dissociation, and conflict: The space where psychoanalysis, cognitive science, and neuroscience overlap. *Psychoanalytic Psychology*, *20*(3), 558–574.

Damasio, A. R. (1999). *The feeling of what happens: Body and emotion and the making of consciousness*. New York: Hartcourt.

Dillon, J., Johnstone, L., & Longden, E. (2014). Trauma, dissociation, attachment and neuroscience: A new paradigm for understanding severe mental distress. In E. Speed, J. Moncrieff, & M. Rapley (Eds.), *De-medicalizing misery II* (pp. 145–155). London: Palgrave Macmillan.

Esman, A. H. (1983). The "stimulus barrier". *Psychoanalytic Study of the Child*, *38*, 193–207.

Ferenczi, S. (1933) 1955. Confusion of tongues between adults and the child. In *Final contributions* (pp. 156–167). London: The Hogarth Press.

Ferenczi, S. (1932) 1995. *The clinical diary of Sándor Ferenczi*. Cambridge, MA: Harvard University Press.

Foa, E. B., & Riggs, D. S. (1993). Posttraumatic stress disorder in rape victims. In J. Oldham, M. B. Riba, & A. Tasman (Eds.), *American psychiatric press review of psychiatry* (Vol. 12, pp. 273–303). Washington, DC: American Psychiatric Press.

Foa, E. B., Steketee, G., & Rothbaum, B. O. (1989). Behavioral/cognitive conceptualization of post-traumatic stress disorder. *Behavior Therapy*, *20*, 155–176.

Frankel, J. (2002). Exploring Ferenczi's concept of identification with the aggressor: Its role in trauma, everyday life, and the therapeutic relationship. *Psychoanalytic Dialogues*, *12*(1), 101–139.

Frewen, P., & Lanius, R. (2014). Trauma-related altered states of consciousness: Exploring the 4-D model. *Journal of Trauma & Dissociation*, *15*, 436–456.

Frewen, P., & Lanius, R. A. (2015). *Healing the traumatized self*. London and New York: W. W. Norton.

Fuchs, T. (2018). *Ecology of the brain. The phenomenology and biology of the embodied mind*. Oxford: Oxford University Press.

Giesbrecht, T., Lynn, S. J., Lilienfeld, S. O., & Merckelbach, H. (2008). Cognitive processes in dissociation: An analysis of core theoretical assumptions. *Psychological Bulletin*, *134*, 617–647.

Gullestad, S. E. (2005). Who is "who" in dissociation? A plea for psychodynamics in a time of trauma. *International Journal of Psychoanalysis*, *86*(3), 639–656.

Heidegger, M. (1927) 1962. *Being and time*. New York: Harper and Row.

Holmes, E., Brown, R., Mansell, W., Fearon, R., Hunter, E., Frasquilho, F., & Oakley, D. (2005). Are there two qualitatively distinct forms of dissociation? A review and some clinical implications. *Clinical Psychology Review*, *25*(1), 1–23.

James, W. (1890) 1950. *The principles of psychology*. New York: Dover Publications.

Janet, P. (1889) 2005. *L'automatisme psychologique: Essai de psychologie expérimentale sur les formes inférieures de lactivité humaine*. Paris: L. Harmattan.

Janet, P. (1919). *Les medications psychologiques: Etudes historiques, psychologiques et cliniques sur les methodes de la psychotherapie*. Paris: Felix Alcan.

Kohut, H. (1971). *The analysis of the self: A systematic approach to the psychoanalytic treatment of narcissistic personality disorders*. New York, NY: International Universities Press.

Langer, J., Wapner, S., & Werner, H. (1961). The effect of danger upon the experience of time. *The American Journal of Psychology*, *74*(1), 94.

Lanius, R. A. (2015). Trauma-related dissociation and altered states of consciousness: A call for clinical, treatment, and neuroscience research. *European Journal of Psychotraumatology*, *6*, 1–9.

Lanius, R. A., Vermetten, E., Loewenstein, R. J., Brand, B. L., Schmahl, C. G., Bremner, J. D., & Spiegel, D. (2010). Emotion modulation in PTSD: Clinical and neurobiological evidence for a dissociative subtype. *American Journal of Psychiatry*, *167*(6), 640–647.

Lapassade, G. (1996). *Transe e dissociazione*. Roma: Sensibili alle foglie.

Laplanche, J. (1999). *Essays on otherness*. New York: Routledge.

Liotti, G. (2004). Trauma, dissociation, and disorganized attachment: Three strands of a single braid. *Psychotherapy: Theory, Research, Practice, Training*, *41*(4), 472–486.

Martín Cabré, L. J. (2008). The psychoanalytic conception of trauma in Ferenczi and the question of temporality. *American Journal of Psychoanalysis*, *68*, 43–49.

Marx, B. P., & Sloan, D. M. (2005). Peritraumatic dissociation and experiential avoidance as predictors of posttraumatic stress symptomatology. *Behaviour Research and Therapy*, *43*(5), 569–583.

Nagel, T. (1974). What is it like to be a bat? *Philosophical Review*, *83*(4), 435–450.

Nemiah, J. C. (1998). Early concepts of trauma, dissociation, and the unconscious: Their history and current implications. In J. D. Bremner & C. R. Marmar (Eds.), *Trauma, memory, and dissociation* (pp. 1–26). Washington, DC: American Psychiatric Press.

Nietzsche, F. W. (1883–1885) 2009. *Thus spoke Zarathustra*. Wilder Publications: Thrifty Books.

Nijenhuis, E., van der Hart, O., & Steele, K. (2010). Trauma-related structural dissociation of the personality. *Activitas Nervosa Superior*, *52*(1), 1–23.

Northoff, G., Heinzel, A., de Greck, M., Bermpohl, F., Dobrowolny, H., & Panksepp, J. (2006). Self-referential processing in our brain: A meta-analysis of imaging studies on the self, *NeuroImage*, *31*(1), 440–457.

O'kearney, R., & Perrott, K. (2006). Trauma narratives in posttraumatic stress disorder: A review. *Journal of Traumatic Stress*, *19*(1), 81–93.

Ogawa, J. R., Sroufe, L. A., Weinfield, N. S., Carlson, E. A., & Egeland, B. (1997). Development and the fragmented self: Longitudinal study of dissociative symptomatology in a nonclinical sample. *Development and Psychopathology*, 9(4), 855–879.

Ozer, E. J., Best, S. R., Lipsey, T. L., & Weiss, D. S. (2003). Predictors of posttraumatic stress disorder and symptoms in adults: A meta-analysis. *Psychological Bulletin*, 129(1), 52–73.

Phillips, M. L., Medford, N., Senior, C., Bullmore, E. T., Brammer, M. J., & Andrew, C. (2001). Depersonalization disorder: Thinking without feeling. *Psychiatry Research. Neuroimaging*, 108, 145–160.

Sar, V., & Rhoades, G. F. (2005). *Trauma and dissociation in a cross-cultural perspective: Not just a North American phenomenon*. London: Routledge.

Schiavone, F., Frewen, P., McKinnon, M., & Lanius, R. A. (2018). The dissociative subtype of PTSD: An update of the literature. *PTSD Research Quarterly*, 29(3), 1–13.

Shapiro, T., & Stern, D. (1980). Psychoanalytic perspectives on the first year of life. In *The course of life* (Vol. 1, pp. 113–128). Washington: NIMH.

Simeon, D., & Abugel, J. (2006). *Feeling unreal: Depersonalization disorder and the loss of the self*. Oxford: Oxford University Press.

Stanghellini, G. (2009). Trauma. In G. Stanghellini & M. Rossi Monti (Eds.), *Psicologia del patologico: Una prospettiva fenomenologico-dinamica* (pp. 235–262). Milano: Raffaello Cortina.

Stein, M. H. (1953). Premonition as a defense. *Psychoanalytic Quarterly*, 22, 69–74.

Stern, D. B. (2017). *Unformulated experience: From dissociation to imagination in psychoanalysis*. Hillsdale, NJ: Analytic Press.

Stolorow, R. (2011). *World, affectivity, trauma*. New York: Routledge.

Terr, L. C. (1984). Time and trauma. *The Psychoanalytic Study of The Child*, 39(1), 633–665.

Thompson, E., & Zahavi, D. (2007). Philosophical issues: Phenomenology. In P. D. Zelaso, M. Moscovitch, & E. Thompson (Eds.), *Cambridge handbook of consciousness studies* (pp. 67–87). New York: Cambridge University Press.

Tulving, E. (2002). Episodic memory: From mind to brain. *Annual Review of Psychology*, 53, 1–25.

Van der Hart, O., Nijenhuis, E., Steele, K., & Brown, D. (2004). Trauma-related dissociation: Conceptual clarity lost and found. *Australian and New Zealand Journal of Psychiatry*, 38(11–12), 906–914.

Van der Kolk, B. A. (2000). Posttraumatic stress disorder and the nature of trauma. *Dialogues in Clinical Neuroscience*, 2(1), 7–22.

Van der Kolk, B. A., Hopper, J. W., & Osterman, J. E. (2001). Exploring the nature of traumatic memory. *Journal of Aggression, Maltreatment & Trauma*, 4(2), 9–31.

Van der Kolk, B., & van der Hart, O. (1995). The intrusive past: The flexibility of memory and the engraving of trauma. In C. Caruth (Ed.), *Trauma: Explorations in memory*. Baltimore: Johns Hopkins University Press.

Varela, F. J. (1996). Neurophenomenology: A methodological remedy for the hard problem. *Journal of Consciousness Studies*, 3(4), 330–349.

Waller, G., Hamilton, K., Elliott, P., Lewendon, J., Stopa, L., Waters, A., & Chalkley, J. (2001). Somatoform dissociation, psychological dissociation, and specific forms of trauma. *Journal of Trauma & Dissociation*, 1(4), 81–98.

Chapter 6

Time, Trauma, and Memory

This chapter focuses on the effects that trauma produces on the subjective organization of memory. Psychological trauma leads to altered memory functioning, expressed in distorted recall of events. To experience temporal continuity, the Self must be able to construct a narrative where the "here and now" is dynamically related with past and future horizons. A stable sense of identity emerges when the individual perceives the "here and now" as an integral part of a temporal continuum. Trauma hinders the continuity of the sense of Self in time, as traumatic memories are not integrated within the structure of the subject's narrative memory. Trauma breaks the experience of time, as it shatters the person's sense of Self. Experimental affective and cognitive neuroscience confirmed that trauma can be regarded as a "disorder of memory," whereby the intersubjectively constituted world turns into a world of alienation.

Time, Trauma, and Memory Fragmentation

Memory is currently being regarded as a "dynamic" process rather than a "static" storage (Dekel & Bonanno, 2013), and is typically divided into explicit or declarative memory and implicit or non-declarative memory. Whereas the former is the memory of which we are often consciously aware, the latter refers to different subtypes of memory, all of which are unconscious, require multiple trials to be acquired, and might not involve a fully developed Self. Explicit and implicit memory are also correlated to the activation of different brain regions. More specifically, explicit memory depends on brain regions located in the temporal lobe, whereas the areas that subserve implicit memory vary depending on the subtype of memory involved. The difference between the two types of memory is also expressed by whether we are able to recall events or not. For instance, the reason why we tend to be unable to recall events dated back to the first years of life lies in the fact that the explicit memory system emerges at circa one year of age, and the cortical systems involved in long-term memory storage and retrieval mature only after two years of age.

DOI: 10.4324/9781003230601-7

Psychological trauma can produce not only dissociation, but also altered memory functions (Krystal et al., 1995). Meares (1995) had already observed that human memory unifies the manifold of experienced inputs, thus making up the flow of inner consciousness. Time experience is thus closely related to memory, so that in the presence of memory dysfunctions, temporal disruptions follow. Essential to self-identity is therefore the unifying recalling of past and present experiences in relation to future expectations. Human beings are not (only) determined by their past: they are (also) the very creators of their present and future. In order to heal, the traumatized person's goal must consist of taking responsibility for the past as *his* or *her* past – and of the future as *his* or *her* future. Traumatized individuals must literally make up their own life every moment (Sacks, [1970] 1998). They must "recollect" their story to create a coherent narrative, which in turn aids in maintaining a self-identity embedded in memory. As Schrag (1999) put it:

> [T]he self exists as *temporalized*. Temporality enters into the very constitution of who the self is. . . . Narrative temporality enriches rather than impoverishes the self. . . . The story of the self is a developing story . . . wherein the past is . . . a text, an inscription of events and experiences that stands open to new interpretations and new perspectives of meaning. . . . The future of narrative time is the self as possibility, as the power to be able to provide new readings of the script that has already been inscribed and to mark out new inscriptions of a script in the making.
>
> (p. 37)

In order to grasp its continuity through the constitution of a narrative, the Self must establish a relationship with both past and future experience, that is, memory and expectations, retentions and protentions. Self-narrative is achieved through the organization of experience according to the individuals's temporal dimensions. In Damasio's (1999) words, "extended consciousness goes beyond the here and now of core consciousness, both backward and forward" (p. 295). A stable sense of identity emerges when the individual becomes able to perceive the "here and now" as an integral part of a continuum that represents his or her whole life. It is in this continuum that the person can recall past events "with an appropriate sense of guilt" (Hartocollis, 1986, p. 219), as well as nurture expectations "with an appropriate sense of anxiety" (p. 219). When such a continuum makes up the background of the individual's autobiography, the subject's experience of time can eventually resemble a stream of consciousness where the Self moves along with intersubjective time.

Typically, individuals retain their sense of Self despite changes in their lives, and even the sense of Self can change without a loss of sameness

(Kohut, 1977). However, trauma hinders the maintenance of the continuity of the sense of Self over time (Ornstein, 1994). The goal is for the trauma patient to restore the integration of scattered memories into the rest of the whole psyche. Therapeutic dialogue helps patients to construct alternative self-narratives through a process that has been called "recontextualization" (Schafer, 1983). The construction of a self-narrative is a process whereby the Self becomes *structured* (Gerhart & Stinson, 1994): it is the narratively structured unity of the person's life as a whole that provides the individual with personal identity. Disconnectedness with the past results in a loss of identity, where experience becomes a sequence of events, a mere "chronicle" (Polkinghorne, 1991). In Kohut's (1977) view, the maintenance of the sense of continuity depends on the establishment of a cohesive Self. According to Stern (1985), the process aimed at integrating the features of the subject's overall experience is carried out by memory. The individual's affective dimension seems also to guarantee the continuity of experience in spite of the changes that the Self experiences during development.

Once language develops, the sensorimotor acts that were used to communicate become "symbols," which represent the building blocks of autobiographical semantic memory. However, whereas language is extremely powerful in terms of constructing a narrative, it can also break down the subject's lived experience as verbally represented. The person's ability to observe what is happening during trauma is possible only via a mechanism that provides emotional detachment without altering one's state of consciousness (Ornstein, 1994). "Disavowal" (Basch, 1983) produces mental processes whereby emotional numbness makes survival possible:

> [D]isavowal manages to avoid painful reality not by vitiating or denying the percept, but by creating two currents in mental life, a split that permits reality to be acknowledged while at the same time allowing a belief in a wished-for situation to co-exist.
>
> (p. 131)

The act of re-presenting traumatic memories plays a crucial role in reintegrating them into a unified whole, thus allowing the Self to reestablish its temporal continuity. Ultimately, the integration of traumatic memories into a unified whole depends on the healing of "split" experiences.

According to Ornstein (1994), one of the most essential functions required in order to establish a sense of self-continuity over time is the ability to distinguish *lived* affects from *remembered* experiences. This is why trauma patients must be able to accept aspects of them that existed also (or only) under the traumatic circumstances. This means acceptance of one's emotional reactions at the time of the trauma, and recognition that affects present in the "here and now" are different from those originally experienced. In other words, cohesiveness of the Self can be achieved only if the subject is able to accept thoughts, attitudes, and behaviors that were present at the time of the traumatic event, and persist because of a compulsion to repeat. Once disavowal becomes less intense, trauma-related symptoms will progressively diminish, and increased self-cohesiveness will make it possible to accommodate affects that had previously fragmented the Self (Ornstein, 1994).

Traumatic memories are primarily imprinted in sensory and emotional modes; also, in particular circumstances, the semantic representations of memories go hand in hand with somatic flashbacks (Van der Kolk, 2000). These sensory experiences tend to remain stable over time, even when other experiences take over the subject's present awareness. Furthermore, they tend to come back when triggered by present stimuli that remind the traumatized subject of the original shock. Traumatic memories are different from other memories in that they do not go through transformation of day-to-day experience, but seem to be never "updated." As a result, traumatic memories can be relived over and over again, with such emotional intensity that the subject thinks they are happening in the "here and now."

When trauma is present, the mind becomes split or dissociated, and is unable to register the memory of the event. As a result, the traumatized individual is unable to consciously recollect and integrate the traumatic experience, and is haunted by intrusive memories. The experience of trauma becomes *frozen in time*: it is not represented as *past*, but rather reexperienced over and over again as a traumatic event *in the present*. High levels of emotional activation can lead to strong conditioned responses while also impairing memory processes. PTSD is a *timeless* phenomenon, which interrupts the ordinary continuum of past, present, and future (Leys, 2000).

In PTSD patients, intense memories of the trauma coexist with disorganized and incomplete narrative memory (Brewin, 2001). The most common kind of recall of traumatic memories consists of flashbacks, which are usually vivid, and yet involve a disruption of the sense of time. They are usually triggered involuntarily and imply the person's avoidance of stimuli that can be reminders of the trauma. Trauma seems to be preserved in memory in a *timeless* fashion – a fact that might account for the long-term effects of PTSD (Van der Kolk, 2014). Trauma is not part of declarative or narrative memory, but remains implicit and non-declarative, encoded in bodily memories and conditioned responses lying outside the verbal domain of cognitive functioning.

Traumatic events escape the subject's ability to understand and internalize them, because of the inability to translate the somatic memories of the shocking event into words: "trauma comprises an event or experience which overwhelms the individual and resists language and representation" (Whitehead, 2011, p. 3). After the traumatic episode, individuals are often deprived of their defenses and are left with a lack of a linear perception of time. In most cases, traumatic memories become dissociated and stored in the unconscious mind where they remain stuck, at least until a further event can bring them to consciousness. These memories usually return and haunt the traumatized individual in the form of compulsive reenactments of the original trauma, even though the person itself cannot understand the origin of his or her symptoms (Romero-Jódar, 2012).

Time, Trauma, and the Dis-Unity of Memory

In his conceptualization of trauma, Janet ([1889] 2005) distinguished "narrative memory" from "traumatic memory." The former refers to a type of memory that allows the individual to recall past events in an organized fashion, that is, as arranged sequentially, thus granting a narrative and a coherent sense of the continuity of the Self. However, the mind cannot assimilate overwhelming or shocking events, which surface to the conscious mind as dissociated images that find no logical place in the linear structure of narrative memory. This is the reason why traumatized individuals are not able to integrate traumatic memories within the structure of narrative memory. These memories further shatter the conception of time as a progressive continuum in the individual's life. Because these memories escape from the possibility to be placed in time, Caruth (1996) concluded that trauma breaks the individual's experience of time: traumatized individuals experience their traumatic memories as unprocessed experiences that are continually relived and reenacted.

Fragmented memories also shatter the unity and identity of the Self. If identity is linked to a coherent narrative that stands as the individual's biographical narrative, traumatized persons can give sense to their own identity only by means of a meaningful narrative of their experience – a process that can be accomplished through narrative memory. Romero-Jódar (2012) argued that the subject's biography is exactly what brings a sequentially arranged narration of its life events together. Accordingly, traumatic memories destroy the perception of the Self as a unified whole, which has a defined past and present, and moves forward in the progression of time. In this view, traumatized individuals must deal with two different timelines: the narrative time of their ordinary life, and the fragmented memories of traumatic time.

Traumatic events make intersubjective relationships collapse as well (Herman, 2015). This is not a secondary effect of trauma: in fact, trauma has crucial consequences not only on the individuals' sense of safety, but also on the attachment system that connects them to others. A secure sense of safety can be acquired early in life in the context of good-enough relationships with one's caregivers. In traumatic situations, however, children seek their first source of protection in the acquired patterns of safety, even though their request for safety is likely to find no answer. As a result, a sense of alienation and disconnection arises, also pervading later relationships. When the sense of connection with caring others is disrupted, the person loses his or her sense of Self. If memories are retranscribed as a result of subsequent experiences, then a lack of developmental memory retranscription ultimately leads to psychopathology (Modell, 1990).

According to Brewin (2001), PTSD patients exhibit two distinct types of memory for trauma. Narrative memory reflects a "verbally accessible memory" (VAM) system, which consists of memories that can be voluntarily retrieved when required. In contrast, phenomena such as flashbacks constitute a different kind of memory, the so-called situationally accessible memory (SAM) system. As Brewin (2001) proposed, "both VAM and SAM systems would ordinarily contain information about the traumatic event, so that there would be two forms of emotional memory representation rather than one" (p. 160). Because the SAM system does not encode spatial and temporal context, it does not discriminate between past trauma and present, actual threat. This is why the individual tends to reexperience threat as if it were happening in the present. In contrast, the VAM system is supposed to encode memories in their spatial and temporal location, so that they can be retrieved when required.

Considering the social dimension of trauma is essential to fully understand why trauma patients exhibit dissociation, intrusive memories, and/or repression. In fact, the social context contributes to shape registration, rehearsal, and recall of memories, narratives, and life stories. Repressing, ignoring, and dissociating are all forms of forgetting, that is, ways to evade memories associated with shocking social circumstances (Kirmayer, 1996). All forms of memory show great plasticity, and the effects of imagination on reconstruction and recall are pervasive (Payne et al., 2004). This is why memory is often prone to distortions (Schacter et al., 2011). Therefore, PTSD might be considered as a "disorder of memory" (Leys, 2000). Traumatic memories are far from being immutable (McNally, 2005). The living brain is dynamic, and even the most vivid memories are never "literal," that is, unchanged reproductions of what happened. If memory does not operate like a videotape machine, then recalling past events always amounts to reconstructing them from several pieces of information distributed throughout the brain. In fact, recollection always means reconstruction. As Foehl (2020) argued:

> [S]elf-reflection is a fugue-like process that is structured in the form of *après-coup*. Memories and meanings of the past are created anew given our present investments and concerns. They are further shaped in relation to our ways of intending multiple futures lived in those investments, futures that we find and create in relation to a meaningful present and past (*avant-coup*). Thus, self-experience is far

from linear. Memory and anticipation (desire) have a dynamic structure in which the depth of the present moment continually forms
and transforms in relation to a spatiotemporal ground that is lived
rather than known. We only find ourselves in reflection after the
fact, and we never quite catch up to ourselves in the experience of
self-understanding.

(p. 131)

Time, Trauma, and the Disruption of Temporal Experience

The ability to remember past events is a cornerstone for one's feeling of
temporal continuity (Staniloiu & Markowitsch, 2012). Episodic or autobiographical memory, as enriched through the acquisition of language,
represents the conjunction of subjective time, consciousness, and the
Self, and is supposed to play a key role in the maintenance of a consistent feeling of self-identity over time. It is vulnerable to both neurological and environmental factors, and subject to distortions and reshaping
in the presence of threatening situations. Each act of recalling might be
viewed as a retranscription of an event into the autobiographical memory,
which involves an action of recategorization and, to some degree, imagination. Trauma can lead not only to impairments in episodic and autobiographical memory, but also to deep changes in personality and ability for
self-consciousness, self-projection, and the feeling of being with others.
Episodic and autobiographical memory are context-specific with respect
to time and place. They are acquired during childhood and enable mental
time travel through past events by attaching emotional aspects to them.
Besides being closely connected to the Self, a central feature of episodic
and autobiographical memory is their intimate connection with emotions.

As it involves reflective awareness, James ([1890] 1950) thought of
episodic memory as the basis of the human "stream of consciousness,"
that is, the constant flux of experience, that endlessly changes and never
repeats itself. The stream of consciousness is therefore intertwined with
the narrative Self. In this view, the Self depends on a specific form of mental activity, which is "associational" and not linear. When this activity is
verbally expressed, it is called "self-narrative," and can be interrupted by
another (traumatic) form of mental activity, which appears as fixed and
associated with negative affect, rather than with dynamic, prospective
feelings. The person's well-being will then depend on the integration of
this form of memory into the more mature episodic and autobiographical
memory system of the Self (Meares, 2003).

We have seen how the experiences encoded during high levels of stress
are often fragmented. The pieces of a traumatic experience are not connected, and do not form a dynamic whole: they do not produce a *Gestalt*

or a coherent episode. The fact that most trauma patients recall their trauma very well, although a very significant minority of patients is not able to remember it at all, has been a matter of debate (McNally, 2005). The function of episodic and autobiographical memory is to bind together and integrate personal events within the Self's narrative. However, the inability to recollect personal information also impairs one's openness to experience new situations and relationships. According to McNally (2005), compartmentalization might be helpful to distance oneself from highly emotionally charged stimuli even in our ordinary life. The mechanism of distancing from traumatic events might take the form of a "third person" narrative. However, the ability to retrieve autobiographical information is state-dependent, and repeatedly different retrieval conditions might modify or even distort the narrative of an event.

Upon retrieval, memories enter in fact a state of lability, after which they are consolidated: in this phase, memories are subject to modifications and can weaken, strengthen, or become distorted. Edelman (2004) regarded memory as the "remembered present" (p. 99), because the past is never retrieved unmodified in the "here and now." Far from being stable single units, memory traces are moments unfolding in an ever-mobile "now" (Johnston, 2005). Kirmayer (1996) argued that the difference between trauma narratives might also be understood as a difference in the "culturally constructed *landscapes of memory*" (p. 5). In this view, trauma narratives are thought of as *cultural constructions* of personal and historical memory. Memory is not like a photographic record of experience: memory storage is highly selective and subject to interpretation and semantic encoding at the moment when a specific event is either consciously experienced or else prereflectively lived. Imaginative elaboration and processing are part of this process, which makes every piece of memory something that resembles more a *construction*, rather than a "snapshot" of experience (Friedman, 1993).

Time, Trauma, and Memory Reconstruction

Memory is not a perfect reconstruction of past events. On the contrary, each act of recalling involves a series of processes that piece together different details, and make inferences to fill in the gaps and create a coherent whole. Drives, biases, stereotypes, and expectations can all affect this inferential process, resulting in constant modifications of what the individual actually remembers. Memory distortions following trauma appear to follow a particular pattern, whereby individuals tend to remember *even more trauma* than what they actually experienced (King et al., 2000). This usually translates into greater severity of PTSD symptoms over time, as the remembered trauma "grows" (Wyshak, 1994). Over-remembering trauma is also associated with poorer mental health outcomes. In fact, as PTSD symptoms increase, so does the amplification of memory for traumatic events (Southwick et al., 2006). From an evolutionary point of view, it would seem far from adaptive to remember an event as more traumatic than it really was, as this would increase pain and PTSD symptoms, thus delaying recovery from trauma. However, as Southwick et al. (2006) speculated, while the error itself is not adaptive, it would nonetheless represent a by-product of an otherwise strong and flexible memory system.

Far from storing in memory the details of experience by means of some kind of "labels" that specify their origins, we rather rely on heuristics to determine whether a mnestic trace of the event is accurate, or else merely suggested or imagined (Newman & Lindsay, 2009). Furthermore, post-event processing can increase the familiarity of new details, so that people may mistakenly think of those details as authentic mnestic traces. The adaptive aspect of this process might consist of the fact that through the "growth" of traumatic memories, individuals can protect themselves from being triggered again by further harmful stimuli. This trauma-related fear conditioning would make the person more resilient than in the case he or she was not overly fearful of triggers following trauma. Ultimately, the tendency to "over-remember" trauma might be a natural way to avoid the reexperiencing of a similar trauma in the future (Newman & Lindsay, 2009).

Memory accuracy depends on several factors: the level of attention paid to the event, the time passed after it, and the presence of interfering information in memory retrieval (Bernstein & Loftus, 2008). As memory is constructive in nature – that is, it undergoes transformation over time – encoding, storage, and retrieval are all prone to memory distortions (Bartlett, 1932). Growing evidence points to the fact that all traumatic memories undergo similar distortion processes (Strange & Takarangi, 2015). People misplace information available *after* a traumatic event by mixing it with what actually happened. This phenomenon might occur both intentionally, for example, through speaking to others, and unintentionally, for example, because of intrusions and flashbacks. After a traumatic event, both intentional recall and unintentional retrieval of details can interfere with the reconstruction of the person's memory of the trauma, resulting in memory distortions.

Interestingly, many brain regions supporting the encoding of true memories also serve to the encoding of false memories (Baym & Gonsalve, 2010; Okado & Stark, 2005). How people represent or misrepresent their traumatic experiences is both theoretically and practically relevant for traumatic psychopathology assessment and treatment. Recalled details that did not occur are likely to mask more important features of the trauma, on which therapy must also focus. Contextual associations occur when individuals relate objects that typically feature together on the stage. They help predict what will occur in the future, but can also produce memory "distortions." In other words, they can represent adaptive processes that have memory distortions as their side effects, which can result in false recognition (Bartlett, 1932).

Time, Self, and Affect

Recent research has shown that "the phenomenology of temporal perception covaries with the phenomenology of affect" (Frewen & Lanius, 2015, p. 74). As Gostecnik (1997) argued, "early interaction with the caregiver is the most essential component in early affect formation" (p. 53). Indeed, changes in the sense of time are associated with changes in affective states (Meissner, 2007). As Hartocollis (1983) put it: "a person's emotional experience has a great deal to do with the way he experiences the flow of time and vice-versa, without necessarily the one being the cause of the other" (p. 139). Time is not a function of space, but rather of subjective experience (Bell & Provins, 1963). As an example, "*objectively different* time spans can be *subjectively equivalent*" (Kafka, 1989, p. 53), and vice versa. Furthermore, the development of the experience of time is also associated with the development of the consciousness of affect.

In Hartocollis's (1974) view, it is the superego that, by warning the ego of the consequences of its wishes, contributes to produce the sense of the future; in turn, by condemning the ego's failure to resist its needs, the superego would contribute to the development of a sense of the past. In this view, affects develop as self-consciousness surfaces in subjective experience. The sense of time varies according to the individual's affective state, and reflects the Self's sense of integrity: "self-consciousness is born out of tension arising from internal object representations that threaten the integrity of the self" (Hartocollis, 1983, pp. 52–53). In turn, this process would also contribute to the emerging sense of being "other" from objects.

As Hartocollis (1983) elaborated, affects are produced when a discontinuity (a "break") occurs in self-awareness: "affect is the end result of a perceptual-cognitive process involving the awareness of uncertainty in relation to the possibility of coping with a novel situation" (p. 53). In human beings, action is associated with the capacity to place oneself within a chain of temporally intertwined events. In this process, imagining possible actions allows the individual to develop a notion of the future. Affects are defined in terms of the dichotomy between time on the one hand and pain and pleasure on the other. The intertwining between time, affect, and the Self defines the human condition as unique and different from that of other animals (Hartocollis, 1986):

> [T]ime and timelessness and all the varieties of temporal experience in-between have intrigued the human mind ever since we discovered the secret of existence: transience, death. . . . The fear of death and

the fear of time are one and the same. . . . To control time is to control oneself and others.

(p. 227)

As Kümmel (1966) pointed out, time is relevant to human beings inasmuch as it is subject to *historical* interpretations. In this view, far from being a "container" of all experiences, time is always conditioned by our biographical understanding of it. From a psychoanalytical perspective, time can be described as an intuitive concept that finds its origins in the affective dimension of early object relations, where the anticipation of the wish-fulfillment gives rise to anxiety on the one hand, and to the sense of time on the other. As Frewen and Lanius (2015) elaborated, the *anticipation* of threat, as opposed to its *presence*, leads to temporal overestimations. For instance, it has been shown that anxiety is associated with perception of longer temporal intervals in the presence of threatening stimuli (Bar-Haim et al., 2010). Also, depression correlates with underestimation of the passage of time (Gil & Droit-Volet, 2009), whereas maniac states point to a sense of being "stuck" in the present (Gruber et al., 2012).

Now, time as duration seems to be "a function of the strength of our instinctual wishes and a metaphor for the integrity of the self in relation to the world of internal objects" (Hartocollis, 1976, pp. 363–364). Time as duration seems to move slowly when instinctual wishes remain unfulfilled or repressed, and to move quickly when wishes are converted to superego demands. Overall, the sense of time as duration is inscribed in the tension generated by the psychic processes deriving from early object relations. In this sense, "time becomes an affect of its own" (Hartocollis, 1976, p. 368). When individuals become preoccupied with the idea of time, they lose the ability to experience affects. Time is experienced as moving slowly or quickly according to the forces that influence the ego. The stronger the wish, the slower the time seems to be, as the subject becomes "impatient" to the temporal unfolding of experience; in turn, the weaker the wish, the faster time seems to go by (Hartocollis, 1986). In other words, time is experienced as moving faster when the primary instinctual wishes become weaker and the superego takes over; vice versa, when the individual overcomes all wishes, time seems to stop existing, that is, it becomes *timeless*. When time seems no longer moving, consciousness becomes overwhelmed by the sense of time: time becomes wish and wish becomes time (Meissner, 2007).

Hartocollis's (1976) conclusion is that the feeling of "one-ness" between mother and child, characterized by a complete wish-fulfillment, becomes one with *timelessness*. The appreciation of duration seems, thus, to refer to the extent to which the person's consciousness is close to his or her instinctual wishes. Time is experienced as moving or stationary according to whether wishes are fulfilled or are pressing for discharge, thus threatening the cohesiveness of the ego. Whereas, under ordinary conditions, the sense of time accompanies our everyday experience without us being aware of it, in psychopathological situations, time becomes the center of the individual's awareness. This exaggerated sense of time goes along with heightened affective pressure, which can in turn be experienced as an affectless state. This apparent paradox leads to time distortions concomitant to variations that threaten the integrity of ego organization. In this view, psychopathology implies that the sense of time is detached from one's sense of Self. In turn, inasmuch as affects are concerned, the subjective loss of affect goes along with a sense that time is slowing down or even arresting. As a result, the ego regresses to a poorly integrated world of object relations. Timelessness evokes a state in which the ego loses connection with the objective world, resulting in an objectless experience (Hartocollis, 1975).

Distortions in the experience of time point to defensive mechanisms that refer to the person's inner dimension of object relations. Trauma-related regret and fear of (imagined or real) threat are associated with disruptions of temporal awareness (Fuchs, 2010). The elaboration of a sense of time is a unique maturation process that impacts the development of human personality. The representation and perception of time is a dynamic process unfolding throughout the individual's life cycle. Distortions in the sense of time and avoidance of the temporal features of existence can therefore be understood as traumatic defense mechanisms. Psychological distortions set individuals in disequilibrium as to their representations of time, and can emerge as depression or anxiety in trauma patients (Fuchs, 2010). Furthermore, psychic conflict can be the consequence of internal representations of the Self that contrast with perceived external stimuli. Anxiety-provoking representations of the world are perceived as "unreal" when the Self is insufficiently prepared to utilize its defensive mechanisms.

The perception of duration goes along with emotional experience (Melges, 1982). Also, the perception of one's Self is relative to time and is mediated through psychic reality. This can also lead to cognitive and temporal distortions, as traumatic anxiety and depression are present. Psychic reality, in turn, depends on the individual's developmental history, that is, on how the individual is able to process the representations of present, past, and possible future trauma. Ultimately, understanding the patient's temporal dynamics seems to be necessary to limit the evolution of depression and anxiety in trauma patients. This, in turn, might enable trauma patients to approach their story from a new perspective and, most importantly, can help to reduce the potential for psychic conflict and, as a consequence, for depression and anxiety (Fuchs, 2010).

Time, Trauma, and Memory in Cognitive Neuroscience

Building back upon Schore's (1994) and Siegel's (1999) works, Wilkinson (2003) analyzed the effects of trauma on the emotional, intellectual, and imaginative experience of the Self. Positive experiences in the infant–caregiver dyad stimulate healthy development. However, traumatic experiences lived in early caregiving relationships adversely affect the development of the child's brain. Unconscious processing is more associated with the right rather than with the left hemisphere (Schore, 2002). In fact, the latter is interconnected with limbic regions, and is therefore closely linked to emotion regulation processes. Whether trauma has physical, psychological, or sexual characteristics, it causes several neurobiological and hormonal changes that force the brain to reorganize in order to face a hostile world. From an attachment theory point of view, trauma modifies the internal working models that operate in order for the individual to be able to adaptively function in relation to others.

As to why trauma patients show diminished positive affect, Fonzo (2018) pointed out that these subjects show abnormalities in the so-called "reward circuit,"[1] which involves areas in the midbrain, striatum, and orbital and medial prefrontal cortex. Biological abnormalities in the reward circuit of traumatized individuals are then supposed to underlie what the *DSM-5* presents as the "negative alterations in cognition and mood" (APA, 2013, p. 271) characterizing PTSD symptomatology, also referred to as "emotional numbing." Research has also focused on the possible linkage between specific PTSD symptoms (e.g., diminished positive affect, diminished interest in pleasurable activities, and inability to have loving feelings in relation to significant others) and reward-related biological processes (e.g., Frewen et al., 2012; Lieberman et al., 2017). As Ford (2015) stated, "it is not just memory (or memories) of traumatic events that are altered in PTSD, but also fundamental aspects of the cognitive processing of the memories associated with autobiographical identity and social and affective information processing" (pp. 70–71).

Findings from the field of affective cognitive neuroscience demonstrated that implicit cognitive schemas, which individuals are often unaware of, can affect the quality of subjectively experienced emotions, and play a crucial role in emotion regulation (Ford, 2015). Emotional arousal can be reduced through intentional appraisal of the significance of emotion-eliciting experiences affecting the person. Emotion regulation is also important when using cognitive tactics to cope with post-traumatic stress (Raio et al., 2013). For instance, refocusing makes use of "attentional processes that might allow individuals to disengage from rigid patterns of regulation" (Aldao & Nolen-Hoeksema, 2012, p. 498), thus reducing psychopathology and enhancing emotion regulation.

Within the framework of cognitive therapy for PTSD, one of the most effective types of treatment for trauma patients (Chard & Healy, 2020), cognitive restructuring is made possible through cognitive psychotherapy techniques directly addressing emotion dysregulation and mobilization of intense negative affect.

In experimental cognitive neuroscience, stress is supposed to impact neural circuits that partly overlap with those that subserve memory (Good, 2013). Nelson and Carver (1998) argued that the neural mechanisms underlying functional plasticity, which are adaptive in typically developing children, tend to become dysfunctional in children exposed to traumatic stress, for whom "opportunity" turns into "vulnerability." Stress is well-known to cause long-lasting impairment in several brain regions. The link between brain, stress, and memory is therefore paramount to consider to achieve a better understanding of traumatic stress and its effects on trauma patients. Therefore, PTSD can be considered as a "disorder of memory" also from a neuroscientific point of view (Van Marle, 2015). Among the various stages of memory storage, the consolidation phase seems to play a crucial role in traumatic psychopathology. When initially fragile memory traces are integrated into long-term storage, their consolidation is made possible by gradual transfer of information from initial hippocampal-cortical links to cortico-cortical connections, which serve to categorize and conceptualize life events (Frankland & Bontempi, 2005). Therefore, a failure in consolidation and depotentiation of traumatic memories might be closely correlated with core PTSD symptomatology (van Marle, 2015).

Early-life trauma can involve disturbances in self-referential processing and social cognition (Lanius et al., 2014), which seem to be underlain by the same "default mode network" in the brain. In fact, individuals suffering from PTSD exhibit deep relational problems, ranging from intimacy disturbances to interpersonal violence. The theory of mind is especially relevant to empathic attunement, which requires the ability to recognize the emotions of others. Empathy-related impairments, as well as difficulties in sharing affective states, are indeed signs of PTSD psychopathology (Nietlisbach et al., 2010). As Van der Kolk (2006) argued:

> [T]he discovery that sensory input can automatically stimulate hormonal secretions and influence the activation of brain regions involved in attention and memory once again confronts psychology with the limitations of conscious control over our actions and emotions.
>
> (p. 277)

In fact, traumatized individuals often react with apparently irrational, subcortically initiated responses to present triggers of past stressful situations: the rationale for this behavior might lie in the neurobiological activation in the "here and now" of brain regions associated with the coping mechanisms that have been mobilized to deal with the past shocking occurrence. When exposed to triggers of their trauma, the cerebral blood flow of trauma patients increases in the right medial orbitofrontal cortex, insula, amygdala, and anterior temporal pole, and decreases in the left anterior prefrontal cortex, specifically in Broca's area. Accordingly, when PTSD individuals are triggered by reminders of their trauma, they tend to experience intense emotions, while being often unable to translate their experience into verbal language.

One of the main features that distinguish human beings from other animals is the flexibility that characterizes their responses to environmental stimuli, also provided by their unique neural plasticity. This flexibility emerges slowly in human development and can be easily disrupted. In fact, it is

> the result of the property of the human neocortex to integrate a large variety of different pieces of information, to attach meaning to both the incoming input and the physical urges (tendencies) that these evoke, and to apply logical thought to calculate the long-term effect of their actions.
>
> (Van der Kolk, 2006, p. 281)

Accordingly, trauma is closely associated with physical helplessness, that is, the sensation that nothing can be done to prevent the harmful situation from happening. From this point of view, trauma can also be thought of as originating from a failure of the person's physiological responses to effectively respond to threat.

Based on the distinction between different types of memory, which seem to be associated with different neural regions, behaviors, and symptoms, Brewin (2001) pointed out that the hippocampus is crucial in the process of "binding" together different aspects of an event, which amounts to making a coherent and integrated whole of it.[2] The author drew also attention to "the paradoxical nature of trauma memories, which may be vague or vivid, intrusive or quiescent, under or out of control, and experienced in the present or the past" (p. 388). Kensinger (2007) provided neuroimaging evidence of the fact that negative emotions enhance not only the vividness of subjective memories, but also the probability of remembering the details of the event. Furthermore, some of the brain areas subserving the processing of emotions (specifically, the amygdala and the orbitofrontal cortex) are also associated with the encoding and retrieval of details related to negative events. Finally, Deffenbacher et al. (2004) pointed out that high levels of stress negatively impact different features of eyewitness memory, where the increased interest toward threatening material ought to be distinguished from the stress response the individual sets in motion to defend him- or herself from harmful stimuli.

Notes

1. An interesting distinction has been drawn between reward, positive emotion, and positive affect: whereas reward processing refers to "the whole organismic response to obtaining, consuming, or learning about a subjectively pleasing or positive valence stimulus or experience" (Fonzo, 2018, p. 218), positive emotion is regarded as a set of "multicomponent response tendencies that unfold over a relatively short period of time and typically occur in response to some antecedent event, involve some conscious or unconscious appraisal of the event, and trigger a cascade of responses including changes in subjective experience, facial expression, physiology, and cognitive processes" (*ibid.*). Finally, and more generally, positive affect comprises "pleasant consciously accessible feeling states, which may or may not have an object or event attached to them and tend to be less multi-component in their constitution" (*ibid.*).
2. PTSD has been supposed to affect the three main features of memory – "capacity," "content," and "process" (Brewin, 2011): "capacity refers to individual variability in the amount of information that can be learned, manipulated, and either recalled or used in some other way . . . content refers to what can be remembered from the past. . . . Memory processes may be described at a number of levels, including the molecular, neuropsychological, cognitive, and social" (pp. 206–207).

References

Aldao, A., & Nolen-Hoeksema, S. (2012). The influence of context on the implementation of adaptive emotion regulation strategies. *Behaviour Research and Therapy, 50*(7–8), 493–501.

American Psychiatric Association. (2013). *Diagnostic and statistical manual of mental disorders* (5th ed.). Washington, DC: Author.

Bar-Haim, Y., Kerem, A., Lamy, D., & Zakay, D. (2010). When time slows down: The influence of threat on time perception in anxiety. *Cognition and Emotion, 24*(2), 255–263.

Bartlett, F. C. (1932). *Remembering*. Cambridge: Cambridge University Press.

Basch, M. F. (1983). The perception of reality and the disavowal of meaning. *Annual of Psychoanalysis, 11*, 125–153.

Baym, C. L., Gonsalve, B. (2010). Comparison of neural activity that leads to true memories, false memories, and forgetting: An fMRI study of the misinformation effect. *Cognitive, Affective, and Behavioral Neuroscience, 10*, 339–348.

Bell, C. R., Provins, K. A. (1963). Relation between physiological responses to environmental heat and time judgments. *Journal of Experimental Psychology, 66*, 572–579.

Bernstein, D. M., & Loftus, E. F. (2008). Memory distortion. *Encyclopedia of Neuroscience, 2325*–2328.

Brewin, C. R. (2001). Memory processes in post-traumatic stress disorder. *International Review of Psychiatry, 13*(3), 159–163.

Brewin, C. R. (2011). The nature and significance of memory disturbance in post-traumatic stress disorder. *Annual Review of Clinical Psychology, 7*, 203–227.

Caruth, C. (1996). *Unclaimed experience: Trauma, narrative, and history*. Baltimore: Johns Hopkins University Press.

Chard, K. M., & Healy, E. T. (2020). Cognitive processing therapy for PTSD. In L. F. Bufka, C. V. Wright, & R. W. Halfond (Eds.), *Casebook to the APA clinical practice guideline for the treatment of PTSD* (pp. 69–90). American Psychological Association.

Damasio, A. R. (1999). *The feeling of what happens: Body and emotion and the making of consciousness*. New York: Hartcourt.

Deffenbacher, K. A., Bornstein, B. H., Penrod, S. D., & McGorty, E. K. (2004). A meta-analytic review of the effects of high stress on eyewitness memory. *Law & Human Behavior, 28*, 687–706.

Dekel, S., & Bonanno, G. A. (2013). Changes in trauma memory and patterns of posttraumatic stress. *Psychological Trauma: Theory, Research, Practice, and Policy, 5*(1), 26–34.

Edelman, G. (2004). *Wider than the sky: The phenomenal gift of consciousness*. New Haven: Yale University Press.

Foehl, J. C. (2020). Lived depth: A phenomenology of psychoanalytic process and identity. *Psychoanalytic Inquiry, 40*(2), 131–146.

Fonzo, G. A. (2018). Diminished positive affect and traumatic stress: A biobehavioral review and commentary on trauma affective neuroscience, *Neurobiology of Stress, 9*, 214–230.

Ford, J. D. (2015). An affective cognitive neuroscience-based approach to PTSD psychotherapy: The TARGET model. *Journal of Cognitive Psychotherapy, 29*(1), 68–91.

Frankland, P. W., & Bontempi, B. (2005). The organization of recent and remote memories. *Nature Reviews Neuroscience, 6*(2), 119–130.

Frewen, P. A., Dozois, D. J., Neufeld, R. W., Lane, R. D., Densmore, M., Stevens, T. K., Lanius, R. A. (2012). Emotional numbing in post-traumatic stress disorder: A functional magnetic resonance imaging study. *Journal of Clinical Psychiatry, 73*, 431–436.

Frewen, P., & Lanius, R. A. (2015). *Healing the traumatized self*. London and New York: W. W. Norton.

Friedman, W. J. (1993). Memory for the time of past events. *Psychological Bulletin, 113*(1), 44–66.

Fuchs, T. (2010). Temporality and psychopathology. *Phenomenology and the Cognitive Sciences, 12*(1), 75–104.

Gerhart, J., & Stinson, C. (1994). The nature of therapeutic discourse: Accounts of the self. *Journal of Narrative and Life History, 4*(3), 151–191.

Gil, S., & Droit-Volet, S. (2009). "Time flies in the presence of angry faces" . . . depending on the temporal task used. *Acta Psychologica, 136*(3), 354–362.

Good, M.-J. (2013). Perspectives on trauma and healing from anthropology and social and affective neuroscience. *Transcultural Psychiatry, 50*(5), 744–752.

Gostecnik, C. (1997). Chronos versus kairos in psychotherapy. *American Journal of Pastoral Counseling, 1*(1), 49–60.

Gruber, J., Cunningham, W. A., Kirkland, T., & Hay, A. C. (2012). Feeling stuck in the present? Mania proneness and history associated with present-oriented time perspective. *Emotion, 2*(1), 13–17.

Hartocollis, P. (1974). Origins of time: A reconstruction of the ontogenetic development of the sense of time based on object-relations theory. *Psychoanalytic Quarterly, 43*, 243–260.

Hartocollis, P. (1975). Time and affect in psychopathology. *Journal of the American Psychoanalytic Association, 23*(2), 383–395.

Hartocollis, P. (1976). On the experience of time and its dynamics, with special reference to affects. *Journal of the American Psychoanalytic Association, 24*, 363–375.

Hartocollis, P. (1983). *Time and timelessness, or the varieties of temporal experience.* International Universities Press.

Hartocollis, P. (1986). *Time and timelessness or the varieties of temporal experience: A psychoanalytic inquiry.* Madison, CT: International University Press.

Herman, J. L. (2015). *Trauma and recovery: The aftermath of violence. From domestic abuse to political terror.* New York: Basic Books.

James, W. (1890) 1950. *The principles of psychology.* New York: Dover Publications.

Janet, P. (1889) 2005. *L'automatisme psychologique: Essai de psychologie expérimentale sur les formes inférieures de lactivité humaine.* Paris: L. Harmattan.

Johnston, A. (2005). *Time driven: Metapsychology and the splitting of the drive.* Evanston: Northwestern University Press.

Kafka, J. (1989). *Multiple realities in clinical practice.* New Haven: Yale University Press.

Kensinger, E. A. (2007). Negative emotion enhances memory accuracy: Behavioral and neuroimaging evidence. *Current Directions in Psychological Science, 16*, 213–218.

King, D. W., King, L. A., Erickson, D. J., Huang, M. T., Sharkansky, E. J., & Wolfe, J. (2000). Posttraumatic stress disorder and retrospectively reported stressor exposure: A longitudinal prediction model. *Journal of Abnormal Psychology, 109*(4), 624–633.

Kirmayer, L. J. (1996). Landscapes of memory: Trauma, narrative and dissociation. In P. Antze & M. Lambek (Eds.), *Tense past: Cultural essays on memory and trauma* (pp. 173–198). London: Routledge.

Kohut, H. (1977). *The restoration of the self.* New York: International University Press.

Krystal, J. H., Bennett, A. L., Bremner, J. D., Southwick, S. M., & Charney, D. S. (1995). Toward a cognitive neuroscience of dissociation and altered memory functions in post-traumatic stress disorder. In M. J. Friedman, D. S. Charney, & A. Y. Deutch (Eds.), *Neurobiological and clinical consequences of stress: From normal adaptation to post-traumatic stress disorder* (pp. 239–269). Lippincott Williams & Wilkins Publishers.

Kümmel, F. (1966). Time as succession and the problem of duration. In J. T. Fraser (Ed.), *The voices of time* (pp. 31–55). New York: G. Braziller.

Lanius, R., Frewen, P., Nazarov, A., & McKinnon, M. C. (2014). A social-cognitive-neuroscience approach to PTSD. In U. F. Lanius, S. L. Paulsen, & F. M. Corrigan (Eds.), *Neurobiology and treatment of traumatic dissociation: Towards an embodied self* (pp. 69–80). New York, NY: Springer.

Leys, R. (2000). *Trauma: A genealogy.* Chicago: University of Chicago Press.

Lieberman, L., Gorka, S. M., Funkhouser, C. J., Shankman, S. A., & Phan, K. L. (2017). Impact of post-traumatic stress symptom dimensions on psychophysiological reactivity to threat and reward. *Journal of Psychiatric Research, 92*, 55–63.

McNally, R. J. (2005). Debunking myths about trauma and memory. *The Canadian Journal of Psychiatry, 50*(13), 817–822.

Meares, R. (1995). Episodic Memory, trauma, and the narrative of self. *Contemporary Psychoanalysis, 31*(4), 541–556.

Meares, R. (2003). *Intimacy and alienation. Memory, trauma and personal being.* New York: Brunner-Routledge.

Meissner, W. W. (2007). *Time, self and psychoanalysis.* Plymouth: Jason Aronson.

Melges, F. T. (1982). *Time and the inner future: A temporal approach to psychiatric disorders.* New York: John Wiley & Sons.

Modell, A. H. (1990). *Other times, other realities: Toward a theory of psychoanalytic treatment.* Cambridge, MA: Harvard University Press.

Nelson, C. A., and Carver, L. J. (1998). The effects of stress and trauma on brain and memory: A view from developmental cognitive neuroscience. *Development and Psychopathology, 10*(4), 793–809.

Newman, E. J., & Lindsay, D. S. (2009). False memories: What the hell are they for? *Applied Cognitive Psychology, 23*, 1105–1121.

Nietlisbach, G., Maercker, A., Rösler, W., & Haker, H. (2010). Are empathic abilities impaired in posttraumatic stress disorder? *Psychological Reports, 106*(3), 832–844.

Okado, Y., & Stark, C. (2005). Neural activity during encoding predicts false memories created by misinformation. *Learning and Memory, 12*, 3–11.

Ornstein, A. (1994). Trauma, memory, and psychic continuity. *Progress in Self Psychology, 10*, 131–146.

Payne, J. D., Nadel, L., Britton, W. B., & Jacobs, W. J. (2004). The biopsychology of trauma and memory. In D. Reisberg & P. Hertel (Eds.), *Memory and emotion* (pp. 76–128). Oxford: Oxford University Press.

Polkinghorne, D. E. (1991). Narrative and self-concept. *Journal of Narrative and Life History, 1*(2–3), 135–153.

Raio, C. M., Orederu, T. A., Palazzolo, L., Shurick, A. A., & Phelps, E. A. (2013). Cognitive emotion regulation fails the stress test. *Proceedings of the National Academy of Sciences of the United States of America, 110*(37), 15139–15144.

Romero-Jódar, A. (2012). When the life giver dies, all around is laid waste: Structural trauma and the splitting of time in *Signal to noise*, a graphic novel. *Journal of Popular Culture, 45*(5).

Sacks, O. (1970) 1998. *The man who mistook his wife for a hat.* New York: Simon & Schuster.

Schacter, D. L., Guerin, S. A., & Jacques, P. L. (2011). Memory distortion: An adaptive perspective. *Trends in Cognitive Sciences, 15*(10), 467–474.

Schafer, R. (1983). Psychoanalytic interpretation. In R. Schafer (Ed.), *The analytic attitude* (Vol. 11). New York: Routledge.

Schore, A. N. (1994). *Affect regulation and the origin of the self.* New York, NJ: Lawrence Erlbaum Associates.

Schore, A. N. (2002). Dysregulation of the right brain: A fundamental mechanism of traumatic attachment and the psychopathogenesis of posttraumatic stress disorder. *Australia and New Zealand Journal of Psychiatry, 36*(1), 9–30.

Schrag, C. O. (1999). *The self after postmodernity.* New Haven: Yale University Press.

Siegel, D. J. (1999). *The developing mind. Toward a neurobiology of interpersonal experience.* New York: The Guilford Press.

Southwick, S. M., Morgan, C. A., Nicolaou, A. L., & Charney, D. S. (2006). Consistency of memory for combat-related traumatic events in veterans of Operation Desert Storm. *The American Journal of Psychiatry, 154*(2), 173–177.

Staniloiu, A., & Markowitsch, H. J. (2012). Dissociation, memory, and trauma narrative. *Journal of Literary Theory, 6*(1).

Stern, D. (1985). *The interpersonal world of the infant.* New York: Basic Books.

Strange, D., & Takarangi, M. K. (2015). Memory distortion for traumatic events: The role of mental imagery. *Frontiers in Psychiatry, 6,* 1–4.

Van der Kolk, B. A. (2014). *The body keeps the score.* London: Penguin Books.

Van der Kolk, B. A. (2000). Posttraumatic stress disorder and the nature of trauma. *Dialogues in Clinical Neuroscience, 2*(1), 7–22.

Van der Kolk, B. A. (2006). Clinical implications of neuroscience research in PTSD. *Annals of the New York Academy of Sciences, 1071*(1), 277–293.

Van Marle, H. (2015). PTSD as a memory disorder. *European Journal of Psychotraumatology, 6,* 1–3.

Whitehead, A. (2011). *Trauma fiction.* Edinburgh: Edinburgh University Press.

Wilkinson, M. (2003). Undoing trauma: Contemporary neuroscience. *Journal of Analytical Psychology, 48,* 235–253.

Wyshak, G. (1994). The relation between change in reports of traumatic events and symptoms of psychiatric distress. *General Hospital Psychiatry, 16*(2), 290–297.

Chapter 7

Time, Trauma, and Neural (Dis-)Integration

This chapter tackles the problem as to whether a single or multiple mechanisms exist in the brain, which would represent the neural basis of human temporal perception. Traumatic stress consists of a biological, psychological, and social shocking experience. Chronic adversities produce lasting scars in the brain, especially when endured during early developmental stages. PTSD is also associated with inflammation of the immune system, which renders trauma patients more prone to psychological and physical pathology. Stress is particularly damaging when it is unpredictable, as it becomes associated with a sense of helplessness and hopelessness. Fear conditioning, emotional circuits, memory consolidation, epigenetics, and genetic factors are all involved in the etiology of PTSD symptomatology. The brain of PTSD patients seems to lose the ability to integrate experience into a unified whole. At the core of trauma resolution lies the reestablishment of the processes of psychic and neural integration and self-organization.

Neural Correlates of Temporal Perception

Different models of time perception set the ground for the debate on whether and, if so, how and where in the brain it is processed (Wittman, 2009). Recent neuroscientific studies have shown that certain brain regions are specifically associated with the experience of past and future, and that these areas are located in the same regions (Nyberg et al., 2010). However, the neural basis of time perception is still a matter of debate, and to a large extent obscure. First, different processes and brain areas might be involved in time sense, depending on the length of the intervals to be measured. Second, different cognitive processes might become activated when trying to estimate the duration of an event, and these processes are supposed to influence but not to be necessary conditions to the experience of time.

If perceived time represents the mental status of the beholder, then time becomes a function of the Self, that is, "$t = f\,(\mathrm{self})$" (Wittman, 2009,

DOI: 10.4324/9781003230601-8

p. 1955). Research has shown that attention, mood, emotion, working memory, and long-term memory all play a crucial role in time estimation (Zakay & Block, 2004; Droit-Volet et al., 2007; Taatgen et al., 2007). For instance, time intervals are judged as longer when we pay more attention to time, whereas time seems to speed up when we are engaged in pleasant activities. Therefore, our sense of time is a result of the intertwined play of different cognitive functions as well as of our inner states. All these factors are supposed to influence time perception, but a single mechanism for this process is yet to be found in the brain.

Among other regions, the cerebellum, the right posterior parietal cortex, the right prefrontal cortex, and fronto-striatal circuits appear to be the substrates of a potential "time machine" in the brain. Moreover, dopamine seems critical to our experience of time, and might represent the basis for a primary timekeeping mechanism. A main difficulty in finding a neural substrate for time perception consists in the fact that many other brain areas seem to be activated during temporal judgment tasks, but they don't seem *per se* essential to human experience of time. Mauk and Buonomano (2004) tried to demonstrate the existence of distributed neural networks, whose neural populations would allow the subject to encode duration. This means that many different brain areas might contribute to human time perception, without there being a specific location in the brain underlying temporal experience. In other words, these network-dependent processes do not involve a single dedicated time system for temporal encoding. However, these processes seem to work at best for very short lapses of time (up to a few hundred milliseconds), whereas the estimation of longer durations seems to require additional processes in the central nervous system.

Time-processing functions seem to be embedded in several interacting neural circuits that lack a single substrate for human experience of time. As a result, the experience of time would not rely on chronological processes only, but would rather be an epiphenomenon arising from cognitive and emotional responses to the environment. A multiplicity of models for time perception have been proposed, without resolution as to what specific mechanism underlies our perception of time (Eagleman, 2008). In fact, it is very unlikely that one single mechanism for temporal processing exists in the brain. Instead, it is more intuitive to think of different temporal processing mechanisms involved on different timescales. This seems plausible especially given the results of research showing how an automatic timing system for shorter intervals (up to circa 1 second) exists, as opposed to a cognitively controlled time system for intervals lasting more than a second (Lewis & Miall, 2003).

We never perceive events in isolation. Also, a mechanism seems to exist, which allows individuals to perceive a succession of stimuli as a unitary *Gestalt*, which integrates such stimuli into perceptual units with a duration of circa 2–3 seconds (Pöppel, 2009). A *Gestalt* is a mental construct that does not exist in the physical world. In fact, the so-called "subjective present" (Fraisse, 1984), that is, the lapse of time in which one can perceive different events as a single occurrence, seems to be limited to 2–3 seconds. Accordingly, there seem to exist several cognitive processes entangled with our perception of time, so that no single area in the brain can be found on which our experience of time might rely. A variability always exists, for example, based on whether attention is paid to an event or not, which leads in turn to different time estimations for the same chronological interval.

Body states as a whole might in fact underlie a timekeeping mechanism (Craig, 2008). In this view, it seems that the insula, which is the substrate of the integration of body signals, underlies the generation of emotions and the person's sense of time as well. The relationship between emotion and time perception has also been investigated (Droit-Volet et al., 2011). Strong awareness of one's emotions and body processes would lead to longer perceived intervals. The insula is involved in temporal processing at different levels. Indeed, it is possible that the rate of body signals accumulated in the insula contributes to the creation of our perception of duration (Craig, 2008). The idea that time and awareness are inextricably intertwined is in line with the Western philosophical (phenomenological) and psychological (psychoanalytical) tradition, according to which time is a creation of the Self (Wittman, 2009). In fact, the experience of the Self is only possible as a unified entity unfolding in time.

Neurobiologically, body signals create a "material Self" that feels a vast array of emotions and can also become self-aware. Because the pathways to the insula constantly inform us about our inner states, this brain area might also be one of the substrates of a supposed timekeeping mechanism. It is indeed in the insula that the accumulation of inner states over time is registered. This signaling of body states is an ongoing temporal process, and might underlie our temporal perception. Ultimately, because affective states are entangled with emotions, the insula might be one of the neural correlates of the human perception of time (Wittman, 2009).

Trauma, Stress, and Inflammation

Far from being separate, the cortex, the limbic system, and the brain stem are rather deeply intertwined. The *cortex* is the most recently evolved part of our brain; the *limbic system* is the center of the brain, where emotions arise in the first place; the *brain stem* controls basic survival functions (Cozolino, 2006). Research has shown that trauma actually changes the structures and functions of the brain, exactly at the intersection where its major parts tend to converge (Solomon & Siegel, 2003). Now, a healthy stress response would consist of responding quickly and appropriately to the stressor, dampening down the stress response shortly after the activation of the flight-or-fight response, thanks to the neural system that can recover and return to baseline, that is, a state of dynamic rest (Nakazawa, 2015). However, the experience of chronic adversities can produce lasting physical scars in the brain. Sudden rushes of alertness mark the traumatized individual's everyday life. When this occurs, the hypothalamus releases hormones that stimulate the pituitary and adrenal glands to pump chemicals throughout the body. Adrenaline and cortisol trigger immune cells to secrete messenger molecules, which in turn lead the body's immune system to activate.

As Nakazawa (2015) pointed out, there is a powerful linkage between mental stress and physical inflammation. During stressful situations, the hypothalamic-pituitary-adrenal (HPA) axis releases stress hormones that promote inflammation. Besides ordinary inflammation, which occurs when the immune system fights a viral or bacterial infection, there are other types of tissue damage that occur slowly in response to chronic stress. When the person's system is chronically overstimulated, it ends up downshifting its response to stress, which appears to never really shut off (Nakazawa, 2015): "chronic stress leads to a dysregulation of our stress hormones – which leads to unregulated inflammation. And inflammation translates into symptoms and disease" (p. 30). Overall, neuroscientific findings demonstrated that PTSD is associated with inflammation of the immune system, so that there would be a bidirectional causal relationship between PTSD and inflammation (Neylan & O'Donovan, 2018).

Stress can be defined as an environmental situation that has the power of disrupting the ordinary functioning of the person (Nelson & Carver, 1998). Trauma involves stress that exceeds the subject's resources for coping (Hubbard et al., 1995). Traumatic stress has also been defined as "a biological, psychological, communal/social, and spiritual shock" (Ford, 2009, p. 1), which individuals have no resources to face. When the brain is not able to moderate the person's stress levels, it enters a state of constant hyperarousal. Of note, stress is more damaging to a child than to an adult. For a young brain, being repeatedly overstimulated means for its immune system to disable the genes that regulate the stress response, thus preventing it from regulating this response also later in life. Individuals who went through a so-called "adverse childhood experience" tend to react so similarly precisely because of the *unpredictability* that often characterizes early traumatic stress. In fact, when even stronger stress is in place, but is nonetheless predictable, it does not produce the negative effects that unpredictable stress shows (Nakazawa, 2015): it is indeed "the unpredictability of stress that is particularly damaging" (p. 42). It has also been shown that there is a high correlation between adverse childhood experiences and health disorders in adulthood (Naka-zawa, 2015). For instance, anxiety problems during childhood can lead to major depression in adult life.

PTSD results from unresolved trauma and reflects the dysregula-tion and dissociation of multiple neural networks. Talking through the trauma, that is, constructing narratives in a supporting environment, fos-ters psychological and neurobiological integration involving cognition, affect, sensation, and behavior. When the system involved in the regula-tion of neurobiological processes aimed at appraising and responding to threat becomes dysregulated, the body keeps reacting as if the trauma were constantly present. As a result, trauma appears to the individual as continuously occurring. However, it has not been proven that the abnor-malities observed in the brain of trauma patients represent the *causes* of PTSD. In fact, it is equally possible that preexisting anomalies might have served as risk factors for the development of PTSD following trauma exposure (Stein et al., 1997).

Neurobiological Symptoms and Neurochemistry of PTSD

PTSD is one of the disorders for which there is the most compelling evi-dence as to the underlying neurobiology (Ross et al., 2017): in this view, "any contemporary neuroscience formulation of PTSD should include an understanding of fear conditioning, dysregulated circuits, memory recon-solidation, epigenetics, and genetic factors" (p. 407). Ross et al. (2017) addressed the genetic and epigenetic factors that are at stake in the origin of PTSD. Epigenetics refers to the mechanisms through which environ-mental factors can influence gene expression. Trauma can epigenetically influence the stress response system, leading to prolonged and maladap-tive responses to later triggers of the original trauma. As to genetics, even though PTSD is closely associated with external stimuli, the disposition towards it has been shown to be highly inheritable. Findings in this field of research are mixed, and mainly focused on genes involved in neural plasticity, neural inhibition, and stress response (Almli et al., 2014).

Along with its main characteristic symptoms – hyperarousal, intrusion symptoms related to the traumatic occurrence, and avoid-ance of trauma-related stimuli – PTSD reflects the loss of integration of cognitive, sensory, and behavioral systems (Nakazawa, 2015). First, hyperarousal is associated with a stress-induced dysregulation of the amygdala and the nervous system, which results in anxious behaviors. As a result, hyperaroused individuals perceive the world as threatening and dangerous. Furthermore, intrusion symptoms related to the trau-matic occurrence consist of traumatic experiences breaking into con-scious awareness and being experienced as if they were happening in the "here and now." This is due to the fact that hippocampal activity fails in contextualizing traumatic memories of the trauma, and in turning them into a coherent narrative. Finally, avoidance of trauma-related stimuli consists of the attempt to defend oneself against dangerous stimuli by limiting contact with the external environment, withdrawing from others, and escaping from painful thoughts, feelings, and emotions. The memory of the trauma and the experience of it in the present moment is then possibly caught up in a cycle of self-traumatization, coping, and exhaustion. This cycle tends to repeat itself and to trigger ongoing frightening emotional responses, rather than to mobilize the body to deal with an actual, present threat.

Structural and functional brain changes are also associated with PTSD (Nutt & Malizia, 2004). Norepinephrine, dopamine, endorphins, and glucocorticoids increase during acute stress, whereas serotonin decreases. When stress becomes chronic, the baseline production and availability of these neurochemicals continue to change, resulting in long-term behavioral and psychological symptomatology. Norepinephrine is involved in the fight-or-flight response and reinforces the encoding of traumatic memories. Long-term high levels of norepinephrine contribute to increased arousal, anxiety, and irritability. Analogously, high levels of dopamine are associated with hypervigilance, paranoia, and perceptual distortions when under stress. High levels of glucocorticoids affect the nervous system, for example, they decrease hippocampal volume and produce memory deficits. It is well-known that hippocampal size in PTSD patients is to some degree smaller than that in persons without this condition (Schacter et al., 1996). In fact, it has been shown that glucocorticoids allow for short-term survival (Karl et al., 2006). However, prolonged high levels of glucocorticoids negatively affect the immune system, resulting in learning impairments and physical illnesses, which go hand in hand with emotional dysfunction, social withdrawal, and compromised adaptive functioning in several life domains.

There is consistent evidence that trauma is not limited to life-threatening experiences, as the *DSM-5* (APA, 2013) seems to suggest (Nakazawa, 2015). Trauma takes on different forms based on the moment when it is experienced, how much it lasts, and how it is perceived. Stress can also affect the infant before birth, for example, when it is accompanied by maternal depression. The most dramatic traumatic experiences occur when the parents or caregivers enact the trauma. When a child experiences trauma by the hand of its caregivers, dissociation may occur as a result of fear and hyperarousal. Prolonged or chronic stress leads individuals to react more strongly to subsequent stress (Solomon & Siegel, 2003). Dissociation allows the mind–body system to escape from trauma through various biological and psychological processes. Dissociation and derealization processes confer trauma patients the opportunity to avoid the experience and memory of the traumatic occurrence, or else to watch it as external observers, as it might be too painful to live the traumatic event from within one's own body. Dissociation and disconnection from events occurring in reality results in a less integrated information processing in conscious awareness, affect, and behavior.

The integration of memories is impaired in persons who suffer from PTSD (Vasterling et al., 1998). The modulation of traumatic memories relies on the activation of the amygdala and the related physiological and biological brain regions. In PTSD patients, memories are difficult to bring together and integrate, resulting in a decreased attention to (and processing of) external stimuli. This might be due to subcortical processes that inhibit the activation of the hippocampus and cortex in memory processes. In fact, "traumatic memories can disrupt the storage (encoding) of information and the integration of the various system of attention and memory" (Cozolino, 2010, p. 273). Conscious explicit memory encoding can be impaired when hippocampal activity is blocked or inhibited by glucocorticoids or high levels of activation of the amygdala, which in turn can lead to a lack of conscious memory for the traumatic episode. In other words, memory integration can be hindered by lower hippocampal activity, which results in a lack of integration of new memories into already existing neural networks. Ultimately, "unresolved trauma disrupts integrated neural processing, so that conscious awareness is split from emotional and physiological experiences" (Cozolino, 2010, p. 283).

Neurobiology of Trauma

Neurotransmitters that regulate arousal and attention function abnormally in PTSD patients, who show high levels of cortisol (Van der Kolk, 2002). Cortisol is also called the "stress hormone," as it becomes activated in the negative feedback loop that aims at reestablishing the stress levels that were present before the traumatic episode. Now, the person's primary goal when facing a traumatic experience is survival and self-protection. Some individuals try to cope by taking actions ("fight" response), whereas other dissociate ("freeze" response). As we have seen, dissociation is a basic predictor of the development of PTSD following trauma (Van der Kolk, 2003). In this view, the longer the experience, the more likely the person is to dissociate during or in the immediate aftermath of the traumatic event. Furthermore, when it is a family member that perpetrates the abuse, the child is more likely to become even more dependent upon the abuser and to get paralyzed in its decision-making processes.

As opposed to the actual trauma, which has a beginning, a middle, and an end, the symptoms of PTSD seem to be "timeless." They do not allow to freely remember the past, attend present activities, or make future plans. Van der Kolk (2000) called PTSD a "physioneurosis" (p. 12), that is, a mental condition characterized by persistent biological emergency responses. This is the reason why PTSD individuals perceive and categorize the world differently from people who do not suffer from traumatic psychopathology. Indeed, it has been shown that PTSD patients, just like clinical samples of subjects suffering from anxiety and depression, are overall significantly more prone to psychopathology than non-clinical subjects (Muran & Motta, 1993). For instance, Najavits et al. (2004) evaluated cognitive distortions in a dual diagnosis sample (a population with PTSD and substance use disorder) compared to a single diagnosis sample (a population with PTSD only), finding that the dual diagnosis sample reported higher levels of cognitive distortions than the single diagnosis sample, and that there seemed to be specificity for dual diagnosis types of distortions.

PTSD subjects experience abnormal psychophysiological reactions on (at least) two levels (Solomon & Siegel, 2003): in response to specific reminders of the traumatic event, and also in response to intense but neutral stimuli (e.g., loud noises). This results in a loss of stimulus discrimination, which goes hand in hand with a heightened physiological arousal in response to trauma-related stimuli. The process through which traumatic triggers following the shock, even if less strong, produce increasing effects over time is referred to as "kindling" (Post et al., 1997). An example is the well-known abnormal startle response seen in PTSD patients. Compared to other individuals, these subjects suffer from a specific type of desensitization due to the inhibition of the stress response as a result of chronic and persistent stress. In this sense, PTSD develops after a traumatic event overwhelms the individual, whose stress response progressively "kindles" instead of returning to baseline.

In PTSD, the brain loses its ability to integrate experience into a unified whole (Van der Kolk, 2003). Several structures in the central nervous system contribute to these integrative processes. For example, the parietal lobes integrate information of different associative areas; the hippocampus creates a cognitive map, where experience is categorized and integrated in its emotional and cognitive aspects; the cingulate gyrus amplifies and filters information so that emotional and cognitive aspects of the traumatic experience are integrated; the dorsolateral frontal cortex helps to "keep in mind" sensations and impulses, and compares them with previous information to plan effective actions. As previously mentioned, people suffering from chronic PTSD have decreased hippocampal volumes, but this change may not be irreversible. In other animals, decreased hippocampal volume is associated with behavioral disinhibition and with flight-or-fight responses to threatening stimuli. As Kesner (1998) noted, not only the hippocampus mediates our memory for the duration of temporal events, but also both the hippocampus and the prefrontal cortex subserve memory (specifically, memory based on new information) for the temporal order of events. Also, whereas the hippocampus mediates memory for past events, the prefrontal cortex supports the prospective openness to future occurrences. In human subjects, it is likely that decreased hippocampal volumes play a key role in dissociation and misinterpretation of information, and in vulnerability to interpret stimuli as threatening. Hippocampal involvement in the regulation of the stress response is critically important to any discussion of stress and memory, because this structure is also implicated in explicit memory (Payne et al., 2004).

During exposure to the script of their traumatic experiences, the traumatized individuals' brain shows heightened activation only in the right hemisphere, particularly in areas closely involved in emotional arousal, such as the amygdala, the insula, and the medial temporal lobe (Payne et al., 2004). As opposed to the activation of the right hemisphere, the left one shows decreased activity, particularly in the Broca's area, which is involved in our capacity to translate personal experiences into a coherent narrative. This is why it is difficult for traumatized individuals to verbalize their experience. In trauma patients, the translation of the traumatic experience into a signifying narrative chain is in fact impaired. This might also explain why traumatic experiences are lived in a *timeless* and *ego-alien* fashion. During exposure to traumatic scripts, the activation of the autonomic nervous system of PTSD patients is not surprising. Indeed, reminders of traumatic exposure elicit higher cortisol levels in trauma patients (Elzinga et al., 2003). The amygdala seems particularly affected by trauma, given its involvement in emotional responses, through the process of translating sensory stimuli into emotional and hormonal signals. High activation of the amygdala also interferes with proper hippocampal functioning. Extreme emotional arousal interferes with hippocampal functioning by preventing proper categorization and evaluation of the experience. Localization of information in time and space is thus hindered, causing further fragmentation of experience. Finally, decreased dorsolateral frontal cortex activation might explain why PTSD individuals show only limited conscious awareness when reexperiencing traumatic events.

Dense concentrations of cortisol in the hippocampus appears to be paired with a modulation of hippocampal activity by means of this hormone, which underlies the damaging effects of stress (Van der Kolk, 2000). Increases in stress hormones not only inhibit the HPA activity via hippocampal mediation but, at high levels, they might also impair the neural structure and function of the hippocampus. It is possible that sensory inputs are still stored in memory, but they are not combined into a unified whole. Neural death associated with glucocorticoid release might thus underlie severe memory impairment, as manifested by PTSD patients. Furthermore, the processing of traumatic information goes along with hemispheric "lateralization." The right hemisphere is involved in understanding non-verbal cues of information, and allows for the integration of different sensory inputs. The right hemisphere is associated with amygdala activation, which is involved in assigning emotional significance to incoming stimuli. In traumatized individuals, the left hemisphere, which is involved in the interpretation of verbal information, seems to be less active. As a result, persons suffering from PTSD are more likely to dissociate or derealize from the present experience than non-PTSD individuals. Finally, PTSD patients seem to suffer from impaired control over subcortical areas associated with learning, habituation, and stimulus discrimination (Payne et al., 2004).

Time, Trauma, and Brain Dis-Integration

The interpersonal perspective in neurobiology put forward by Solomon and Siegel (2003) drew on a broad range of disciplines to create an integrated picture of human experience. Such word-based frameworks often focus on moment-to-moment experiences, thus allowing us to gain a bigger picture than what the sensory–motor apparatus permits us to produce. However, these frameworks make it difficult for the traumatized individual to experience the "lived" aspects of his or her existence, which are best available through sensation. The core idea of contemporary interpersonal neurobiology is that *integration* is the key component of human well-being. Here, "integration" means the connection of differentiated elements into a functional whole. It has been argued that the human mind has a natural instinct toward integration, which becomes disrupted by traumatic occurrences: "neural integration, a coherent mind, and empathic relationships form the three sides of a triangle of mental health that can be seen as the focus of healing in the process of psychotherapy" (Siegel, 2003, p. xiv).

The adult brain is typically predisposed to respond to external stimuli through relatively stable action patterns (Siegel, 2003). The function of the mind is to inhibit, organize, and modulate these automatic responses. At times, however, it is hard for the mind to entirely exclude unacceptable emotions, thoughts, and sensations from consciousness. As a result, individuals are often better at finding a rationale for their irrational beliefs than at finding a way to master them. Emotional responses do not occur by rational choice, as limbic brain structures, such as the amygdala, "tag" incoming stimuli and determine their emotional significance. At times, when the stimuli are particularly strong, it seems that the person *does not have a choice*, but is *compelled* to act in a certain way; in other words, the mind–body system is massively *inclined* to take a certain action after receiving specific stimuli from the environment (Van der Kolk, 2003).

Both Darwinian and Pavlovian theories suggested that the goal of emotions is to trigger physical responses. To move effectively in the world, individuals need to be able to temporally predict what is coming next, and move their bodies accordingly. Such *temporal prediction* occurs when the body forms a sensorimotor image that contextualizes the external world by comparing it with its previous representations. Emotions are meant to be such guides for action, like "maps" that lead the traveler to navigate an unknown reality. What distinguishes human beings from other animals is the possibility to choose *how* to respond to specific situations. This ability is subserved by the development of the neocortex. However, this same ability becomes easily disrupted, especially when in an emergency or when trauma is present. For instance, traumatized individuals are prone to respond to reminders of trauma by automatically engaging in physical actions intended to respond to the threatening situation as if it was occurring in the present. Once sensory triggers of past trauma engage the emotional brain, higher brain functions have less control over behavior, and can thus trigger a behavioral "regression" (Van der Kolk, 2003).

The *DSM-5* (APA, 2013) definition of PTSD features physiological hyperarousal in response to traumatic sensory triggers. However, trauma cannot be reduced to a physiological response: "the essence of trauma is utter helplessness combined with abandonment by potentially protective caregivers" (Van der Kolk, 2003, p. xxi). As a result of trauma, children and adults seem to lose their ability to use their emotions to navigate the world and take action effectively. Sometimes, individuals do not use their mind to discover things, but rather to hide them. According to the concept of a "hierarchical" information processing, there are intertwined functional relationships among different levels of information processing. Cognitive, emotional, and sensorimotor processing are mutually dependent, they work simultaneously, and give rise to a unified information processing system. The ongoing experience of sensory fragments in PTSD might find an explanation also in thalamic dysfunctions, which interfere with the integration of limbic and cortical information. The thalamus is likely to facilitate the integration of different areas of the brain. Its structure plays a key role in integrating sensory information by connecting the limbic system to the neocortex, and has thus been called the "sensory gateway to the cortex" (Lanius et al., 2003, p. 141). Dysfunctions in the thalamic functions lead to a failure in the integration of sensory information. The thalamus might thus play a key role in the interaction between cognition, emotion, and behavior. Thalamus dysfunctions would then force sensory information to become "stuck" in lower processing levels, which never reach the level of integration provided by the neocortex. Thoughts, emotions, and physical sensation would thus remain separated and not integrated into a unified whole.

Thalamic dysfunctions might therefore underlie the *timeless* nature of flashbacks of the original traumatic experience, by interfering with the relay of information to the limbic system and the neocortex. In other words, higher brain structures would become temporarily disconnected from lower brain areas, interfering with bottom-up as well as top-down processing. Finally, thalamic dysfunction might account for the inability to contextualize past memories into the present situation. When temporal binding does not occur, individuals cannot integrate what is happening in the totality of their biography and, as a result, memory fragments remain dissociated from autobiographical memory and identity (Lanius et al., 2003).

Neuroimaging studies demonstrated that trauma is associated with differences in brain lateralization. Indeed, the right hemisphere has been shown to activate more than the left while recalling traumatic experiences (Lanius et al., 2003). More specifically, non-PTSD subjects tend to show brain activation patterns consistent with verbal episodic memory retrieval, as well as more activation in the left prefrontal areas, whereas PTSD patients show that the right posterior areas of their brain are more activated, resulting in more non-verbal patterns of memory retrieval. This difference might help to explain the sensory-based and non-verbal flashbacks in individuals suffering from PTSD. In fact, PTSD patients exhibit patterns of lateralization that support a right-hemispheric dominance. As Lanius et al. (2001) demonstrated, PTSD patients show "lower levels of brain activation than comparison subjects in the thalamus, the medial frontal cortex (Brodmann's area 11), and the anterior cingulate gyrus (Brodmann's area 32)" (pp. 1921–1922).

As Dillon et al. (2014) argued:

> [T]he brain encodes different types of memory (sensory, emotional, verbal, pre-verbal) in different ways and in various cortical areas. If the trauma is severe, the memory is more likely to be stored in the right brain, split off from the conscious linguistic functions of the left hemisphere.
>
> (p. 149)

Studies using PET and fMRI in subjects with PTSD revealed several brain areas associated with the recalling of traumatic experiences. PTSD involves a disruption of episodic memory, along with an experience of extreme anxiety apparently lacking any determinable cause. As previously mentioned, trauma patients exhibit high activation of the amygdala, which might be the reason for their frequent fearful behaviors, especially when triggered by trauma-related stimuli (Brewin, 2001, 2011). As part of the cognitive processing system, the medial prefrontal cortex is supposed to play a key role in the modulation of fear responses by inhibiting the limbic system and therefore the amygdala. The amygdala is supposed to process and perhaps even store emotional memories, which are highly resistant to forgetting. This capacity of the amygdala is partly mediated by norepinephrine, which also reaches high levels in stressful situations. High levels of cortisol disrupt hippocampal function, impairing episodic and spatial memory, whereas high levels of both norepinephrine and cortisol facilitate amygdala function and the related emotional memories.

Traumatized individuals show medial prefrontal cortex dysfunction along with abnormal suppression of the stress response mediated by the HPA axis (Payne et al., 2004). Notably, the medial prefrontal cortex plays an important role in the retrieval of episodic memories, and might be involved in the segregation of traumatic memories. Also, altered levels of medial prefrontal cortex activation might be responsible for the *timeless* nature of perceived traumatic memories. The anterior cingulate gyrus is involved in several functions, such as the representation of subjective experience, the integration of bodily responses with behavioral demands, and emotional awareness. This brain region is closely involved in the modulation of emotions. Individuals suffering from PTSD, who show a disruption in this system, present indeed emotion dysregulation, including avoidance of trauma-related triggers and emotional numbing.

The hippocampus, which is commonly associated with memory functions, is essential to human declarative memory, and is connected to the amygdala and the cortex. The hippocampus is supposed to play a crucial role in the formation of conscious memories that bear spatial and temporal details (Brewin, 2001, 2011). It is also involved in traumatic behaviors, such as vivid reexperiencing traumatic memories as well as traumatic amnesia. Decreased hippocampal volume is associated with trauma exposure or memory deficit. From a developmental point of view, when a child faces adversity or stressors, the size of the developing hippocampus shrinks, altering the child's ability to process emotions and manage stress. The hippocampus and adjacent medial temporal regions seem to be critical in binding disparate fragments of information into a unified memory trace. At the same time, the hippocampus is crucial in placing autobiographical memory in time, place, and context. It is not surprising, then, that disruptions in the hippocampal functions due to high levels of stress negatively influence the storage of information about place, time, and context of a traumatic event.

Emotional memories can continuously enter awareness in the form of "body memories" (Van der Kolk, 1996), that is, generalized feelings of anger, fear, and uneasiness, unbound to the traumatic episode that seemed to have caused them. Without a contextual framework where a linkage between emotional memories and the corresponding traumatic events can be established, these emotional memories surface as vague and troublesome disconnected feelings. As a consequence, anxiety will be experienced as "generalized." Trauma affects all layers of the brain, from the autonomic responses to trauma-related triggers up to distortions of trauma-related cognitive functioning. For instance, the orbitofrontal cortex is connected to a vast array of cortical and subcortical areas, and is affected by what occurs in the surroundings, thus influencing a variety of behaviors and physiological responses. This brain region is supposed to mediate the communication between cortical and subcortical systems. It might also play a role in the regulation of arousal, keeping it within the limits of our "window of tolerance." It seems that abuse or neglect in the first years of life negatively impacts the orbitofrontal cortex maturation, which does not allow traumatized children to form secure attachment patterns. Furthermore, a dysregulation in the orbitofrontal cortex might account for the autonomic, emotional, and cognitive dysregulation exhibited by PTSD patients (Payne et al., 2004).

As Fragkaki et al. (2016) pointed out, even though several studies have investigated the neurobiology and neuroendocrinology of PTSD after finished traumas, little literature exists as to which PTSD symptoms are manifested by PTSD patients who undergo *ongoing threat*, and it is still a matter of debate whether these individuals present similar abnormalities. Fragkaki et al. (2016) examined the brain functioning and cortisol levels in relation to PTSD in individuals exposed to ongoing threat, such as police officers, fire fighters, and people going through intimate partner violence. They were able to show that ongoing threat is associated with decreased hippocampal volume, although this is not significantly associated with symptom severity, nor with reduced volume of the amygdala or parahippocampal gyrus. Both PTSD patients who underwent finished trauma and PTSD individuals who undergo ongoing threat showed hyperactivation of the amygdala and hypoactivation of the prefrontal cortex and hippocampus (Fragkaki et al., 2016).

To sum up, it seems that PTSD patients who are asked to recall their trauma exhibit brain patterns of activity that are strikingly different from those that non-PTSD patients show when asked to recall ordinary autobiographical memories. The brain connection patterns of the trauma patient's brain are lateralized on the right hemisphere, which is consistent with a non-verbal pattern of memory recall. On the contrary, when non-PTSD patients are asked to recall non-traumatic memories, their left brain is more active, which points to verbal patterns of memory retrieval (Lanius et al., 2003). Ultimately, trauma may induce the separation of the two hemispheres. In other words, impairment in the integration between the right and the left hemisphere is a core deficit in unresolved trauma patients. Therefore, healing from trauma also requires the integration of both hemispheres, which can be achieved through the creation of a coherent narrative (Solomon & Siegel, 2003).

According to the interpersonal approach to neurobiology put forward by Siegel (2003), one of the hallmarks of trauma is that it creates incoherent narratives, along with impairments in neural integration. The application of the complexity theory to the brain allows us to see the latter as a system that has innate tendencies toward complexity and self-organization, which can be achieved by bringing together two intertwined processes: integration and differentiation. The concept of self-organization, if applied to the brain, might amount to what psychologists call "self-regulation" for the person as a whole. Mental health and well-being are thus defined as the brain capacity to determine itself according to the principles of integration and differentiation – where "integration" means that neural circuits are functionally clustered into a working whole, and "differentiation" refers to the fact that neural circuits become specialized in their functions (Solomon & Siegel, 2003).

Emotion represents the ground of neural integration. Balanced emotion means integration of affects, whereas unbalanced emotion can be seen as chaotic and inflexible states of mind, as manifested by PTSD individuals. Emotion is also part of self-regulation. This is why the lack of resolution for trauma patients results in self-dysregulation and emotional disequilibrium. In PTSD patients, the lack of integration between emotional states and self-regulation ultimately leads to chaotic states of mind. Therapy for these individuals should consist of focusing on the integration of neural functioning, both inside (within the psyche) and outside (in interpersonal relationships). One of the most important therapeutic outcomes is indeed the creation of coherent autobiographical narratives, both for specific traumatic events and for one's own life as a whole. The mind itself can be seen as a "system" with an innate tendency to heal itself (Solomon & Siegel, 2003), a process that becomes frozen in the presence of trauma. Trauma can hinder the mental process related to self-organization, and the movement toward ever higher degrees of complexity. It blocks the natural process of the brain to reach ever more complex states of self-organization. Therefore, at the core of the resolution of trauma lies the reestablishment of the processes of neural integration and self-organization.

References

Almli, L. M., Fani, N., Smith, A. K., & Ressler, K. J. (2014). Genetic approaches to understanding post-traumatic stress disorder. *International Journal of Neuropsychopharmacology*, *17*(2), 355–370.

American Psychiatric Association. (2013). *Diagnostic and statistical manual of mental disorders* (5th ed.). Washington, DC: Author.

Brewin, C. R. (2001). Memory processes in post-traumatic stress disorder. *International Review of Psychiatry*, *13*(3), 159–163.

Brewin, C. R. (2011). The nature and significance of memory disturbance in post-traumatic stress disorder. *Annual Review of Clinical Psychology*, *7*, 203–227.

Cozolino, L. J. (2006). *The neuroscience of human relationships: Attachment and the developing social brain*. New York: W. W. Norton.

Cozolino, L. J. (2010). *The neuroscience of psychotherapy: Healing the social brain*. New York: W. W. Norton.

Craig, A. D. (2008). Interoception and emotion: A neuroanatomical perspective. In M. Lewis, J. M. Haviland-Jones, & L. F. Barrett (Eds.), *Handbook of emotions* (pp. 272–292). New York, NY: The Guilford Press.

Dillon, J., Johnstone, L., & Longden, E. (2014). Trauma, dissociation, attachment and neuroscience: A new paradigm for understanding severe mental distress. In E. Speed, J. Moncrieff, & M. Rapley (Eds.), *De-medicalizing misery II* (pp. 145–155). London: Palgrave Macmillan.

Droit-Volet, S., Fayolle, S. L., & Gil, S. (2011). Emotion and time perception: Effects of film-induced mood. *Frontiers in Integrative Neuroscience, 5*, 33.

Droit-Volet, S., Meck, W. H., & Penney, T. B. (2007). Sensory modality and time perception in children and adults. *Behavioural Processes, 74*(2), 244–250.

Eagleman, D. M. (2008). Human time perception and its illusions. *Current Opinion in Neurobiology, 18*(2), 131–136.

Elzinga, B., Schmahl, C., Vermetten, E., van Dyck, R., & Bremner, J. D. (2003). Higher cortisol levels following exposure to traumatic reminders in abuse-related PTSD. *Neuropsychopharmacology, 28*, 1656–1665.

Ford, J. D. (2009). Understanding psychological trauma and posttraumatic stress disorder (PTSD). In J. D. Ford, D. J. Grasso, J. D. Elhai, & C. A. Courtois (Eds.), *Posttraumatic Stress Disorder* (pp. 1–30). Oxford: Oxford Academic Press.

Fragkaki, I., Thomaes, K., & Sijbrandij, M. (2016). Posttraumatic stress disorder under ongoing threat: A review of neurobiological and neuroendocrine findings. *European Journal of Psychotraumatology, 7*(1), 30915.

Fraisse, P. (1984). Perception and estimation of time. *Annual Review of Psychology, 35*, 1–36.

Hubbard, J., Realmuto, G., Northwood, A., & Masten, A. (1995). Comorbidity of psychiatric diagnoses with post-traumatic stress disorder in survivors of childhood trauma. *Journal of the American Academy of Child and Adolescent Psychiatry, 34*, 1167–1173.

Karl, A., Schaefer, M., Malta, L. S., Dörfel, D., Rohleder, N., & Werner, A. (2006). A meta-analysis of structural brain abnormalities in PTSD, *Neuroscience & Biobehavioral Reviews, 30*(7), 1004–1031.

Kesner, R. P. (1998). Neural mediation of memory for time: Role of the hippocampus and medial prefrontal cortex. *Psychonomic Bulletin and Review, 5*, 585–596.

Lanius, R. A., Lanius, U., Fisher, J., & Ogden, P. (2003). Psychological trauma and the brain: Toward a neurobiological treatment model. In M. F. Solomon & D. J. Siegel (Eds.), *Healing trauma: Attachment, mind, body, and brain* (pp. 139–162). New York: W. W. Norton.

Lanius, R. A., Williamson, P. C., Densmore, M., Boksman, K., Gupta, M. A., Neufeld, R. W., Gati, J. S., & Menon, R. S. (2001). Neural correlates of traumatic memories in posttraumatic stress disorder: A functional MRI investigation. *American Journal of Psychiatry, 158*(11), 1920–1922.

Lewis, P. A., & Miall, R. C. (2003). Brain activation patterns during measurement of sub- and supra-second intervals. *Neuropsychologia, 41*, 1583–1592.

Mauk, M. D., & Buonomano, D. V. (2004). The neural basis of temporal processing. *Annual Review of Neuroscience*, 27, 307–340.

Muran, E. M., & Motta, R. W. (1993). Cognitive distortions and irrational beliefs in post-traumatic stress, anxiety, and depressive disorders. *Journal of Clinical Psychology*, 49(2), 166–176.

Najavits, L. M., Gotthardt, S., Weiss, R. D., & Epstein, M. (2004). Cognitive distortions in the dual diagnosis of PTSD and substance use disorder. *Cognitive Therapy and Research*, 28(2), 159–172.

Nakazawa, D. J. (2015). *Childhood disrupted: How your biography becomes your biology, and how you can heal.* New York: Atria Books.

Nelson, C. A., & Carver, L. J. (1998). The effects of stress and trauma on brain and memory: A view from developmental cognitive neuroscience. *Development and Psychopathology*, 10(4), 793–809.

Neylan, T. C., & O'Donovan, A. (2018). Inflammation and PTSD. *PTSD Research Quarterly*, 29(4), 1–10.

Nutt, D. J., & Malizia, A. L. (2004). Structural and functional brain changes in posttraumatic stress disorder. *The Journal of Clinical Psychiatry*, 65(supplement 1), 11–17.

Nyberg, L., Kim, A. S. N., Habib, R., Levine, B., & Tulving, E. (2010). Consciousness of subjective time in the brain. *Proceedings of the National Academy of Sciences*, 107(51), 22356–22359.

Payne, J. D., Nadel, L., Britton, W. B., & Jacobs, W. J. (2004). The biopsychology of trauma and memory. In D. Reisberg & P. Hertel (Eds.), *Memory and emotion* (pp. 76–128). Oxford: Oxford University Press.

Pöppel, E. (2009). Pre-semantically defined temporal windows for cognitive processing. *Philosophical Transactions of the Royal Society B*, 364, 1887–1896.

Post, R. M., Weiss, S. R. B., Smith, M., Li, H., & McCann, U. (1997). Kindling versus quenching. *Annals of the New York Academy of Sciences*, 821, 285–295.

Ross, D. A., Arbuckle, M. R., Travis, M. J., Dwyer, J. B., van Schalkwyk, G. I., & Ressler, K. J. (2017). An integrated neuroscience perspective on formulation and treatment planning for posttraumatic stress disorder: An educational review. *JAMA Psychiatry*, 74(4), 407–415.

Schacter, D. L., Savage, C. R., Alpert, N. M., Rauch, S. L., & Albert, M. S. (1996). Conscious recollection and the human hippocampal formation: Evidence from positron emission tomography. *Proceedings of the National Academy of Sciences of the United States of America*, 93, 321–325.

Siegel, D. J. (2003). Foreword. In M. F. Solomon & D. J. Siegel (Eds.), *Healing trauma: Attachment, mind, body, and brain* (pp. xiii–xvi). New York: W.W. Norton.

Solomon, M. F., & Siegel, D. J. (2003). *Healing trauma: Attachment, mind, body, and brain.* New York: W. W. Norton.

Stein, M. B., Hanna, C., Koverola, C., Torchia, M., & McClarty, B. (1997). Structural brain changes in PTSD. Does trauma alter neuroanatomy? *Annals of the New York Academy of Sciences*, 821, 76–82.

Taatgen, N. A., van Rijn, H., & Anderson, J. R. (2007). An integrated theory of prospective time interval estimation: The role of cognition, attention and learning. *Psychological Review*, 114, 577–598.

Van der Kolk, B. A. (1996). Trauma and memory. In B. A Van der Kolk, A. C. McFarlane, & L. Weisaeth (Eds.), *Traumatic stress*. London: The Guilford Press.

Van der Kolk, B. A. (2000). Posttraumatic stress disorder and the nature of trauma. *Dialogues in Clinical Neuroscience, 2*(1), 7–22.

Van der Kolk, B. A. (2002). Post-traumatic therapy in the age of neuroscience. *Psychoanalytic Dialogues, 12*(3), 381–392.

Van der Kolk, B. A. (2003). Foreword. In M. F. Solomon & D. J. Siegel (Eds.), *Healing trauma: Attachment, mind, body, and brain* (pp. xvii–xxvi). New York: W.W. Norton.

Vasterling, J. J., Brailey, K., Constans, J. I., & Sutker, P. B. (1998). Attention and memory dysfunction in posttraumatic stress disorder. *Neuropsychology, 12*, 125–133.

Wittman, M. (2009). The inner experience of time. *Philosophical Transactions of the Royal Society B, 364*, 1955–1967.

Zakay, D., & Block, R. A. (2004). Prospective and retrospective duration judgments: An executive-control perspective. *Acta Neurobiologiae Experimentalis, 64*, 319–328.

Chapter 8

Time, Trauma, and Therapeutic Change

This chapter refers to the dialectical intertwining between *Chronos* and *Kairos*. *Kairos* points to the trauma patient's tentative efforts to create a "kairotic" space as a defense against *Chronos*. Trauma patients build their experience upon a "denial of time," which is intrinsic to resistance to change and transformation. Trauma results in a sense of "extended time," whereby a shifting back and forth between outer perception and self-awareness occurs. Trauma patients seem to lack a sense of temporal identity. They live in a universe devoid of object relations, and feel "alone in eternity." Human feelings about time and timelessness may be either constructive or destructive, depending on their relationship to the pleasure principle (*Eros*) and the death drive (*Thanatos*), respectively. Finding an adaptive dialectic between these two poles is the scope and goal of human existence.

Therapeutic Time as a "Kairotic" Space

We have seen how the concepts of *Chronos* and *Kairos* refer to objective, chronological time on the one hand, and subjective, lived time, on the other. *Chronos* refers to time as measure, "the quantity of duration, the length of periodicity, the age of an object or artifact, and the rate of acceleration as applied to the movements of identifiable bodies" (Smith, 1969, p. 1). On the contrary, *Kairos* points

> to a qualitative character of time, to the special position an event or action occupies in a series, to a season when something appropriately happens that cannot happen at "any" time, but only at "that time," to a time that marks an opportunity which may not recur.
>
> (*ibid.*)

Besides the two concepts of *Chronos* and *Kairos*, Roberts (2003) analyzed the notion of "chaos" as underlying human creativity:

> [A]ll creative processes, it seems, emerge in the quasi-magical place between order and disorder. This "ultimate crucible" in which

DOI: 10.4324/9781003230601-9

self-ordering of structures occurs is the domain which lies between order and disorder. This is the domain of "chaos" wherein lies creativity. . . . [C]reativity is a property of chaos itself.

(p. 214)

As the youngest son of the god Zeus, *Kairos* represented in Greek mythology the "auspicious moment" (Kelman, 1969), a unique moment that can never repeat. Later on, *Kairos* acquired the meaning of "the right time," "the decisive moment," or "the inspiration of the moment" (Goldwert, 1991, p. 553). In the medical lexicon of the followers of Hippocrates, *Kairos* was the "crucial" moment in treatment – "that point in the course of an illness when a physician exercised all of his skills to determine the outcome" (*ibid.*). *Kairos* is "the moment or occasion of making meaning" (Roberts, 2003, p. 209). In the psychoanalytical tradition, the concept of *Kairos* can be found as far back as in Freud's thinking, where this notion, regarded as the time of trauma, appeared to be associated with psychic functioning and history. In this view, *Kairos* is "that crucial time in the past that is decisive for what then must come after" (Rieff, 1971, pp. 25–26). In Jungian psychology (see Jung, 1958), *Kairos* represented "the feminine sense of time, a conception or pregnancy of the moment, a sudden birth of feeling" (Ulanov, 1971, p. 177). *Kairos* is also associated with Erik Erikson's (1950) idea of human personal identities, which develop through resolutions of conflicts and crises.

These identities are neither a linear progression of phases of growth, nor a doomed waxing and waning which produces the general arc of life. They are individualized solutions to problems which are both common and unique, calling for moments of reflection and decision. They occur in time seen as *kairos*. And each *Kairos* is a crisis or an opportunity in which interpersonal relations are assessed and realigned.

(Pruyser, 1968, p. 215)

Rose (1997, 2007) further wondered whether the concept of *Kairos* allows us to understand the patient's tentative efforts to create a "*kairotic*" space as a defense against *Chronos*. Notably, *Chronos* and *Kairos* are not irreconcilable opposites, but rather dialectically intertwined dimensions. Rose (1997, 2007) further linked to psychic reality the second law of thermodynamics, according to which "in a closed system entropy never decreases" (p. 463). When the person as an organizationally closed system is forced to open, anxiety arises. In therapy, the finitude of the therapeutic setting may threaten several internal structures that are built upon a "denial of time" (Rose, 2007, p. 23).

The complex process that trauma patients must go through "takes place by bringing together affect, representation, sensorial and somatic experiences, dreams, associations and enactments as they are gathered and given meaning *après coup* through analytic work" (Perelberg, 2015, p. 1453). From a psychoanalytical point of view, trauma-related dissociative experiences can be changed and undone through repeated transference and countertransference processes (Wilkinson, 2003). In transference, patients set in action specific modes of perceiving time (Meissner, 2007). In this view, when thinking about the temporal dynamics of internal objects, one might wonder whether looking for temporal and spatial disruptions of the transferential process might help to better understand the therapeutic process, which involves a transformation of the patient's internal object relations.

As Kalsched (2015) argued, unremembered trauma tends to be "repeated in the transference, leading to mutual 'enactments' between the analytic partners and, hopefully, to a new outcome" (p. 477). The question put forward by Rose (1997, 2007) is whether patients utilize the structure of *Kairos* to protect themselves from the structure of *Chronos*. Now, the denial of the temporal unfolding of existence is intrinsic to resistance to change and death. The attempt to transcend time (and death) and to limit the termination of the analytical process seems to go hand in hand with the patient's wish to eliminate separateness or distance from the analyst. However, the denial of time also amounts to a wish to stop development and growth.

Patient and therapist are in fact continually confronted with the issue of time (Arlow, 1984). Reifying and anthropomorphizing time may serve to represent unconscious wishes, which find their way into the transferential process. These two processes, that is, reification and anthropomorphization of time, are associated with intrapsychic conflict, and point to the influence of time in human experience. This experience underlies the interplay between the immediate perception of objects and self-observation. A sense of *extended time* seems to result from such painful experiences. This shifting back and forth between outer perception and self-awareness lies at the core of therapy, especially psychoanalysis. When an undesirable element emerges in the patient, then self-consciousness also arises, along with a shift from the attention paid to narration of the person's experience (Arlow, 1984).

Time is associated with psychic self-narrative. "Narratives are structuralisations of happenings and courses of events, and are of fundamental importance for one's identity and self-structure [. . .] timelessness signifies here that narrative time is suspended" (Varvin, 1997, p. 90). The scope and goal of trauma therapy is supposed to allow the person to gain mastery over his or her existential narrative, and what the psychotherapist ought to pay attention to is how the patient's unconscious wishes determine his or her present experience. Patients respond to sensory present in a way that influences the probable modes of future response, that is, in modes that "shape [their] future" (Arlow, 1986, p. 519). In psychoanalysis, it is in the process of free association that the analyst can record a succession of the analysand's thoughts, feelings, and emotions. Therefore, this same succession of told experiences is the cornerstone of the individual's experience of time, from which new meanings are open to stem. Insofar as the therapist is concerned, he or she is able to reorganize the patient's experience of time through interpretation, thus expanding the person's concept of Self (Kafka, 1977).

Accordingly, Hinton (2015) viewed psychoanalysis as

> a complex temporal process, a future that may alter the past, a past that may become the future, simultaneously existing along with an evanescent present as the pulsating intersection of past and future. This aspect of time is syncopated, multifaceted and non-linear.
>
> (p. 365)

Far from considering time as a sequential linear arrow, psychoanalysis aims at understanding what lies at the core of our subjective experience (Loewald, 1980). The intertwining between present, past, and future points to an experienced "now" whose nature is made up of perception, memory, action, affect, and existential value. In this view, subjective time can be thought of as "the deep organizing activity of the mind that links mental elements forging meaningful wholes from which we create historical accounts" (Auerbach, 2014, p. 200). According to Loewald (1980), trauma brings about an

> experience of fragmentation, where one's world is in bits and pieces none of which have any meaning. The time continuum by which we hold our world together, the interrelatedness and the connections between a past, present, and future disintegrate, are broken in the most elementary sense, so that each instant loses its relation to any other instant and stands by itself, not embraced in a time continuum.
>
> (pp. 141–142)

Trauma, Arousal, and the "Here and Now"

According to Freud (1937), the therapist's

> task is to make out what has been forgotten from the traces which it has left behind or, more correctly, to *construct* it. . . . His work of construction, or, if it is preferred, of reconstruction, resembles to a great extent an archeologist's excavation of some dwelling-place that has been destroyed and buried or of some ancient edifice.
>
> (pp. 258–259)

Smith (1988) borrowed Freud's definition of "reconstruction" to explain what happens between patient and therapist, as the former's experience is brought back to life, or "reconstructed." In the therapeutic setting, patients are sometimes so close to their memories that they lack the ability to recognize those mnestic traces as *their* memories (Griffin, 2013). The "sense of time" can be defined as the combination and integration of several psychophysiological functions that form a cluster of "related components" (Meerloo, 1966, p. 236). Traumatized individuals seem indeed to lack a sense of continuity in their lives. They live in an empty universe, and are "alone in eternity" (p. 246).

Persons who went through trauma tend to show dysregulated arousal states. They often oscillate between being hyper- and hypoaroused. While adaptive in certain situations, these two extreme poles become maladaptive if they turn to long-term coping strategies. The optimal arousal zone is otherwise called "window of tolerance," which must be maintained in order for the person to be able to process and integrate traumatic experiences. Within the window of tolerance, arousal naturally fluctuates and is context-specific, as sympathetic and parasympathetic activities relatively balance each other. The width of the window of tolerance is directly associated with how much stimulation is required to trigger the "threshold of response." In trauma patients, the window of tolerance is normally narrower than that in other people, showing unusually low or high threshold, or both. Expanding the window of tolerance is therefore one of the main goals of therapy (Levine, 1997).

When one has survived trauma, his or her inability to maintain arousal within the window of tolerance might prevent future adaptive responses, thus activating dysfunctional coping strategies even in the absence of threatening situations. In traumatized individuals, even minor stressors can activate extreme arousal levels, *as if* the threat were still present and occurring again, in the "here and now." As they also become unable to regulate their window of tolerance by keeping it within optimal limits, they become more vulnerable to further traumatization, in a vicious cycle that tends to repeat itself and never ends. Hyperarousal leads to the fragmentation of experience, especially in relation to its emotional and sensory components. Because they become hyperaroused even when facing apparently innocuous stimuli, trauma patients find it hard to give sense to their emotions and check the reality of their perceptions. This results in a deficit to respond adaptively to potential subsequent threat, behaving impulsively rather than reflectively.

The behavior of hyper- or hypoaroused individuals tends to be less structured when compared to the behavior of other persons, as in these individuals "reflexive defensive tendencies appear to be random and disorganized" (Ogden et al., 2006, p. 36). This results in a lack of organization of experience into a unified sense of Self, which in turn produces further difficulties in modulating the arousal. Instead of turning back to the window of tolerance, traumatized individuals tend to remain hyper-activated even in the absence of threat. They also tend to become hyper-aroused when facing innocuous triggers without being able to integrate them into the wholeness of their experience. Dissociation occurs when a reaction to trauma-related triggers cannot be integrated within one's whole experience, thus hindering the individual's ability to process new information even when within the optimal window of tolerance. A primary goal of psychotherapy is indeed to help trauma patients to integrate the dissociated aspects of their Self, by reengaging traumatic reminders within the window of tolerance (Ogden et al., 2006).

The therapist ought to facilitate the person's focus on current experience by attending to the flow of present inner states through awareness and attention paid to the "here and now" as it unfolds over time, thus reinforcing the person's ability to maintain and expand his or her focus on the present. The goal is to welcome every sensation rather than to escape *a priori* from it, by allowing difficult thoughts to simply "be there" in a non-judgmental attitude. This requires individuals to "step back" from traumatic memories, and observe what happens in the "here and now" of their body as they recall them. By narrating their experience, individuals no longer *are* their experience but *have* it (Ogden & Minton, 2000).

Trauma and Human Embodiment

PTSD goes hand in hand with disturbing body sensations, and trauma can be regarded as a psychophysical experience (Rothschild, 2000). Trauma therapy aims at understanding how the body processes, remembers, and perpetuates stressful events. In PTSD, traumatic occurrences are not relegated to the past as other life events, but keep intruding in the person's everyday life as body sensations and reenactments. Traumatized individuals cannot do anything but bodily reliving over and over again the life-threatening situation, and the emotional and physical reactions to it. Usually, individuals affected by PTSD cannot recall the temporal order or the specific time of their trauma, even though they continue to have somatic reactions that remind their body of it. It is as if traumatized individuals were lacking explicit memory for the trauma, and were left with only implicit and somatic fragments of it (Rothschild, 2000).

Awareness of the body sensations is a central focus in somatic approaches to PTSD, insofar as consciousness of actual sensory stimuli is the first link to the "here and now." In the therapeutic setting, as Rothschild (2000) argued, "simple body awareness makes it possible to gauge, slow down, and halt traumatic hyperarousal, and to separate past from present" (pp. 100–101), thus allowing to move the first steps toward a deep transformation of somatic memories. The awareness of one's own body is comprised of the consciousness of inner and outer stimuli, and can be nurtured and therefore utilized for self-soothing. PTSD individuals tend to identify some of their body sensations as dangerous, especially when these are reminders of previous trauma. Nonetheless, the more PTSD patients become familiar with their emotions, the less scary these become. When trauma patients deny the very existence of their emotions, it might be useful noticing in-session changes in the body posture, facial expression, and tone of voice, for example, by asking questions such as "Which body parts are you aware of right now?" "Did you notice that you began swinging as I raised my question?" It is always the body that grounds the individual in the "here and now." As Rothschild (2000) stated, "sensing the body is a current-time activity" (p. 107). The therapeutic setting is made up of the intertwining between the therapist's observations and the patient's narrative, which find their root in psychophysiological processes. In this view, the body would therefore have in itself the resources to identify, access, and resolve traumatic experiences.

In PTSD patients, inner stimuli tend to take over the "emotional body" hiding the external world, which is interpreted on the basis of inner sensations only. At the same time, perception narrows down, as the ability to simultaneously process different stimuli diminishes, leading to perceptual distortions of reality and further distress. By being hypervigilant to dangerous stimuli, trauma patients also lose the ability to discern them, as the *realization* of them being safe is hindered or becomes impossible. Here, by "realization" is meant both "to find out" and "to produce" traumatic symptomatology, which affects not only the person as a foreign body, but is also produced by the individual's internal psychosomatic processes. Spotting danger everywhere amounts to being constantly scared of everything. Becoming aware of the difference between safe and dangerous stimuli, and between past and present, is therefore one of the primary goals of trauma therapy. PTSD patients ought to come to terms with the fact that, even though they might experience the trauma as if it were happening in the "here and now," it is only a memory that belongs to the past. When this is not the case, retraumatization can occur, as the person might delve into flashbacks and become trapped in hyperaroused states of mind.

Trauma patients can only process trauma in a safe and trauma-free environment, such as that provided by a good-enough therapeutic relationship. The body remembers traumatic events by encoding in the brain only some of the features of the threatening situation. Healing from trauma involves both working on the mind *and* on the body: "somatic memory becomes personal history when the impact of traumatic events is so weakened that the events can finally be placed in their proper point in the client's past" (Rothschild, 2000, p. 173). As Dietrich (2001) argued:

[E]xposure, desensitization, and cognitive-emotional processing are active mechanisms of therapeutic change for symptoms of PTSD. . . .

[E]xposure, desensitization, and processing are key mechanisms for particularly chronic and complicated forms of PTSD and associated features; however, additional mechanisms of change are likely required for complete and successful treatment in the latter.

(pp. 38–39)

Finally, for severely traumatized individuals, teaching the right skills to manage traumatic symptomatology might be the most effective type of treatment. In this view, it is possible that targeting risk factors might help both treating PTSD and preventing recurrences of the condition over time.

Awakening the mind to the wisdom of the body is a primary goal of trauma therapy (Levine, 2012). Its aim is to develop the individual's awareness of the "here and now," that is, the present moment, moving from chaos and rigidity into a more stable and harmonic way of living. The preverbal, interpersonal asset of this kind of body-focused psychotherapy allows the person to articulate the multidimensional features of trauma, by integrating sensory and motoric states of the body that had previously been held captive outside the realm of conscious awareness. As previously mentioned, what distinguishes human beings from other animals is the *flexibility* of their responses to environmental challenges. However, traumatized individuals tend to respond to reminders of past trauma by automatically and unconsciously activating bodily responses that were adaptive only at that time, but are irrelevant or even harmful in the present context.

The regressive movement that can go along with trauma and dissociation leads the person to take a step back and embrace rigid action patterns, that is, flight-fight-freeze responses, which are meant to protect or defend the individual from threatening situations. Far from being, alternately, either psychic or physical, trauma represents a combination of helplessness and abandonment that are felt by both the psyche *and* the body. Upon failure to use emotions to communicate with other human beings, traumatized individuals seemingly lose their ability to utilize their emotions as guides for effective action. They also fail in verbally identifying what they are feeling (a condition called "alexithymia"), as well as in recognizing their needs and take care of themselves (Meissner, 2007). Also, traumatic stress worsens when perpetrated in the context of interpersonal relationships, where the person can respond to threat with compliance or submission. Boundary violations and loss of self-regulation make people vulnerable to ongoing physical and emotional dysregulation, which can become a habit in the long term.

Past trauma keeps affecting the ways in which traumatized individuals perceive themselves and their surroundings. Past experiences find their place in the present, and are reenacted in breath, sensory perceptions, and bodily sensations, thus forming a gestaltic whole (Naranjo, 2000).

The therapist must facilitate self-awareness and self-regulation by help-ing the person to regain a sense of control over his or her own life. Indi-viduals need to recognize that having feelings is "safe." Reorienting the individual to the present experience is helpful to overcome the impression or, worse, the belief to be trapped in the past, and acknowledge instead that emotions are in constant flux, and never remain the same or neces-sarily become overwhelming (Ogden et al., 2006). Trauma patients must be allowed to grow in self-mastery at a pace that helps them to stay with each and every moment of their past trauma without surrendering, compensating, or dissociating. In this sense, delving into the body and getting in touch with one's physiological experience is the way out of the person's distressing symptoms. In this sense, the way "in" is the way "out" (Levine, 2012).

Time, Trauma, and Therapeutic Change

Given the connection between time and the Self, the goal of trauma ther-apy rests on the ability to perceive memories as *one's own* memories, the past as *one's own* past. As Emde (2005) pointed out, on the one hand human beings seek to establish a sense of discontinuity in their existence, for example, by detaching the past from the present; on the other hand, they try to create a sense of continuity, for example, by gaining a sense of ownership over past experiences – a process that Emde (2005) referred to as "affirmative empathy" (p. 124). Another goal of therapy is, there-fore, to develop empathy toward one's own past, to look at oneself as the same person from past to future, and to accept previously repudiated affects (Beres & Arlow, 2004). The therapeutic work would then consist of bringing past repressed material into consciousness, and owning it as a part of one's narrative. As a result, not only the past will be remembered, but it will also become part of the present.

In the therapeutic setting, both patient and therapist are engaged "in reviewing and reconstructing the temporality of the self. . . . The reconstruc-tion of the past takes place in the present and is influenced by the present in the form of *Nachträglichkeit*" (Meissner, 2007, p. 244). As a result, indi-viduals become able to reshape their memories, modifying the influence of the past on the present and reconfiguring their self-narrative as well. In fact, therapeutic change consists of reorganizing the experience of reality in time (Modell, 1990). Critical to increasingly seeing reality as a shared world of object relations is the development of the ability to tolerate affects, self-soothe, and manage intrapsychic conflicts. The patient's ability to engage in the therapeutic relationship without dissociating fosters his or her capac-ity to test reality and have a more accurate sense of time. In other words, therapy seeks to bring about a change that fosters a different relation to the temporality of existence. If time disturbances have defensive purposes for the traumatized person, then the healing process will entail a reorganization of perceived time in relation to endured trauma (Terr, 1984).

The therapeutic process consists of symptom reduction and reintegration of the individual's temporal dimensions. The psychotherapist's role is to draw the patient's attention to the present, giving him or her the opportunity to place the trauma somewhere in the past. A further goal of therapy involves reowning the time that has been "lost" because of the trauma. The therapist's work aims at helping the patient to view the traumatic memories in perspective, which then become narrative memories instead of flashbacks, nightmares, and events that jeopardize the present. A positive outcome of therapy becomes then integration and unification of the Self, where the patient gains a sense of safety in his or her life.

The collision of the patient's desires with the temporal boundaries of the setting makes much of the therapeutic alliance (Rose, 1997, 2007). In this view, the patient's demands are manifested in the transference through his or her temporal psychic structure. The interpretation of the patient's distortions of time are deeply linked to the patient's transference (Wilkinson, 2003). The therapeutic setting should thus make it possible for the patient's temporal processing to become conscious and be explicitly tracked, so that they can be analyzed and articulated. In this view, the patient's sense of time is created as a result of the time boundaries of the session, which would work just like a superego. In this sense, the end of a session might be experienced as a "Thou shalt not . . . continue" (Rose, 1997, p. 464), whose injunction creates a sense of imminent past and future.

Trauma therapy facilitates regression to more primitive mental states, whereby objective time becomes subjectively "personified" (Hägglund, 2001, p. 85). What emerges is then the manifold of unstructured representations related to a primary logic and unconscious functioning, which take shape in associations that are free from any temporal boundary – free to be "expressed" (Semi, 2011). The analytic regression and the weakening of the ego defenses not only enable a freer expression of the unconscious mind but also a more primary relationship to temporal experience. Within the analytic boundaries, chronological time gives way to a *timeless* reality, where past and present mix up, as do wishes and memories (Sabbadini, 1989a, 1989b). Therefore, time plays a key role in therapy, both because it brings about change as its most fundamental function and because transference operates through temporally determined mechanisms, such as regression and repetition, involving the reenactment of the past in the present. The Freudian notion of

> *Nachträglichkeit* represents the specific temporal motion of the session and of the analytic process, and the typical state of mind of the analyst at work, which is established retrospectively, differentiating

transference movement from simple, reductive repetitions of archaic internalized object relations.

(Marion, 2011, p. 40)

Time and Timelessness as Psychic Organization Principles

Hägglund (2001) elaborated on the concept of timelessness as the correlate of the experience of a "true Self," on which the therapist can act in order to co-create an authentically creative experience. Deeply experiencing one's Self as such is associated with the experience of the present moment in all its fullness, which in turn reinforces the integration of the Self. Human feelings about time and timelessness may serve opposite ends, that is, constructive or destructive, depending on their relationship to the pleasure principle (*Eros*) and the death drive (*Thanatos*), respectively. Central to human psychic functioning in the psychoanalytic process is inscribing time in the process of articulating and symbolizing repressed material into verbal forms of communication. In this view, time is involved in change, development, and growth, as well as in the awareness of one's own temporal limits, that is, mortality.

Therefore, time and timelessness may have opposite connotations, according to their relationship to the subject's mental state. On the one hand, they can relate to a "frozen stasis" (Levine, 2009, p. 336) of a life that remains stuck in the illusion of an infantile omnipotence, where denial of reality takes place. On the other hand, they can be associated with primary object relations, where the sources of life, energy, and love are to be found. At the erotic pole (*Eros*), timelessness is associated with temporal differentiation. At the opposite pole (*Thanatos*), one can find the atemporal stasis of the repetition compulsion that mirrors the death drive. As a result, the relationship between time and timelessness is dialectical and apparently contradictory at the same time, and ultimately paradoxical in nature. It is linked to reality as loss and limitation on the one hand, and as hope and possibility on the other. As Levine (2009) concluded, life, and especially "psychoanalysis, is all about time" (p. 337).

Trauma contains the pressure of unbound affects that threaten to emerge as experiences of annihilation out of repressed unconscious material. For the traumatized individual, healing means to *historicize* existence and accept time as a sequence that makes the past something that no longer is, and the present something different from the past. In fact, trauma patients need to learn that the past is part of their life story *as* memory and not as something that continues to be perceived in the present. In this view, the not-yet-represented traumatic memories must be given a voice, in order to no longer influence the experience of the "here and now." They must be historically turned into memories *of the past*, and unbound from the eternal "now" in which they seem to exist. This process occurs when traumatic memories are verbally expressed and temporally inscribed. In other words, unrepresented mental states need to be transformed and reconstructed for the very first time through verbalization and historization. According to Levine (2009), what must be recognized is "*a powerful psychic imperative to historicize, retranscribe, and even create the past*" (p. 341) through the articulation of mental events that places them into a coherent narrative.

This process allows the person to construct a meaningful narrative and a sense of identity of his or her own Self in time. The ego has the power to signify, resignify, and organize unconscious material through recall and association, despite the timeless character of the endured trauma. Healing from trauma implies going through inscription, articulation, and historization of traumatic memories into a coherent life narrative. As long as this process does not take place, traumatic memories remain not only unrepresented and unmentalized, but also frozen "outside" time (Levine, 2009). Therefore, the association between the psyche and the spoken word "inserts time into psychic process and psychic process into time" (p. 353). Here lies also the association between language, time, and psychic differentiation, as well as the role of the therapist in helping the patient create his or her past out of the "unpast."

Notwithstanding, this seems in contrast to the statement, attributed to the German philosopher G.W.F. Hegel (1770–1831), according to which "words murder time," which Joannidis (2005) tried to make sense of by understanding the timeless nature of the unconscious mind. In this view, the understanding of the sentence involves acknowledging that the conceptualization of the notion of time moving from outside its nature runs the risk of destroying the active structuring of that concept, that is, the "lived" experience of it. In the therapeutic setting, what patients bring into therapy is their particular ways of ordering experience, and also their modes of understanding personal history. In other words, patients bring their (understanding of) time into the therapeutic setting, so that it can be brought to life in the interaction with the therapist (Joannidis, 2005).

Harasemovitch (2011) also explored the "dialectical relationship" (p. 1185) between time and timelessness, regarding them as "vital counterparts of one another" (p. 1184). The *relationship* between time and timelessness would function as the *trait d'union* that allows new forms of psychic experience to be born to life through differentiation, disorganization, and reintegration. Freud's (1915) definition of the timelessness of the unconscious mind is in fact diminished by the statement that "the *Ucs.* [Unconscious] is alive and capable of development" (p. 190). To use Harasemovitch's (2011) words, psychic structures can also work toward an "emotional bridge" (p. 1197) between time and timelessness, thus creating new meanings in human experience. When temporality breaks up, the intertwining between its dimensions becomes open to new modes of integration, thanks to what Green (2009) called "*le temps éclaté*," that is, an "explosion" of time.

References

Arlow, J. A. (1984). Disturbances of the sense of time – With special reference to the experience of timelessness. *Psychoanalytic Quarterly, 53*, 13–37.

Arlow, J. A. (1986). Psychoanalysis and time. *Journal of the American Psychoanalytic Association, 34*(3), 507–528.

Auerbach, W. (2014). Time and timelessness in the psychoanalysis of an adult with severe childhood trauma. *Studies in Gender and Sexuality, 15*(3), 199–213.

Beres, D., & Arlow, J. A. (2004). Fantasme et identification dans l'empathie. *Revue française de psychanalyse, 68*(3), 771–790.

Dietrich, A. M. (2001). Risk factors in PTSD and related disorders: Theoretical, treatment, and research implications. *Traumatology, 7*(1), 23–50.

Emde, R. N. (2005). A developmental orientation for contemporary psychoanalysis. In E. S. Person, A. M. Cooper, & G. O. Gabbard (Eds.), *Textbook of psychoanalysis* (pp. 117–130). Washington, DC: American Psychiatric Publishing.

Erikson, E. H. (1950). *Childhood and society*. New York: W. W. Norton.

Freud, S. (1915). The unconscious. In J. Strachey (Ed.), *The standard edition of the complete psychological works of Sigmund Freud* (vol. 14, pp. 159–215). London: Hogarth Press.

Freud, S. (1937). Constructions in analysis. In J. Strachey (Ed.), *The standard edition of the complete psychological works of Sigmund Freud* (vol. 23, pp. 255–269). London: Hogarth Press.

Goldwert, M. (1991). Kairos and Eriksonian psychology. *Perceptual and Motor Skills, 72*(2), 553–554.

Green, A. (2009). From the ignorance of time to the murder of time. From the murder of time to the misrecognition of time in psychoanalysis. In L. T. Fiorini & J. Canestri (Eds.), *The experience of time: Psychoanalytic perspectives*. London: Karnac Books.

Griffin, F. L. (2013). In search of lost time in psychological space. *American Imago, 70*(1), 69–106.

Hägglund, T. (2001). Timelessness as a positive and negative experience. *Scandinavian Psychoanalytical Review, 24*(2), 83–92.

Harasemovitch, J. C. (2011). (A)temporal dialectic: Creative conversations between timelessness/time and transference. *Journal of the American Psychoanalytic Association, 59*(6), 1183–1200.

Hinton, L. (2015). Temporality and the torments of time. *Journal of Analytical Psychology, 60*(3), 353–370.

Joannidis, C. (2005). Words murder time. *International Journal of Applied Psychoanalytic Studies, 2*(2), 164–173.

Jung, C. G. (1958). *The undiscovered self*. New York: New American Library.

Kafka, J. (1977). On reality: An examination of object constancy, ambiguity, paradox, and time. In J. H. Smith (Ed.), *Thought, consciousness, and reality* (pp. 133–158). New Haven: Yale University Press.

Kalsched, D. E. (2015). Revisioning Fordham's "Defences of the self" in light of modern relational theory and contemporary neuroscience. *Journal of Analytical Psychology, 60*, 477–496.

Kelman, H. (1969). Kairos: The auspicious moment. *American Journal of Psychoanalysis, 29*, 59–83.

Levine, H. B. (2009). Time and timelessness: Inscription and representation. *Journal of The American Psychoanalytic Association, 57*(2), 333–355.

Levine, P. A. (1997). *Waking the tiger: Healing trauma: The innate capacity to transform overwhelming experiences.* Berkeley, CA: North Atlantic Books.

Levine, P. A. (2012). *Healing trauma: A pioneering program for restoring the wisdom of your body.* Lexington, KY: ReadHowYouWant.

Loewald, H. W. (1980). The experience of time. In H. W. Loewald (Ed.), *Papers on psychoanalysis.* New Haven, CT: Yale University Press.

Marion, P. (2011). The time of Nachträglichkeit. *The Italian Psychoanalytic Annual, 5*, 23–40.

Meerloo, J. A. M. (1966). The time sense in psychiatry. In J. T. Fraser (Ed.), *The voices of time* (pp. 235–252). New York: G. Braziller.

Meissner, W. W. (2007). *Time, self and psychoanalysis.* Plymouth: Jason Aronson.

Modell, A. H. (1990). *Other times, other realities: Toward a theory of psychoanalytic treatment.* Cambridge, MA: Harvard University Press.

Naranjo, C. (2000). *Gestalt therapy: The attitude and practice of an atheoretical experientialism.* Carmarthen: Crown House Pub.

Ogden, P., & Minton, K. (2000). Sensorimotor psychotherapy: One method for processing traumatic memory. *Traumatology, 6*(3), 149–173.

Ogden, P., Minton, K., & Pain, C. (2006). *Trauma and the body: A sensorimotor approach to psychotherapy.* New York: W.W. Norton.

Perelberg, R. J. (2015). On excess, trauma and helplessness: Repetitions and transformations. *International Journal of Psycho-Analysis, 96*(6), 1453–1476.

Pruyser, P. W. (1968). A *dynamic psychology of religion.* New York: Harper & Row.

Rieff, P. (1971). The meaning of history and religion in Freud's thought. In B. Mazlish (Ed.), *Psychoanalysis and history* (pp. 23–44). New York: Grosset & Dunlap.

Roberts, J. (2003). Kairos, chronos and chaos. *Group Analysis, 36*(2), 202–217.

Rose, J. (1997). Distortions of time in the transference. *International Journal of Psycho-Analysis, 78*, 453–468.

Rose, J. (2007). Distortions of time in the transference: Some clinical and theoretical implications. In R. J. Perelberg (Ed.), *Time and memory* (pp. 23–46). London: Karnac Books.

Rothschild, B. (2000). *The body remembers: The psychophysiology of trauma and trauma treatment.* New York: W. W. Norton.

Sabbadini, A. (1989a). Boundaries of timelessness. Some thoughts about the temporal dimension of the psychoanalytic space. *International Journal of Psycho-Analysis, 70*, 305–313.

Sabbadini, A. (1989b). How the infant develops a sense of time. *British Journal of Psychotherapy, 5*(4), 475–484.

Semi, A. A. (2011). *Il metodo delle libere associazioni.* Milano: Raffaello Cortina.

Smith, H. F. (1988). Time, reconstruction, and psychic reality. *Journal of The American Academy of Psychoanalysis, 16*(1), 71–81.

Smith, J. (1969). Time, times, and the "right time;" "chronos" and "kairos." *The Monist, 53*(1), 1–13.

Terr, L. C. (1984). Time and trauma. *The Psychoanalytic Study of The Child, 39*(1), 633–665.

Ulanov, A. B. (1971). *The feminine in Jungian psychology and Christian theology.* Evanston, IL: Northwestern University Press.

Varvin, S. (1997). Time, space and causality. *Scandinavian Psychoanalytical Review, 20,* 89–96.

Wilkinson, M. (2003). Undoing trauma: Contemporary neuroscience. *Journal of Analytical Psychology, 48,* 235–253.

Conclusion
Healing From Trauma

The psychoanalytical concepts of *Nachträglichkeit* and *après-coup* show that psychic time is complex and nonlinear. As Varvin (1997) argued, "simple linear causality therefore does not exist in the psyche" (p. 89). These concepts allow us to understand how what is not yet symbolized can act in the psyche. Here, "both temporality and causality are reversed, and that it is not a question of a relation between cause and effect, but of an interaction between two modes of representing experiences" (Varvin, 1997, p. 94): an "iconic/figurative" mode, as we can see in the repetition present in our dreams, and a "symbolic/narrative" mode, as is testified in traumatic experience that has been worked through. Trauma can be seen as a fundamentally impaired integration of the individual's whole life. Post-traumatic states are characterized by rigidity and incapability to organize life in the temporal unfolding of intersubjective existence. In other words, trauma blocks the person's innate movement toward integration and healing. Releasing this blockage is central to psychotherapy, so that one can achieve bodily awareness and adaptive self-regulation.

Meissner (2007) understood time as an entity that is constituted via the intertwining of mind and body, that is, as a property of the person as a whole: "the self is an embodied self" (p. 212). Namely, the sense of time is closely related to the body, and the Self should be considered as a dialectical unity of body and mind. Now, integration, that is, the connection of differentiated elements into a functional whole, lies at the core of the person's well-being. By integrating different domains of experience, one becomes able to develop a new form of consciousness, which leads to a more harmonious life. The development of the sense of time is a lifelong process, which Meissner (2007) suggested to start even in the womb, before the infant is born.

Originally, trauma leads to the splitting of different sensorial modalities and of parts of the ego, generating an effect of "inauthenticity." This is why, in the clinical setting, linking different sensorial modalities with one another amounts to achieving an effect of "authenticity," which lies at the core of the healing process (Soreanu, 2017, p. 235). One might

DOI: 10.4324/9781003230601-10

explain trauma as an event that occurs within a causal connection; here, "explain" (see the Latin expression "*scire per causas*," that is, knowing through the causes) merely means searching and tracing back a possible cause for the traumatic event. In this perspective, time runs monodirectionally from past to present, and from present to future. Alternatively, one can propose a phenomenological-hermeneutic explanation, which inserts trauma in a *synchronic* dimension that takes place within a process of *creation of meaning*. In this perspective, trauma is not understood in relation to its "causes," but rather to its "meaning." The psychological laws that mediate the temporal relationship between events and their psychic processing are not those of physics, but rather of *sense*.

As we have seen, the past is "retention" (Husserl, [1905] 1991), that is, memory of the just-passed; in turn, the future is "protention," that is, expectation of the yet-to-come. This means that past and future are contained in the present not physically, but *intentionally*. The sense of an event is generated in the dialectical relationship between past (retention), present (presentation), and future (protention). Now, only a person owning a *telos* has an *arché* (Ricoeur, [1985] 1988). And the *arché* is "shaped like a past into the future, a *future anterior* . . . it's the *past that will have been*" (Agamben, 2008, pp. 106–107). To understand the meaning of temporal events, it is thus necessary to shift from a diachronic to a *synchronic* dimension, that is, from a *naturalistic* account of temporality, which regards events in a linear, monodirectional succession of cause and effect, to a *hermeneutic* account that captures the sense of events in their dialectical intertwining. Only in this way it becomes possible to understand our present experience, allowing a redefinition of the meaning of past experiences.

The working alliance between patient and therapist is a relationship of "existential engagement" (Herman, 2015, p. 147). The traumatized individual experiences a temporal fragmentation of self-experience, which corresponds to a fragmentation of what Merleau-Ponty ([1945] 1962) called "intentional arc," essential to the coherence of our action, perception, and interaction with others. As a result, *trauma appears as a disruption of subjective and intersubjective temporality*. The discontinuity of the intentional arc generates gaps in the person's experience, precisely where the temporal coherence of a unified conscious awareness is constituted. Traumatic intrusive thoughts and flashbacks disrupt the temporality of the trauma patient's experience, so that the retentional and protentional coherence is also disrupted, producing an "arrest of existential temporality" (Fuchs, 2010, p. 17).

Trauma patients become fixated with time because their experience of time as irreversible points to a past that cannot be changed, and to a future closed to any possibility. The therapist must aim at reestablishing a coherent sense of Self in the patient, by allowing him or her to gain tools to reduce the potential for psychic conflict and anxiety in the face of emotionally charged stimuli (Duportail, 2005). The elimination of traumatic temporal disruptions may eventually provide the means to help the patient anticipate, reduce, or even avoid psychic pain in the form of depression or traumatic anxiety, thus reestablishing a coherent self-narrative. The goal is for the patient to achieve a state of improved ego functioning, which can be considered an important foundation on which clinical success depends. The patient's goal is to find sense and meaning to the trauma he or she endured, which can be achieved through therapeutic dialogue and empathic resonance. In fact, being aware of the temporal dimensions that characterize the traumatic experience allows the therapist to become better conscious of the difficulties trauma patients might be experiencing.

Because the sense of Self and the sense of time are interrelated, temporal distortions occur not only in well-functioning individuals, but also when psychopathology is present (Taatgen et al., 2007). The more individuals can experience the present, the less the past and future have power over them (Loewald, 1972). Accordingly, the loss of the sense of Self is linked to a sense of depersonalization, which involves a perceived lack of being in place in the spatiotemporal continuum. When trauma is present, all psychic processes are disrupted, including the perception of time. Time provides the constant pressure to remembering the past and limiting the future due to its finite nature. Time can therefore be regarded as the pinpoint of the reflection on the traumatized Self. Each event is experienced in its multiple forms of past, present, and future. The present moment is delineated against past experiences and future possibilities. Therefore, improved ego functioning enables a more differentiated potential to gain a deeper insight into the meaning of life.

In traumatic experience, a sense of future is unavailable in its openness, and the past becomes an endless repetition of the same. Also, trauma breaks the chain of memory. Unlike ordinary memories, the mnestic traces of the trauma are not inscribed in the person's coherent biography, and tend to remain unchanged over time. In this sense, trauma is *inscribed*, but not *reinscribed* in the individual's conscious awareness. This is why "imagining new possibilities, not merely the repeatedly retelling of the tragic past, is the essence of post-traumatic therapy" (Van der Kolk, 2002, p. 389). Trauma patients do not experience time as a dimension they truly own. The closure of the future dimension goes hand in hand with a past that cannot be changed. When the future is closed, there is no longer room for change. Trauma patients thus become overwhelmed by thoughts of hopelessness and helplessness. Disturbances in the process of temporization and a sense of inhibition of the temporal "becoming" characterize the traumatized person's suffering. The subjective sense of time is distorted, resulting in temporal perception slowing down or speeding up. The collapse of the traumatic Self's activity goes along with the collapse of time. In this view, the human "becoming" can be regarded as a forbidden dimension of time, an obstacle to the connection with the temporality of others. Psychic pain seems infinite and unbearable. Suffering becomes endless suffering, with a beginning but no end.

The core experience of trauma involves disempowerment and disconnection from others (Taylor et al., 2003). This is why healing requires the establishment of new safe relationships and the empowerment of the individual's capacity to tolerate psychic pain (Herman, 2015). Recovery takes place only within a healing relationship and cannot occur in isolation. In a healing connection with others, the trauma survivor recreates the abilities that were lost due to the trauma. These include the capacity for trust, autonomy, identity, and intimacy. Empowering trauma survivors means helping them to become the authors of their own recovery. Accordingly, therapists must be able to listen carefully and validate the traumatized individuals' experiences, reinstating in them an element of new control. Elliott (2004) suggestively described the relationship between patient and therapist as a "dance," where each individual follows and leads the other, in a mutual collaborative approach characterized by a sense of co-exploration. In this view, a balance between active stimulation and responsive attunement is to be achieved.

As opposed to interpretation, empathy is meant to *evoke* the hidden layers of the traumatized person's emotions, thoughts, sensations, and perceptions by indirectly hinting at them without superimposing a pre-established hermeneutic. As a result, trauma patients are and remain the only true interpreters of their own experience (Frost et al., 2014). Galovski et al. (2015) contended that a good therapeutic relationship allows the therapist to reinstate in trauma patients a gradual ability to grow adaptive coping strategies out of the rigid defenses they have built to protect their ego, and to develop a capacity for self-reflection that includes past, present, and future. The therapeutic bond seems to have the power to open up new emotional memories, that is, new stories and possibilities that, over time, will end up inhibiting the automatic activation of maladaptive behavioral patterns.

The disruption of perceived time coincides, for the traumatized person, with a basic disturbance in the self-narrative, inhibition of lived experience, and a break in the experienced temporal unfolding. Furthermore, desynchronization and lack of spontaneity seem to characterize the trauma patient's experience. Closure to the future and to the past makes the individual fall prey to time and become dominated by it. The therapeutic setting becomes the locus where the person can reexperience the trauma in all its developmental aspects (Van der Hart et al., 2005). In psychotherapy, there may be in fact moments when understanding something amounts to changing the big picture of the representation of life, reorganizing the relationship to past experiences and to object relations. As in a "kaleidoscope" (Sodré, 1997), the elements remain the same, but the overall picture changes. This new understanding comes from insights that do not depend on new information, but rather on an interpretative change of past events.

A transformation in the trauma patient's psychic reality comes about when an aspect of the past, which is still present in the person's mind, is subject to a change in perspective, which in turn brings about a transformation of the overall individual's life story. The aim of the therapeutic process thus consists of recreating a coherent self-narrative, as the subject becomes able to see past events *as such*, and not just as eternal repetitions of the same. In this way, feelings of hopelessness and helplessness will turn to feelings of mastery over the person's life (Anderson & Gold, 2003). Traumatized individuals must "recollect" their story to make up a coherent narrative, which aids in maintaining a self-identity embedded in memory (Schrag, 1999).

The metaphor of "depth" can denote the rhythm of temporality, which is not linear nor monodirectional, but "deepens" as changes in temporal experience occur. In this view, both therapist and patient must enter a "fluid time-state" (Lafarge, 2014, p. 304) in order for change and transformation to occur. Therapy becomes "an island in time" (Torres, 2007, p. 252), where everything lies outside the ordinary flow of experience. It is in this sense that *therapy deals first and foremost with time*. In fact, through psychotherapy, the individual can eventually allow him- or herself to *abandon the past after remembering it*; it is also in therapy that the patient reaches true maturity through the creation of a space of "illusion" that goes beyond mere renunciation of the fulfillment of his or her wishes (Torres, 2007).

To conclude, the link between trauma and temporality is paramount for the therapist to consider, because it allows a reframing of the view that the person has on oneself, within the wholeness of one's own existence. *In traumatic phenomena, temporal linearity is disrupted: the sense of a traumatic event is achieved more in a synchronic than in a diachronic dimension.* Trauma follows the logic of a "rebellious diachrony" (Duportail, 2005). As we have seen, it is only at a further time that the original trauma can be signified: "all we can know directly is what conscious experience becomes; we can never know what it was before that" (Stern, 2017, p. 17). In the therapeutic setting, patients are sometimes so close to their memories that they lack the capacity to recognize those same memories as *their memories* (Griffin, 2013, p. 79), as when we try to see something by placing our eyes too close to the target.

Given the understanding of trauma that can be grasped on the basis of the concept of *Nachträglichkeit*, therapy must act in a temporal reversion that is understandable only by assuming the conflicting contemporaneity of at least two meanings of time, that is, chronological, objective time on the one hand, and phenomenological, subjective time on the other. "We come to know ourselves retrospectively, an act of *après-coup* that momentarily stills a continual shape-shifting process, one part of the lived experience of depth" (Foehl, 2020, p. 131). As a result, the benefits of the therapeutic action are possible precisely because the past is not determined once and for all, but is always *determinable* again by a present that feeds back on it. As it is deposited in the dynamic movements of temporality, the past still remains indeterminate, that is, determinable "*nachträglich*," as Freud would say. To act means not only to predetermine the future, but also to redefine the past. In this sense, the therapeutic process goes from present to past, in order to interpret something that can be grasped only afterward, in the form of the *après-coup* (Lacan, [1955] 1993). Everything the traumatized person recalls is not the same before and after therapy. Even though it *is* the same, it is *known* as different (Wilson & Lindy, 2013). Ultimately, for each of us, the past is resignified and "shaped *après-coup*" (Birksted-Breen, 2003, p. 1504). Ultimately, "remembering, continually re-creating the past, is the living ground of our subjectivity" (Hinton, 2015, p. 354).

References

Agamben, G. (2008). *Signatura rerum: Sul metodo*. Torino: Bollati Boringhieri.

Anderson, F. S., & Gold, J. (2003). Trauma, dissociation, and conflict: The space where neuroscience, cognitive science, and psychoanalysis overlap. *Psychoanalytic Psychology*, 20(3), 536–541.

Birksted-Breen, D. (2003). Time and the après-coup. *International Journal of Psychoanalysis*, 84(6), 1501–1515.

Duportail, G. (2005). *Intentionnalité et trauma: Lévinas et Lacan*. Paris: L'Harmattan.

Elliott, R. (2004). *Learning emotion-focused therapy: The process-experiential approach to change*. Washington, DC: American Psychological Association.

Foehl, J. C. (2020). Lived depth: A phenomenology of psychoanalytic process and identity. *Psychoanalytic Inquiry*, 40(2), 131–146.

Frost, N. D., Laska, K. M., & Wampold, B. E. (2014). The evidence for present-centered therapy as a treatment for posttraumatic stress disorder. *Journal of Traumatic Stress*, 27(1), 1–8.

Fuchs, T. (2010). Temporality and psychopathology. *Phenomenology and the Cognitive Sciences*, 12(1), 75–104.

Galovski, T. E., Wachen, J. S., Chard, K. M., Monson, C. M., & Resick, P. A. (2015). Cognitive processing therapy. In U. Schnyder & M. Cloitre (Eds.), *Evidence based treatments for trauma-related psychological disorders*. Cham: Springer.

Griffin, F. L. (2013). In search of lost time in psychological space. *American Imago*, 70(1), 69–106.

Herman, J. L. (2015). *Trauma and recovery: The aftermath of violence. From domestic abuse to political terror*. New York: Basic Books.

Hinton, L. (2015). Temporality and the torments of time. *Journal of Analytical Psychology*, 60(3), 353–370.

Husserl, E. (1905) 1991. *On the phenomenology of the consciousness of internal time*. The Hague: Nijhoff.

Lacan, J. (1955) 1993. *The seminar of Jacques Lacan: The psychoses (book III, 1955–1956)*. New York: W. W. Norton.

Lafarge, L. (2014). On time and deepening in psychoanalysis. *Psychoanalytic Dialogues*, 24(3), 304–316.

Loewald, H. W. (1972). The experience of time. *The Psychoanalytic Study of the Child*, 27(1), 401–410.

Meissner, W. W. (2007). *Time, self and psychoanalysis*. Plymouth: Jason Aronson.

Merleau-Ponty, M. (1945) 1962. *Phenomenology of perception*. London: Routledge & Kegan Paul.

Ricoeur, P. (1985) 1988. *Time and narrative* (Vol. 3). Chicago: University of Chicago Press.

Schrag, C. O. (1999). *The self after postmodernity*. New Haven: Yale University Press.

Sodré, I. (1997). Insight et après-coup. *Revue française de psychanalyse*, 61(3), 1255.

Soreanu, R. (2017). Something was lost in Freud's beyond the pleasure principle: A Ferenczian reading. *American Journal of Psychoanalysis*, 77(3), 223–238.

Stern, D. B. (2017). *Unformulated experience: From dissociation to imagination in psychoanalysis*. Hillsdale, NJ: Analytic Press.

Taatgen, N. A., van Rijn, H., & Anderson, J. R. (2007). An integrated theory of prospective time interval estimation: The role of cognition, attention and learning. *Psychological Review*, 114, 577–598.

Taylor, S., Thordarson, D. S., Maxfield, L., Fedoroff, I. C., Lovell, K., & Ogrodniczuk, J. (2003). Comparative efficacy, speed, and adverse effects of three PTSD treatments: Exposure therapy, EMDR, and relaxation training. *Journal of Consulting and Clinical Psychology*, 71(2), 330–338.

Torres, M. A. (2007). The time dimension and its relationship to the analytic process. *International Forum of Psychoanalysis*, 16(4), 247–253.

Van der Hart, O., Bolt, H., & Kolk, B. A. (2005). Memory fragmentation in dissociative identity disorder. *Journal of Trauma & Dissociation*, 6(1), 55–70.

Van der Kolk, B. A. (2002). Post-traumatic therapy in the age of neuroscience. *Psychoanalytic Dialogues*, 12(3), 381–392.

Varvin, S. (1997). Time, space and causality. *Scandinavian Psychoanalytical Review*, 20, 89–96.

Wilson, J. P., & Lindy, J. D. (2013). *Trauma, culture, and metaphor: Pathways of transformation and integration*. New York: Routledge.

Index

Note: Page numbers followed by "n" indicate a note on the corresponding page.